P9-CQX-247

West of Then

A Mother,
a Daughter,
and a Journey
Past Paradise

Tara Bray Smith

SIMON & SCHUSTER

New York London Toronto Sydney

SIMON & SCHUSTER
Rockefeller Center
1230 Avenue of the Americas
New York, NY 10020

Copyright © 2004 by Tara Bray Smith

All rights reserved,
including the right of reproduction
in whole or in part in any form.

SIMON & SCHUSTER and colophon are registered trademarks
of Simon & Schuster, Inc.

For information regarding special discounts for bulk purchases,
please contact Simon & Schuster Special Sales at
1-800-456-6798 or business@simonandschuster.com.

Except for the image on page 6, all photographs are courtesy of the author.

Designed by Helene Berinsky

Manufactured in the United States of America

10   9   8   7   6   5   4   3   2   1

Library of Congress Cataloging-in-Publication Data

Smith, Tara Bray.
    West of then : a mother, a daughter, and a journey past paradise / Tara Bray Smith.
        p.   cm.
        1. Adult children of narcotic addicts—Hawaii.   2. Narcotic addicts—Hawaii.
    3. Women—Drug use—Hawaii.   4. Mothers and daughters—Hawaii.   I. Title.
    HV5831.H3S65 2004
362.29'34'092—dc22
[B]
                                                                                    2004048723

ISBN 0-7432-3679-3

*For my sisters
and for Margaret*

Author's Note

I have tried to render the Hawaiian language accurately here, using Mary Kawena Pukui and Samuel H. Elbert's *Hawaiian Dictionary* as a guide. I have also wanted to be true to the way I experienced the language as a child growing up in the islands. After the first reference, Hawaiian and other foreign words and phrases are left unitalicized, without diacritical marks. A pronunciation key and glossary appear at the back of the book.

This is a memoir. Some of the story portrays events and conversations that took place many years ago. I have relied on memory—mine and others'—for help in painting scenes. I have changed a few names. This being said, historical occurrences have been researched, and all errors of fact or interpretation are mine.

"Then the bowsprit got mixed with the rudder sometimes."
—Lewis Carroll, *The Hunting of the Snark*

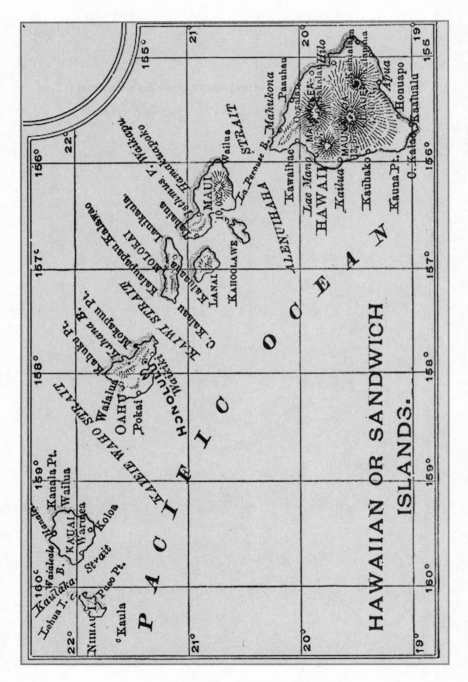

Map of Hawai'i, circa 1890

West of Then

Karen, 1980

Prologue

✄

Thanksgiving 2002   Honolulu

M Y MOTHER LIVES IN A SMALL PARK. IT'S MAYBE TEN thousand feet square, wedge-shaped, and it sits near the entrance to downtown Honolulu. According to the city, it isn't even a park. It is a "mini park": Kamaliʻi Mini Park, which means "Small Child" in Hawaiian. My mother—her name is Karen Morgan—calls it Triangle Park for its shape, slung as it is between the Pali Highway and Fort Street, the former leading to the mountains, the latter to the sea. A fire station occupies Triangle Park's base; other than this, its major features are a few spindly trees girdled by benches and a grassy area crisscrossed by chipped-rock sidewalks. A bus shelter lines its southern flank. An apartment building sits on one side of the park, a municipal parking lot and a methadone clinic on the other. Prostitutes sometimes walk by here; the area is popular with transvestites in particular. Were it not for the junkies like my mother and the occasional hooker, I doubt passersby would pay Triangle Park much heed. One could easily mistake it for a median strip; it is only a little wider.

To me it is huge, or at least big enough to hide my mother, whom I am still trying to find.

But let us orient ourselves:

We are in the middle of the Pacific, at the edge of the Tropic of Cancer in the Torrid Zone. Eight islands rest here, the newest in a string of volcanic seamounts that stretches thirteen hundred miles up to Kure, a coral atoll a third of the way to Japan. O'ahu, where we are, is near the center of the main archipelago. It is the third largest of the islands and the most populous: about one million souls, depending on how many tourists are in town. We are on the most isolated inhabited landmass on the globe; there is nothing as populated for thousands of miles in any direction. East is west; West is east. A city has been built here called Honolulu, "Sheltered Bay," on the natural harbor that formed at the mouth of the Nu'uanu Stream—good not for landing canoes, which preferred the shallow sandy beaches of Waikīkī further south, but for Western ships that docked here with increasing frequency after 1778, when the first Europeans arrived at these islands, led by Captain James Cook.

The year is 2002, the month November, a pleasant one in Honolulu. The heat of summer has passed on to the lower Pacific. Here it is balmy, breezy—Twain's "slumberless Sabbath"—seventy-eight degrees in the shade, and I am looking for my mother.

I have come to Triangle Park the day after Thanksgiving because I wanted to tell her something, news about her older sister, Margaret, who is ill and at this moment lying in a hospital bed a few blocks down the street. My mother and I fought, she walked away from me, and now I am sitting in the sunlit grass waiting for her to reappear. This is how my mother and I operate: we come together and are separated, merge and then are repelled. I know she will always come back, just as I know she will always leave.

She has a quick temper these days, and she has disappeared. So I pick at the grass, smoke a cigarette. I look around. Looking around is a way to steal back the time my mother has stolen from me. I have spent a lot of time waiting for Karen: whole evenings in airports, mornings on curbs, once an afternoon in a deli in Monterey. That time she said she was going to the store. I waited with my younger half sisters—Layla, then five, Lauren, a newborn—for four hours. I was not yet thirteen; I suppose I thought she would come back eventually. I entertained Layla by drawing on a napkin; I fed Lauren from her bottle. I watched the minutes tick by on a black-and-white clock above my head. Where had she gone? Why had she left? When would she come back? What would I do if she didn't? None of these questions had answers; they only yielded more questions. (The biggest of which—what was she doing?—seems clear now, in Triangle Park.) Every so often I took the stroller and Layla and we walked down the street to find her, but all I saw were strangers—I was visiting my mother in California only for the summer—so I set my face into a mask of what I thought might look like calm and continued to wait. With what was left of my money I bought a sugared pretzel for Layla and a coffee. The man behind the counter seemed concerned, but my resolve must have signaled him to stay quiet. Other than commonplaces he never said a word.

Mom returned a few minutes before closing and bought Layla and me caramel apples. While we pushed Lauren's stroller down the Monterey boardwalk she apologized—Karen always apologizes—and I looked at the seagulls. I remember that the wooden planks beneath my feet were wide and pale gray, and that the ocean was gray, too, which seemed strange. Hawai'i's ocean is blue, perfectly blue, like the sky, and that was the only ocean I was familiar with.

I'm thirty-two now. I am unmarried, childless, and untethered. I live in New York, far away from here. I am an adult. Still, when I am waiting for my mother, I feel like that girl in the deli, immobilized by a pose I myself have defined. Cars pass slowly, light on their windshields. Green mountains rise up on my right; white clouds skid across the blue, familiar sky above. Across the street there is a hedge of Tahitian gardenia—*tiare,* it's called here. Always a pretty flower to gaze upon in Hawaii.

And I have become very good at looking.

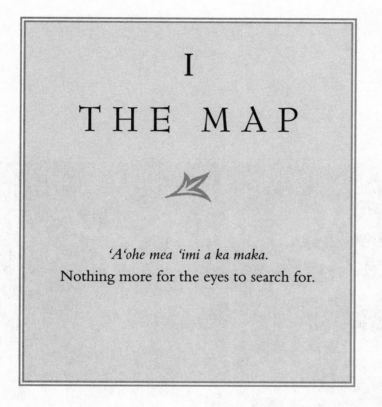

I

THE MAP

'A'ohe mea 'imi a ka maka.
Nothing more for the eyes to search for.

Faye family, ca. 1905. Courtesy of Kauai Museum

The Bounty

Thanksgiving 2002   Honolulu

THE FIRST TIME I SAW SNOW FALLING WAS ON THANKS-
giving. I was in the town of East Barnet, Vermont. It was 1987. I
was seventeen. My ex-stepmother, Debbie, and I were the guests of two
kindly gay innkeepers. We were in New England looking at colleges. I
am from Hawaii. I had never seen snow before. And this wasn't even a
real snow, the men informed me. This was a *dusting.*

"Won't stick." They shook their heads. "More pie, hon?"

It didn't matter. I walked outside and opened my mouth and tried to
eat it. Debbie took a picture of me. I look ridiculous. My arms are out-
stretched. I am wearing yellow padded snowshoes and a stonewashed
denim jacket my friend Kenji Nakano had brought me from Japan.

I felt exhilarated and disappointed both. Snow was supposed to do
something. Cover you up, at least. This snow wasn't even cold.

A year later I went to college down the road from there—Dartmouth.
I felt I was in a J. Crew catalog. I got a boyfriend within a month. Scott
had a good sense of humor, especially when it came to misfortune, and
he was smart, so his stories were good. At Collis Café we ate hummus
and discussed our classes over flavored coffee. That fall he was taking a
course in colonial New England history.

When the Pilgrims came, Scott informed me, they made a mistake about the weather in America. They thought that because their new home was on the same latitude as Spain, winters would be mild. Like what they were familiar with, but better. North America is much colder than Europe, however. The first winter most of the Pilgrims froze and died. Which was why, that second year, when the Indians came with maize and turkey, they celebrated Thanksgiving.

"Ain't that shit-out-of-luck."

Scott was from Texas. I'd been to Texas.

I always remembered this story. How sad, to be so disappointed by a place you thought would change everything.

Fourteen years later to the month, I am in a park in downtown Hono-lulu, waiting for my homeless mother to reappear from wherever she's gone off to. In 1988 I did not think this is where I would end up. Scott liked to think I'd end up in a suit and high heels, at an advertising job. I encouraged the fantasy by joining a sorority. He said I would be the best dancer at the Christmas party. This flattered and depressed me. My own projections were less precise. When I thought of what I'd be doing in 2002 I imagined the reflection of lights on dark windows. I would be in an apartment high off the ground. It would be dark outside and light in-side. My hair would be up. That's as far as I got: apartment, hair up, the reflection of light on windows.

In 1988 my mother had just gotten out of rehab. Though I didn't know how things would turn out for her, I was hopeful. I am usually hopeful.

There were men in jumpsuits here this morning, men whose job it is to clean up this park. They came with hoses and rakes and garbage bags. They cleared out the dead leaves; they emptied the wastebaskets. They picked up the human trash: greasy paper bags, empty beer bottles, toilet paper and Styrofoam plate-lunch containers and cigarette butts and feces. By now, by midmorning, Triangle Park feels sparkly again. The wind sweeps down from the mountains, making the leaves shiver. The sun is on the grass. Near a building hung with Chinese signs a woman crosses the street. She's approaching a car that has stopped and is now idling, waiting for her.

Her name is Serena. She is blond, fiftyish, drug-addict lean. She wears a denim miniskirt and a pale pink tank top. A tattoo wilts down her left bicep. She turns her head to let the wind from the ocean clear the hair from her eyes—in Honolulu the trade winds are constant—and for a moment I can see her face in full: wide high cheeks, bright brown eyes. It could be a pretty face but for the missing teeth. They deflate her jaw, giving her the look of an old baby, elongated and tattooed.

In the past I have seen Serena from a distance and mistaken her for my mother because she is skinny like my mother is, has dyed hair like my mother does, and at times looks hollow and vacant the way I think my mother might look when she's high, though this is largely speculation, because ever since she relapsed four years ago Karen is memorable to my sisters and me mostly for her absence. So really Serena is what I picture my mother might be, or what she might become, a toothless hag, if she stays in Triangle Park any longer.

Karen Morgan gave me up twenty-five years ago, when I was seven. She was a heroin addict and couldn't take care of me. My father and my stepmother raised me, educated me, sent me to college. I don't know why I think my mother is my responsibility, but I do.

She has been beaten up, raped. She's been arrested; she's prostituted. Add to this the long-term effects of opiate addiction, heavy smoking, bouts with pneumonia, and the constant threat of disease—TB, staph, septicemia, hepatitis, and HIV—and perhaps you can understand why I am afraid my mother is going to die out here. I do not know whether this is a real fear or not. But people die on the street, and this is why I am here.

So I wait, look around. Everything is so close on an island. Walk seven or eight blocks *makai*, oceanward, and you're at Aloha Tower, once the tallest building in Hawaii. The steamships used to come in here, the *Lurline* and the *Matsonia*. Members of my own family ate baked Alaska and tomato aspic on those boats, four and a half days out from San Francisco. They bought *lei* from the lei sellers at the docks—

pīkake, plumeria, and double carnation, my great-grandmother's favorite. They threw coins off the decks. A half-dollar tossed might get six local boys to dive.

Two miles south is famously ruined Waikiki. A mile *mauka,* mountainward, is Nuuanu, the tony Honolulu suburb of gardenias and secret green pools and a queen's summer palace. My mother and her three siblings—Margaret, Gail, and Brewster—grew up in Nuuanu in a big house with its own Hawaiian name: Polihiwahiwa, "Nestling in the Bosom of the Hills."

To get from Polihiwahiwa to here you need only follow the Nuuanu Stream. It trickles by my mother's childhood home, ginger gracing its banks, flows through the Buddhist cemetery where Auntie Gail used to take me on walks, trolls inhabiting the underside of every bridge, and empties into Honolulu Harbor, just a few blocks away. Down here the bridges are wide enough for cars. Magenta bougainvillea lines the stream's stone banks and the water is slack, a dark bluish green.

On this side of the river—that's what the stream is called here, despite its modest size—is Chinatown, Honolulu's red-light district. On the other, Iwilei, where in the early 1900s Honolulu's prostitutes had their cribs. Somerset Maugham's Miss Sadie Thompson was imagined to have plied her trade here, in one of the one-room bungalows that lined these streets: remarkably clean, noted the observers of the day. Today the cottages are gone, but the whores remain. They've just moved down the block, to the river, where pimps stand along the banks talking into cell phones and johns prowl the bridges in SUVs. Though the names of the bars on Hotel Street allude to more innocent times—Hubba Hubba Live Nude, Smith's Union Bar, Hana Hou Lounge, which means, loosely, "Do It Again"—downtown bordering Chinatown has long been this way, seedy and sad, with bums and massage parlors and drug dealers in dark alleys. It's been this way since ships stuffed with Hawaiian sandalwood sailed for Canton back in the 1800s, when Fort Street really emptied into a fort—built of coral for Kamehameha, the chief who united these islands and became Hawaii's first king—and sailors sang:

Ship me somewhere west of 'Frisco,
Where the best is like the worst,
Where there ain't no ten commandments,
And a man can raise a thirst.

Foreigners started coming to Hawaii a few years after Cook. They wanted a paradise and here one was. They wanted prostitutes; those could be arranged. Booze, opium, marijuana, cocaine, crack, crystal meth (called *batu* here), Oxy—these would have to be brought in, but there were boats, then steamers, eventually container ships and airplanes. So Chinatown and Iwilei went on like this, a bit salty, a bit squalid, sometimes cleaned up, more often ignored.

But my mother is here now, and everything is different.

Serena laughs at the person in the idling car. Then she waves her arms as if to say "No goal," crouching on her bandy legs. When she leans past the car's tinted window I can't see her face so I don't watch Serena anymore.

A man sitting next to me on the grass offers me a bite of turkey. "Want some?" he says, and extends to me a plastic plate. "No," I say at first, then, "Okay."

His name is Ron. Ron is also fiftyish, also lean, with thinning brown hair and a waxy, deeply grooved face. Ron is from California, where, according to him, the cops aren't as mellow as they are in Hawaii, and being homeless is harder.

Ron has been living on and off the street for a decade. He's a heroin addict, though last year he got his use down to just once a month. "Once a month and I was good," Ron says. "I got my disability on the first and that was it." Lately, though, it's been "real bad." He spends his check the first week he gets it.

But here it is the day after the day of plenty and Ron's plate is loaded with leftover food: ham, turkey, mashed potatoes, and, because we are in Hawaii, macaroni salad, *two scoop* rice, a slice of fried Spam. Ron got the food from Central Intermediate, a school down the block in whose breezeways he sleeps. (In Honolulu even the janitors are kind. They come by, shake him gently in the morning.) Nights are spent at Central Intermediate; days here, at Triangle Park, or along Fort Street Mall, the street-turned-pedestrian-alley where the bums of Honolulu hang out, dozing, chatting, smoking, scheming.

Mark Twain wrote about Fort Street in the 1860s. It was made of crushed white coral, he noted; the low-roofed houses were charming. He remembered a lot of cats.

Ron's got nothing and yet he offers me some. I'm not hungry. I've already had my Thanksgiving. My sister Layla—she's twenty-four now—and I went to Aunt Gail's, in Lanikai, a pretty Honolulu suburb a half hour over the Pali. Lanikai means "Heavenly Ocean," though who knows if that's real; many names in Hawaii were made up by real-estate developers. Still, it's nice in Lanikai. Gail has three towheaded children and a psychiatrist husband and a big house near the beach. Michelle Pfeiffer lives down the road. Layla and I go to Gail's for holidays. If Lauren were here she'd have come, too.

My youngest sister moved away a year and a half ago, when she was seventeen, a junior in high school. Our mother didn't have a place for her to live anymore, so Lauren dropped out and stayed with Layla. Now she's in Houston, living with her father's family. If she were here today she'd make me laugh. Or she'd get me out of here, take me over to Doris Duke's, where she'd jump off the rocks first, calling up from the ocean for me to follow. Lauren is wild, like Mom. I am not, so we make a good pair. Sitting here alone, I miss her company. It's always easier to wait with others.

The fact that I'm outside in a park and it's sunny and food is being offered makes me want to eat it. I take a bit of the ham and half of a roll. "Thanks, Ron," I say, and he grins. He too has lost front teeth, though not as many as Serena.

"Plenty where that came from."

I sort of like Ron, despite everything.

Nate the Blade shuffles by, humping a backpack. I have heard some of Nate's story. He got his name because he threatened some dude with a knife, so a Fort Street bum with a sense of humor dubbed him Nate the Blade. He's a poet who went to Oxford, and he does appear rather sensitive, with his sparse mustache, and his rosebud mouth, and his days spent in the periodicals room of the state library down from 'Iolani Palace, reading.

When he was five, Nate will tell you, his father threw him out into the Minnesota cold without so much as a coat. Now he lives on the streets of sunny Honolulu. Funny how you can end up so far and yet so close to where you started.

Nate lifts a hand out of his pants pocket and waves, nods darkly.

Ron nods back, drags on his cigarette. He wears a sling on the arm he doesn't use for smoking. He got beaten up a week ago, he tells me. Someone mistook him for the guy who stole another guy's drugs. They beat the shit out of him, broke his collarbone, and knocked his front teeth out.

"And I wasn't even doing anything!" Ron shrugs. "Jeez!"

I nod. I'm sympathetic, though it's hard to imagine Ron really "doing anything" except what he's doing right now: sitting on his haunches in Triangle Park, smoking a cigarette, every so often cracking a joke, or going to look for food.

Brenda is out here, too, on a bench among the scant trees. Brenda is Hawaiian, and a man. She wears a cropped baby tee and silky polyester running shorts and has long fingernails and soft little girl-breasts. When Brenda laughs she covers her rotten teeth with her hands and shakes silently.

A woman comes up, pokes around the trash. Lank brown hair frames a ropy face. She wears a peasant skirt. She could be an old rocker chick—a Stevie Nicks type for whom the party has gone on too long—until she opens her mouth. Her teeth are worse than Brenda's. They are brown and they twist like roots. She asks another woman, who has just sat down next to me, whether there are any plastic cups in the bin.

"No. Check that one," this woman says, and waves to a can at the end of the park. An abandoned car sits there, stuck at one of the meters that line the curb.

The trashpicker nods and departs.

"At least I don't look like her," the lady next to me says.

She's wearing a pleated mauve skirt and a tweed jacket, this one. She's quite thin, early fifties, with dyed auburn hair, blue eyes, and intact teeth, though if you looked in back you'd see where they were cracked, chafing against her mouth, causing her words to come out sloppily. Her skinny legs—they used to be shapely, a dancer's legs—stack in front of her, crossed at the ankles. She's barefoot. Black pumps upturn at her side. She got the shoes, the rayon skirt, the tweed jacket too warm for Honolulu from a donations box, along with the Bioré face wash and the sample-sized shampoo and moisturizer she pulls out of a duffel bag and tries to push on me in a confused attempt to give me something, even if it's the last thing she owns. A bandage wraps around the top foot, her right one, concealing a pus-filled abscess she insists is a spider bite, though I suspect it's from shooting up and I tell her so. She waves that top foot back and forth absentmindedly, like a girl. She is a girl, despite the wrinkles. She picks at the grass, digs at it with a stick. She burns the leaves that have fallen from the trees with a lighter, bringing the burning leaves to her nose to smell them because she smells, touches, tastes, needs to see, feel, wrack herself with everything. She was once beautiful. This was all once beautiful.

She's my mother. Ron is her husband, my new stepfather. They got married a year ago. They met at a shelter, or somewhere along Fort Street Mall. They knew each other for three weeks. Serena is one of my mother's best friends, though sometimes Karen will say "Aw, girlfriend!" to Brenda and give Brenda a high five, and sometimes she'll say Nate the Blade is her best friend, though I don't believe it.

Karen lives out here in Small Child Park. She sleeps in the breezeways of Central Intermediate with Ron. She eats at a mission called the River of Life.

In May of 2002 my mother called me in New York and told me she was sleeping in a park. Three weeks after that she disappeared. I came to Hawaii to find her. I left a nascent romance, friends that had become a family, an apartment, and a city that was beginning to feel like home to spend the fall of my thirty-second year looking for my mother among the lost people of downtown Honolulu. I left a life—nothing especially interesting, lights in dark windows, but my own.

Today is the day after Thanksgiving. I'm supposed to be thankful for everything, even sitting in this park. And I am grateful. My mother is here, sitting in front of me. And we're in Hawaii, and it's so lovely: warm, pleasant, tropical, full of *aloha,* welcoming, exotic, spiritual, natural, un-spoiled, spoiled, so I-used-to-go-there-once-that-was-a-long-time-ago.

But I can't help it. I hate it here. I hate Brenda and Nate and Serena. I hate Ron. I hate the cigarette butts in the grass and the woman who digs through the trash. I hate this lady my mother has become.

"At least you don't look like her?"

"Yeah." Karen's pissed, suspicious, and probably high. She doesn't give a fuck what I'm saying.

I speak loud enough for her to hear.

"You will."

In the Land of Make Believe

June 1998   Honolulu

"NOW, TARA DEAR," GAMMA SAID, HANDING ME A GLASS bowl shaped like a lotus flower. The spoon was scratched, but monogrammed. "Mayonnaise? Anyway, listen—"

She readjusted her dark glasses, pursed her lips. Her blond hair swept back from her face in impressive waves. "It's Lauren."

Next to me Auntie Margaret burped. Lupus, I guessed, made you gassy.

"Her eyebrows, dear. She overplucks them."

I laughed. Margaret did, too.

"No really, it's too much!"

My grandmother reached into her pants pocket for a picture she'd cut from a fashion magazine, passed it to me. It showed a brown-haired woman with thick eyebrows. She was pretty, looked like Brooke Shields. She didn't look anything like my fifteen-year-old sister, though, who was blond and sly and whose eyebrows were naturally thin, like lines of dark sand.

I didn't know what else to say so I agreed. "You're right."

"It's the style I guess," Margaret offered through a bite of sandwich. "The style!"

"The style, Mom."

Twenty-five years ago Aunt Margaret lived in a tepee, out in Wai'anae, on the west side of Oahu. She had cut her own album called *These Trails*—folksy and beautiful if heavy on the wind chimes—the cover of which featured the bare foot of a friend named Boogie. She moved to New York then, where she had a flat in the Bowery and decided to test karma by stealing the rent money. She got hepatitis and ended up having to pay it back anyway. Then she went to Japan and Puerto Rico and across the United States, stopping at Arcosanti, the Paolo Soleri retreat in Arizona, where she worked as a cook. That's where her lupus bloomed, brought on, as Margaret will tell you, by a few days spent in the desert eating only sage and cactus fruit. After that she went to Monterey—the reason my mother was there—where her lupus got worse, forcing her to come home. Margaret moved to my grandmother's house when the disease attacked her kidneys. In 1998 she had just started twice-a-week dialysis, so she stayed close to home.

Margaret has been, in her life: a slack-key musician, masseuse, Reiki master, seller of hotel amenities, housesitter, poet, exotic dancer, and touch therapist. She is, as a cousin once called her, the Real Thing. At luncheon the Real Thing was tired and sick but she still helped Gamma set up, putting sweet pickles in a little bowl, setting out salad forks and iced-tea glasses, and gathering a few flowers at the center of the table.

"The style?" My grandmother shook her head. "Well, I don't think so. I think it's common."

"What?" Margaret kept chewing.

"The *style*. I think it's common." Gamma looked at me for backup. I shrugged and nodded at the same time.

Maybe Lauren's eyebrows were common. Overplucked, like a regular teen. She did wear a lot of eyeliner. And she was nearly flunking out of high school. She smoked pot; for most of her life she'd been on food stamps.

Lauren partied in Waikiki hotel rooms with much older rap stars on their way to Japan. Mom told Lauren to clean up her room and then called the cops. Lauren saw Mom in her car in the parking lot of the

Kailua Times supermarket smoking something from a pipe. Mom said, "God, it was just *hash!* So I was smoking a little hash? So *what!*" Karen Morgan was not good on drugs. Sober, she was eccentric and intermittently employed, but on drugs she lost things.

So Lauren needed to grow her eyebrows out.

We were at the point with my mother's family where things were about to get strange.

"A girl should have natural eyebrows." Gamma looked at me and nodded. "Like yours, Tara."

For most of my twenties I kept my armpit hair long.

"Mine?"

"Anyway, I just think she should be told."

My grandmother smiled. Karen's kids. It was true. We were ragamuffins. Gamma's nervous laughter, her desire to see our eyebrows grow out, the haircuts and shampoo for Christmas—they were honest, if confused, attempts to get her middle daughter into line. But she couldn't, so she turned her attention to us, her granddaughters. Lauren should have gone to Dominican, like Gamma did, and been disciplined by the nuns. (With whose money?) Layla shouldn't wear all that eye makeup. (But she wanted to go to cosmetology school.) There was something wrong with me, though no one could put her finger on exactly what. Still, we should all write our thank-you notes.

I was the only one of Karen's kids who ever took the thank-you-note thing seriously.

"I'll call and tell her," I said.

"Well, good then." Gamma tipped her head.

The sad thing is that I probably did.

Most journeys begin with a map. This one outlines a fantasy. What we wanted, and how things turned out to be.

In the summer of 1998, at the end of my twenty-seventh year, I realized my mother was tacking into disaster. The signs were all there: days spent in bed, no money for rent, no job, small cons. I had left a teaching job the fall before, traveled to Europe for the first time that spring, and was moving to New York City at the end of summer. I was looking forward to starting a new life. I liked new lives. Like *Little House on the Prairie*—across the river to build a sod house.

In the meantime, I had come home for a few months. See friends, visit family. Though I wanted to see my mother immediately, circumstance had kept us apart. So I found myself at my grandmother's in Kāhala, the fancy Honolulu neighborhood that used to be a pig farm.

Auntie Margaret, dying of lupus, lived there, in Gamma's add-on, next to the washer-dryer and the back door and the mail basket where private-school bulletins and other where-are-you-nows addressed to my mother collected. It was shady out there—lupus sufferers can't tolerate the sun—and under an awning, my aunt had set up for herself an outdoor kitchen, with a toaster oven and a refrigerator. Pill bottles and vitamins piled up next to the garden hose. Margaret had added a few gypsy touches: a purple orchid near the *pūneʻe,* a throw rug at the foot of the washer-dryer. We could have been in India or the Philippines. The air smelled like dust and leaves, there was a sink right there next to the croton hedge, and Margaret was a natural: pale and thin, dark blue eyes, dark hair, hovering here and there in a loose print dress, batiked overshirt, sandalwood beads.

Call it tropical colonials in reduced circumstances. Gamma, Catherine Deneuve–ish in a white collared shirt, pearls, slacks, tennis tan, served English muffins and canned salmon, sliced tomatoes on the side. She was polite and called me *Tara dear.* There was mint and a wedge of pineapple in the iced tea. Plantation iced tea, which was apt, since all of this, tarnished as it was, had been paid for by plantations: Kekaha and Waimea, both on the far west side of the island of Kauaʻi, stretching ten hot miles from the Waimea River, where Captain Cook first landed, to the end of the road, Polihale, the cliffs from which the spirits of the recently dead were said to have flung themselves in their journey to *pō,* land of darkness under the sea. For a century my mother's family, Norwegian immigrants named Faye, managed Kekaha—in the westernmost

town in the United States—and owned Waimea. They grew and milled
sugar, quite profitably, to ship to California for refining. They were, on
a very small scale, what they used to call King Cane.

Both plantations were nearly gone by the summer of 1998. Kekaha
would close for good in 2000 and Waimea had, in the eighties, added
Cottages to its name and become a hotel. Guests slept in the two- or
three-room board-and-batten houses once built for workers: the several
hundred thousand Chinese, Japanese, Portuguese, Puerto Rican, Korean, and Filipino laborers, among others, who wore around their necks
metal tags called *bango*s, Japanese for "number," engraved with digits that
announced the wearer's ethnicity, and by which they were paid, called
to order, housed, counted, and classified.

This was America, though, the fiftieth state, not *Indochine.* Tom Sel-
leck had once lived right down the road from Gamma. So had Jack Lord.
Other than a few remaining plantations, Hawaiian sugar was gone. Kahala Mall had a Gap and a Banana Republic and a Starbucks. The outdoor kitchen thing was set up so that when Gamma went on a trip she
could lock up the main house. My grandmother didn't trust her kids.
Kid. My mother, the one who never picked up her mail and had undue
influence over the sister with the floaty dress and dreamy eyes.

Normally that's whom we'd have been talking about over lunch:
Karen. Her latest offense (stealing Margaret's guitar or Layla's graduation
money from her father); why she was what she was (genes, drugs, the
sixties); what we could have done about her (nothing); whether she
could or couldn't change. (Yes, she could! No, not ever.)

That day in June, however, my grandmother was begging my aunt to
show me her fistula.

"Oh, come on, Margaret," Gamma cried, nodding at her daughter,
then at me. "This is your niece! Let her *see!*"

I had no idea what a fistula was, but it sounded terrible, and it
resided somewhere on Margaret's body, underneath her batiked shirt. I
shook my head at my aunt: I don't want to see the fistula. At my grandmother I smiled: I do want to see the fistula. Please let me?

Margaret sucked her teeth and sunk into her chair, her shoulders up around her ears.

"Listen to her. 'Show her your fistula! Show her your fistula!' God! I don't want to show everyone my fistula. It's private, Mom. My private business."

Gamma stared at my aunt and blinked. "Now, Margaret, just the other day at group you pulled down your shirt and went, 'Look at my fistula, everybody!' What about that?"

"I did not!"

"You certainly did!"

"I did not!"

"Oh yes you did."

It went on this way for a while. I could have been there or not there; it didn't matter. It was unpleasant, though, like watching lovers fight in public. So I looked past them, at the leafy entrance to the carport. A bell hung on the door that jingled when someone walked through it. When I was in second grade Gamma owned a white Malibu convertible. I don't remember anyone taking it out. It sat in the garage collecting dust. My mother and I slept at Gamma's in those days, when we didn't have anywhere else to stay, in the bachelor's apartment Margaret now inhabited. Gamma's was the first number I memorized; her address, out of all of them, I can still recite by heart.

Inside, Gamma's gold chains pooled in trays. Great-Aunties Mig-and-Ida's (they were never apart) Episcopalian plunder from chaperoned summers in Europe was tucked chastely into corners. White sheets, old perfume, powder in the bathroom. Queen Emma's lilies blocked Gamma's bedroom window so that the room was always in shadow and tinged green.

This was my grandmother: cool and shaded and off-limits.

This was my mother: She cut wires on alarms; she stole silver. She hocked her graduated pearls. She was a thief and a rebel and she was my hero.

Mom wasn't really welcome at Gamma's anymore. The doors were locked; the garage had its bell. Karen had never lived at Gamma's anyway. The rooms of my mother's childhood were gone—which was why, of course, I wanted to walk in them.

Keala'olu, the "Cool Road." Gamma's wasn't a large house—a cottage by mainland standards—and it wasn't on the nicest of streets. Rather, it sat on a street just off the nicest street: Kahala Avenue, running lazily, palm-fringed, along the water; but it was a good address. My great-grandfather, Hans Peter Faye Jr., bought it as a beach house sometime in the fifties, when there was money for such things.

The first Hans Peter Faye had started planting sugar in the swamps and rock fields of Mānā on Kauai in 1884, following an uncle who had come to the island—via Christiania (Oslo), New York City, and the California gold rush—thirty years before. Valdemar Knudsen, my great-great-great-uncle, had gotten a lease from the Hawaiian crown on fifty thousand acres in the mid-1850s. Knudsen's nephew, Hans Sr., my great-great-grandfather, drained the swamps and brought water down from the mountains. By the middle of the twentieth century, Kekaha Planta-tion was considered to be one of the most valuable pieces of land in the territory.*

The eight Faye children—their mother, Margaret Lindsay, was a first-generation Scotswoman from a north-shore plantation—had a privi-leged, if rustic, upbringing. Houses were plain and ample; school was at home. Recreation was found outdoors, on the beaches and in the ocean, supplemented by an occasional game of lawn tennis, a horseback ride, or a visit to one of the other plantation families on the west side. Sum-mer was spent in the mountains, where it was cooler. Hawaiian cow-boys, called *paniolo* after the California Spanish *vaqueros* who taught them

---

*Faye's descendants never owned most of the land they planted. When Hawaii became a ter-ritory in 1900, the lease, held by the Hawaiian crown, passed on to the U.S. government. Kekaha Plantation owned the mill, however, thereby guaranteeing a monopoly on the lease, which had been transferred from the Knudsens to the plantation corporation in 1880, with Valdemar Knudsen's widow, Annie Sinclair Knudsen, receiving a percentage of the sugar proceeds. Eventually the corporation bought the Knudsens out completely. At the time of the buyout, in the late 1910s, Annie Knudsen was being paid about $80,000—$1 million in today's dollars—for 8 percent of the sugar yields.

to ride, wended up the steep ridges of the Waimea Canyon toward Kōke'e with the children on their laps.

There was always help: teachers and governesses from Australia or the mainland; nurses in full kimono; cooks and washerwomen and butlers and handymen looking to get out of the fields. But for a large family with means, the west side was, perhaps, provincial and just too hot. Seeking a European education for his children, Faye moved the bunch of them, including nurses, back to Christiania in the 1910s, where they lived across from the palace and occasionally lent their car to the king. The outbreak of World War I in 1914 sent them back to the States; they settled in Berkeley, California. The 1910s and 1920s were good for sugar: Kekaha's acreage increased, as did the number of homes. There was the Berkeley house, a ranch near Sacramento, a cottage in Tahoe; and back on Kauai, the plantation houses, the Kokee cabin, and a beach house in Hanalei.

H.P. Jr. and his four brothers (Lindsay, Eyvind, Alan, and Alex) attened Choate, with my great-grandfather—we called him Gampa—going on to Yale, where he met my great-grandmother, G.G., from New York. H.P.'s sisters were educated as well. Ida and Isabel went to Wellesley, Mig to the Sorbonne. When they came home to Kauai from the mainland, Kainuma or Toshi would lay out fresh coconut milk and cookies, along with their clothes, washed and pressed and folded. My grandmother claims she never saw her own mother drag a mop, clean a floor, wash a dish.

Gamma and her two sisters, Eleanor and Bubsy, attended Punahou, a private school in Honolulu built in the 1840s for the children of missionaries. When Punahou was occupied by the Army Corps of Engineers during World War II, the girls got shipped by convoy to California to graduate. Gamma and Bubs to Dominican in San Rafael, Eleanor to Stanford. After her own stint on the East Coast, Gamma returned to Hawaii, choosing for a husband a *kama'āina* doctor's son—kamaaina means "old-timer," literally, "child of the land"—with a good pedigree. Brewster Morgan, of *Mayflower* descent, had just come home from the war. He had been shot down over the English Channel and imprisoned at Stalag Luft III, the camp made famous by Steve McQueen and *The Great Escape*—though he was liberated by the Americans before he could dig his way out.

He married my grandmother at his family's home at Polihiwahiwa, where they would then reside, Gamma spending the late forties and early fifties giving birth to four lovely children: Margaret (the Eldest), Karen (the Black Sheep), Gail (the Lost Child), and Brewster Jr. (Brew, "Brew Boy," the Mascot)—all monikers courtesy of Mom's Adult Children of Alcoholics literature. Gamma did amateur theater and modeled for Watumull's; she and Brewster Sr. went to dances at the Royal Hawaiian on weekends or to parties at the estates of the sugar planters. Down at the Outrigger Canoe Club members debated whether to extend club memberships to upwardly mobile Japanese; while up at Polihiwahiwa Brewster's mother, Gamma E., for Elsie, initiated her two eldest granddaughters into the mysteries of Episcopalianism—Polihiwahiwa had its own chapel—and the kids played at Jackass Ginger, the swimming hole across the street. Sometimes in the evenings the whole family would go for a walk.

It was a lovely life in paradise.

In 1952 H.P. Jr. was accused of tax evasion. Some called it a union conspiracy. Though never convicted Gampa resigned. He'd been president of American Factors, Kekaha's agent, and one of the Big Five.*

Everything was changing. Labor, following the success of Harry Bridges and the ILWU in California, got savvy and sent big lawyers to backwater Honolulu to make sure the provisions of the Wagner Act were being followed. Strikes came fast and were more debilitating. Every two years a plantation or dock called for higher wages. In 1946 the plantations had gotten rid of the camp houses, which was deemed a victory for the workers, who received higher wages and were no longer tied to

---

*By the 1930s the Big Five—Castle & Cooke, C. Brewer & Co., American Factors, Alexander & Baldwin, and Theo H. Davies—controlled 96 percent of Hawaii's sugar crop, as well as its major industries. Thirty men, through interlocking directorships, determined the fortunes of well over half of Hawaii's economy. It was said that my great-grandfather took the fall for much more powerful men high in the Republican party.

King Cane's paternalism. Then came the Democratic Revolution of 1954, in which the Republicans' hold on the territorial government was first broken; then statehood in 1959 and America's first Japanese-American senator, Daniel Inouye.

Gampa and G.G. moved back to Kauai to help with the plantation. There was one stoplight in Kekaha, and it was in the middle of a cane field.

Gampa Brewster's first bankruptcy followed. He sold truck-farming equipment to vegetable growers just as Hawaiian agriculture was beginning to be supplanted by tourism. Then another. Gamma and he lost their house at Polihiwahiwa. My grandmother, undone by the fall, sued for divorce. She and the children moved out to a house in Niu Valley that Margaret said smelled like mud, even though it had a pool.

Some time after that, Gamma's second husband, Andy Wuebel, an engineer who favored a Californian look, had the Kahala house remodeled. Until then it had been a typical Honolulu beach bungalow: view of the sixth hole of the Wai'alae golf course, wind-tossed palm trees, and a drainage ditch into which errant golf balls sometimes plopped like stunned birds. When I was a kid I was sent to collect them, a dollar a bag.

Now the house, like nearly everything having to do with my mother's family, seems stuck in time. Positively late sixties, when it was remodeled. It still has the same white-beige shag carpet; the same polished concrete *lānai;* the long-leaved, shiny Japanese grass fashionable with *mu'umu'u*-wearing society ladies and their gardeners. Shades of orange and green still swirl on the floor-to-ceiling drapes, low armchairs still crouch. There are the cantilevered gravel eaves, vaguely ranch style; the Orientalia in the courtyard—a pagoda, a bronze frog; the slatted wooden gates. Except for the mullioned glass cabinets in the kitchen, a trace of what had been, it was once altogether modern.

That day at lunch in 1998 there were signs of wear—Gamma's house is marked by the clutter of the aged—but this was a veneer. Really, the last thirty years could have disappeared, which would mean that I didn't exist. But this is a favorite fantasy of mine: that time could be stopped somewhere before I was born, before everything went sour with the plantation and my family and my mother. The pictures from back then looked so happy. The china was newer.

Back at lunch, Margaret wasn't going to take it any longer. She cupped her hands over her ears.

"Don't yell at me!"

Faulkner had stumbled to Honolulu. Plumeria instead of magnolia, but the set pieces were the same: the Eccentric, the Fading Beauty, the Angsty Grandkid, the mayonnaise salad, the birds moaning in the trees.

"Your voice!" Margaret cried.

Undaunted, my grandmother pushed on. "Margaret, it shows how serious lupus is. Lets people know what they're dealing with." She took a breath. "Not some silly disease."

I was wondering what disease Gamma would have considered silly when Margaret leaned forward in her chair. She was baring her teeth.

"My . . . private . . . business."

Gamma pulled back from the table and smoothed her hair away from her face. She sighed, resigned: a mother's trick.

"All right, Margaret. All right."

My grandmother was in a B movie once: *Seven Women from Hell,* a Cesar Romero flick about female prisoners of war in the Pacific. I haven't seen it but I can imagine. Cleavage spills out of camo; sadistic guards leer. They shot it on Kauai, at the Coco Palms, Guslander's place in Wailua. Tiki torches, monkeys, parrots on the wing. Karen, Margaret, Gail, and Brew ran around the cane fields that bordered the hotel while Gamma struck a pose. Something wide-shouldered, bustily American. Something that fixed attention. Something that required a natural brow.

Around the table we were quiet. Then Margaret pulled up a sleeve.

We all like to see something awful every once in a while, and there's usually someone to oblige us. "That's where the doctor sticks his needles," Margaret said, nodding. Red and purple scabs stippled the soft hollow of her elbow. She pulled aside her collar, turned her cheek.

"And this is my fistula."

A vein, thicker than a garden hose, pulsed from Margaret's neck to her forearm, ending in a patch of needle pricks, as if dammed. It was monstrous and looked very painful. I could see why my grandmother wanted me to see it. I was amazed.

I wanted to touch it. Instead I put my hand on my aunt's knee. "Does it hurt?"

She straightened her collar, rolled down her sleeve. She looked tired. "No. Oh, sometimes."

It was normal, this fistula, a side effect of dialysis. The vein balloons, weakens, and distends. Other people had it, diabetics and the like, Margaret informed me, though I was suspicious. It seemed more metaphorical.

We cleared the dishes, finished our iced teas. I was already telling a story about it. Accursed plantation owners—aunt's fistula—mother heading into ruin—daughter unable to get something she needed from the stuck blood. On islands things tend to get exaggerated. One feels, to be at the center of something—all that ocean around, like a frame. We were once rich; we had servants. We were the Royal Family of Mana. Gampa Great issued his own postage stamp. We took ships places and had summer homes and Chinese cooks. *'Ukulele*-strumming Hawaiians serenaded us at Christmas for *dalas,* and the *Pākē* brought ducks and strings of red firecrackers. Even our fistulas were beautiful.

We were on to dessert. Gamma had retired to her bedroom, to the bed that spread whitely under my favorite thing in my grandmother's house, an old-fashioned map for a child's room that's called "The Land of Make Believe." It's an illustration, something from the thirties. All of the characters from fairy tales are there: the princess, the king, the witch, the Wandering Jew. The castle is there in the middle, and on the outskirts, the dark forest.

And out on the lanai, a different kind of make-believe. Margaret was showing me pictures. The four blond Morgan kids, bucktoothed, arranged at Christmas. Mom and Margaret in matching striped T-shirts under a coconut tree. Mom dressed up in high heels and gloves with paste rings and tin bangles on. ("She liked to be fancy," Gamma says. "She was that kind of girl.") Newspaper clippings about Polihiwahiwa—"Damask table! Supreme hostess!"—various fair-haired and bobbed ancestors in dressing gowns. Gampa Great in plantation puttees and a romantic mustache on a white horse. My sisters and me in various stages of ragamuffinness. Mom with a weird perm.

The stories: How Gampa Brewster became bald. (From flying upside down during the war!) Gamma E. the High Episcopalian and her priest, Father Bray. (She had her own chapel! She carved the wooden crosses herself!) Margaret and Karen's magical childhood beside babbling Nuuanu Stream. The parakeets and hamsters and gardenias. The Pride of India tree in which my aunt started meditating at age five so as to be closer to the sky. The day Margaret lost her mind.

"It happened on this day here," she pointed to a picture. It was my aunt, sitting in lotus on a lava bank, facing the ocean. She's wearing a bikini; her eyes are closed. She looks just like my mother, but more solemn, like my mother's moontwin.

It was just after she started meditating seriously, Margaret told me, the first summer she was home from Dominican. She tried acid for the first time with John Pritchard, my mother's boyfriend. (It's true; the sisters were always, perhaps, too close.) He took Margaret to the Makapu'u lighthouse, on a cliff, to watch the lights spin. He brought along a book, *Crash Pad Chicks,* and a blanket. Not that kind of girl, Margaret commanded, "Take me home!" So they started back down the dark dirt road. A few minutes later she told him to stop the car.

"We were at the edge of a precipice! We would have been killed!"

Margaret sucked her breath in. A few crumbs rested at the corners of her pretty mouth. "It took me ten years to get straight. *Ten years.* Some never came out of it."

"Wow."

"And that's when God died. Poof! Just like that. My left brain was gone. All I could do was ceramics."

"Hmm."

"So this is when you were born." She tapped her finger on the page. "Nineteen sixty-eight."

I was born in 1970, but it's all right. God died in 1968, along with innocence and Bobby Kennedy. My mother had me a few years later. After that John Pritchard died. The hunk. The sandy-blond surfer with a taste for sisters. My mother's first love, blown to bits sometime in the seventies in a *kiawe* explosion. He had been on the Big Island, turning kiawe—Hawaiian mesquite, brought over in the 1800s to feed the cattle that fed the whalers—into charcoal. My mother had wept when she heard the news.

"John Pritchard," she told me once. "I should have married him when I had the chance."

Margaret and Karen. Karen and Margaret. Gamma once called them Siamese twins: born a year apart, always together. Pushed their beds close when they were little girls and in the well between them went fishing. Called each other, inexplicably, "Mare." Mare this, Mare that. Each Mare would be pregnant, husband away fighting a war, like their father had, and each would give birth to a puppy, a doll, what have you. Margaret named the sex. Or they would be lovers, kissing their own hands, running through the Nuuanu woods before the divorce, little Gail running after them. ("That's why Gail is mad at us," worries Margaret. "Poor Gail," Gamma clucks.) Margaret and Karen even grew to look like each other: dark-haired, almond-eyed, almost Spanish, whereas the younger two stayed blond and freckled.

But where Margaret was good, Karen was bad. Where Margaret was pious, Karen was profane. Rose White, Rose Red. One spit pearls, the other toads. At fifty-something, one would end up with her mother, the other on the street. It all got set up a long time ago. "It's been this way since she was seventeen," my grandmother once told me. "Honestly, I'm numb."

I have left my grandmother's house crying many times. That summer day four years ago—the day of Margaret's fistula, at the beginning of my mother's fall—I walked out dry-eyed. Past the door, the one with the bell on it. It was just a door—benign, dusty. Mourning doves cooed.

Past the pink hibiscus hedge along the edge of the golf course, past Aloha gas station. All this land had been owned by the son of the man who ran Lihue Plantation on Kauai. Hans Isenberg, from Bremen, came to Kauai in 1858 and asked my great-great-great-uncle for a job. Knudsen didn't have one, so Isenberg went to Lihue instead. He married a missionary's daughter—the plantation owner's daughter—and made a fortune in sugarcane. Isenberg's son would eventually move to Oahu, buy Waialae-Kahala, and turn it into a ranch. Now it was a golf course, one that I was driving slowly past. The Sony Open is played there for a purse of several million.

Before that, they say, the land wasn't owned by anybody.

Now there's a story.

The Island of Manhattan

August 2002   New York City

I AM GOING HOME. EASIER DONE THAN SAID. I AM PUTTING a bathing suit and a few T-shirts into a bag. I am packing sunglasses, swimming goggles I will never use, books, tennis shoes. People say how lucky I am to be going home to Hawaii, and it's true, but I can't help feeling sad. I am leaving some kind of life.

Seven million people visited Hawaii last year. Probably most did not learn to pronounce the place. How do you, anyway? *Hawayee,* like a tourist? Or Hawai'i—*Ha-vy-ee*—with the catch, the *'okina,* the glottal stop, like a little choking. *You pronouce Hawayee funny.* That's because I'm from there. Well, not really *from* there, only Hawaiians are *from* there, but I can say all the words that scare tourists: *humuhumunukunukuāpua'a, Kā'anapali, Ka'a'awa, Peepayleenay.* Once, for the parents of my best friend, Lauren Nevin, I made up a chant that sounded like real Hawaiian. We were in the Nevins' maroon LeBaron. It was 1985, sophomore year of high school. We had just celebrated Lauren's birthday at the Mauna Lani—"Heavenly Mountain"—hotel. Sweet fifteen. Miranda and Kama, our other best friends, were there. I entertained Rick and Liz Nevin, from Chicago, béarnaise and Frangos in their fridge, by chanting fake Hawaiian all the way back up the dark foothills of the Kohala

31

Mountains to our school, Hawaii Prep. Just sounds I made up: a weird watery voice, lots of glottal stops. Rick and Liz loved me. *One night she even entertained us with an impromptu Hawaiian chant!* This she wrote to the admissions director at Dartmouth College, a personal friend. Liz made me a copy of the letter: broken home, drug-addicted mother. I got in.

Now Lauren runs a homeless shelter for teens in San Francisco, Kama teaches yoga in L.A. Miranda had a baby and lives in Kamuela (Hawaiian for Samuel, the name of a former postmaster), the town where we went to high school. I live in New York. Outside of one childhood home, in the subdivision of 'Ulumahi ("Breadfruit Grove"), in the town of Līhu'e ("Cold Chill"), on the island of Kauai, Hawaii ("It is safest not to attempt translation of such forms," say Pukui, Elbert, and Mookini in *Place Names of Hawaii*), I have never lived in a single place longer. At night I dream about *Ha-vy-ee.*

Ua mau ke ea i ka 'āina i ka pono. The life of the land is perpetuated in righteousness. I am going home to find my mother. Easier said than done.

On Karen Morgan's fifty-second birthday in early May 2002, she called me from a hotel. She was in Honolulu. I was in New York. It was late, two A.M. or so, and I had just come from a party. I was a little stoned.

My mother is a drug addict, though I don't exactly know what kind. People have said heroin; all I have seen her do is coke. She says she's on methadone now. She has done other drugs, but they come up casually, like, *Oh yeah, back when I was doing crack.*

Let it be known: I'm careful around drugs. I have seen what they've done to my mother. And I'm rebellious, like any child, and how does the daughter of hippies rebel against her parents? She can only be punishingly good. So these are the drugs I stay away from: heroin, coke, Oxy, Percocet, Xanax, crack, methadone, hash, black-tar heroin, morphine. I smoked pot occasionally, though. Pot made me laugh and I talked a lot.

Even late at night, which is when my mother usually calls. Probably she had forgotten about the time difference. People from Hawaii often forget about the time difference. Perhaps it's because we have a whole time zone named after us. Hawaiian Standard Time, it's called. Five or six hours behind New York, depending on daylight savings. Hawaii doesn't observe daylight savings. We're too tropical. Winter is wetter; otherwise nothing really changes. This seems much more desirable now than it did when I was growing up, and all I wanted was change. Daylight savings, seasons, state lines to cross, leaves turning, snow, factories, coats, new houses, new people, nuclear plants: it all seemed good. I left at seventeen for school and kept leaving. New Hampshire for college, then Portland, Oregon, then Chicago. I traveled for a while, then New York. The longest I spent in an apartment was two years. Every other year I'd pack up and pare down and move, disburdened.

When you're from paradise, where do you go from there?

The night of her birthday Karen was at the Pagoda, where there's cable TV and double beds and the pantry downstairs sells booze and cigarettes. You can get a kamaaina rate at the Pagoda—eighty bucks a night.

"Ron got the room for me," Mom cooed. I hadn't yet met Ron, but I had seen wedding pictures. Layla sent them to me. She's how I hear about our mother these days. Layla goes to cosmetology school downtown; she used to run into Mom on her lunch break.

In the pictures Ron and Karen are at Honolulu Hale, City Hall, where you can get a Hawaiian priest and a lei for a couple bucks extra. Mom is pale, with surprising red hair. In some pictures she and Ron gaze fondly at their clasped hands, in others, at the Hawaiian priest. They both look very serious, as only drug addicts can.

TV voices tinkled in the background. "Ron's so sweet, Tara, he really is. I can't wait for you to meet him."

I hate talking to my mother when she's high. Not because it's so awful—I was a little high, after all—but because she denies it. She slurs her words or forgets what she's saying or runs on about her schedule or her fake job or how she's "helping people" downtown. And when I confront her, when I say clearly, *Are you doing drugs?* just like that, *Are you doing drugs?* she denies it. "No. God! How can you say that! God!"

She's so convincing I start thinking I'm crazy. And because I want to keep talking to her, because she is my mother and I love her, I start thinking I am.

"We're eating avocado sandwiches and watching television. We're in a hotel."

"You already said that."

I was irritated. Why was she in a hotel on her birthday? What happened to Anita's house, where she was before? Anita always took a few seconds to get the phone up to her mouth after she answered it. Lots of fumbling, heavy breathing, capped by a final depressing, *Hullo?* Once a teenaged boy answered. I asked for Karen. He mumbled, "Aw no, she doesn't come around here anymore."

My mother had become a person who "came around."

I leaned my hand on the wall beside the phone. It was smooth and pale yellow. Its pale yellow smoothness calmed me. I reminded myself of my circumstances: I lived in an apartment on the Upper West Side, which I was subletting from a professor of classics at Barnard. There were translations of Catullus on the bookshelves. I had DSL and a TV and a cell phone. I had a boyfriend, a graduate student in philosophy. He was sweet and smart. We had food in the refrigerator. Expensive food: prosciutto and Pellegrino water and smelly cheese and pâté and little pickles. I bought it with my own money. I paid my rent.

I ventured the question: "Why? Where are you staying?"

Mom took a bite of sandwich. "In the park," she said, chewing. "Downtown. The little triangle park, up by Longs."

It took me a second, but something came out.

"What?"

"Don't worry. It's safe. Gets wet at night though. Last night we covered ourselves with cardboard." She started laughing. "*Cardboard.* God, how pathetic."

Cardboard? In the park?

"How long have you been there?"

She pulled the phone away from her face. She'd always had the habit of talking to someone in the middle of a phone conversation. In the past it had been to Layla and Lauren, and usually it had something to do with getting their clothes off the floor, but they both moved out years ago. Now Mom had only Ron to take care of.

She called out somewhere past the phone. "*Rawn,* how long have we been staying in the park? Three weeks? Huh, *Rawn?*"

I didn't hear the answer.

"Three weeks." I could almost hear her nodding.

It was dark in my apartment. I noticed I was swaying.

"But why didn't you call me?"

"I'm sorry, honey. I'm sorry. My cell phone got stolen and we didn't have it for a long time but then it just got returned to us and the guy wanted twenty dollars. Anyway we paid one bill and now the cell's on for good and I promise I'm going to be in better touch. I promise. I'm eating ice cream every day. I'm a hundred and ten pounds. God I'm skinny. When you're homeless you don't want to eat. Anyway Ron buys me Ensure and we have a schedule—"

It was her voice. It had changed. It was raked over, excitable, the voice of someone who had a lot to explain.

I wished I hadn't smoked that pot.

"Okay. Well, happy birthday." It seemed like a good thing to say. "How are you?"

She cleared her throat. "Things have been rough, but Ron and I are doing better. Getting back on our feet. We went through a terrible time two and a half weeks ago but now our spirits are up. We've got goals now. A schedule. And we're working."

There was no way my mother was working.

"That's great."

"Margaret told you what happened, right?"

"No."

"Ron OD'd. Tried to kill himself. He was sleeping with my methadone counselor and I found out. I was devastated. Crushed. Really crushed. Anyway, we're really strong now. Much better."

I was still on the cardboard. Was it a box? A soda flat?

"Isn't there a shelter?"

She yawned. "Ron and I don't want to be separated, honey."

Something wild came out of my throat. I didn't mean it to. It was a wail. I was wailing. Fuck Ron. Fuck him. Just like always: Mom chose the man. He'd use her and screw her and take her away from her kids. Then he'd dump her or worse, make her crazy, like the last one, Terry, the male nurse.

Ron was a loser, a homeless fucking junkie, and he was going to take her down with him.

Her voice was hoarse. "Honey, don't cry. Don't cry."

"Are you okay though? Are you okay?"

"I'm okay, I'm okay. Ron, aren't we okay?"

This time I heard him.

"We're okay!" He was yelling. He had a bum's voice: pack and a half, at least. The hotel room sounded small, like a closet. "We're on our way up!"

"Did you hear that? We really are. On our way up. I'm eating ice cream every day. I'm going to find a job and Ron's going to find a job— right, Ron?—and things are going to change. We're doing it for our daughters. Ron has a daughter. Eighteen years old. Lives in California. Did you know that?"

I didn't know a fucking thing about Ron. Ron could get run over by a truck for all I cared. In fact, I hoped Ron would get run over by a truck. Then maybe my mother would get out of the park.

"No."

"Yes, he does, and we're doing it for you guys. Now, please don't cry. Don't cry. I can't take it when you cry."

She used to like it. It used to make her feel like I missed her.

I stopped and wiped my eyes and cleared my nose and told her I'd send her money for her birthday. She said, "That sounds good," and started to give me the address of the post office box where she and Ron got mail, but when she got to the number she spaced it. "I've got it in my stuff," she trailed off, and I said, "Okay, call me when you've got it." She said, "I will, honey. I'll call you tomorrow."

The next day I waited for her to call. She didn't, so I went to work. This was in my bedroom. I had just finished a book for recently gradu-

ated college students—a how-to thing. How to get a job, how to deco-
rate your apartment cheaply, how to meet people and get a checking account and a credit card and make macaroni and cheese.

I don't think my mother ever had a credit card.

For a few weeks, I went about my life. I worked distractedly. I made
lunch for my boyfriend; I went to yoga; I got out and smoked cigarettes
and laughed. I thought about the cardboard, but I was used to separat-
ing myself from difficult things. And I was far from Hawaii, five thousand miles away. I did not know whether it was raining there, or sunny,
or hot. In New York it was spring. The trees along the Hudson were in
bud. I watched the mist unrolling in the morning and clearing in the afternoon. I didn't know where Triangle Park was, so I couldn't imagine
it. In New York I was insulated and anonymous. It's what I'd always liked
about the city. Home was too full of ghosts.

Karen finally called on Mother's Day. I had just had brunch with my
boyfriend's mother. We were in the East Village, shopping. I stepped
onto the sidewalk.

"Hi, honey. Hi." My mother was giggling.

I waited till she finished. "Happy Mother's Day."

"Oh, thanks."

Silence, suspicious shuffling.

"What are you doing?"

"Just getting coffee. I have the number."

"What?"

"The number. For the post office box."

I had started paying for my mother's storage in January. Every month
I'd send A-American Storage a hundred dollars. This wasn't a good sign.
My mother never used to ask me for money. Now she was reminding
me about sending more. Fortunately, Ron had a preferred customer number with Western Union so the transfer was made much easier.

I recorded the address on a pink sheet of paper I held in my hand.
Later, when I got home, I transferred it to the book where all of my
mother's addresses and phone numbers are listed under "M," for Morgan, though it's legally Brody now, Ron's name, and before that it was

Daniels, Layla's father's name, and before that it was Smith, my father's name. She never got married to Lauren's. Each address had a line through it, some zigzagged, some straight. I put the post office box number at the end, in pen, next to her on-again-off-again cell number.

Now the post office box has a line through it, and the cell is disconnected.

"Thanks, honey. Thank you so much."

"I hope it helps."

"It helps. It helps to have a family. Layla came today, you know. It was fun."

My sister had made her first visit to Triangle Park that day. She called me later and told me about it, trying to laugh. She sat in the grass with Mom and Ron and someone Layla called Pakalolo Bob, though that wasn't his name. She just made it up for the story because *pakalōlō* means marijuana and Bob seemed like an appropriate name for one of my mother's new friends.

"My friends on the street can't believe I'm from here," Mom said before she hung up. "I'm *from* here."

The packing went so easily this time. I didn't have much—a few boxes. Except for a desk, I don't own any furniture, not even a bed. Which makes two of us.

The Age of Aquarius

1970   Waialua, Oahu

I AM OF TWO MINDS ABOUT THE PAST. PART OF ME BELIEVES it's something to be left behind. This I inherited from my father. In 1966 he left Santa Monica for Hawaii and never looked back. If he ever moves to Mexico like he keeps promising, it will be the same story.

Then there is the part of me that is stuck, like my grandmother with her plantation table manners, or Auntie Margaret sitting in lotus, the lava rock under her thighs leaving its impression like thousands of tiny irregular teeth marks. A living past was my mother's gift to me, the kind of gift that a thirteenth godmother might give: one that draws blood, given by someone who wasn't invited.

Karen Morgan sucked her arm when she was a kid. Lying in bed, sitting at a desk, she sucked at the crook of her arm, inside of her elbow. She bit the skin; she could almost taste blood. She sucked so much her teeth turned buck.

She was a funny-looking kid, outspread teeth and arms and legs, unruly blond hair, deep-set blue eyes. She liked to dress up. She liked to wear eyeshadow and gloves and stockings. My great-aunt Eleanor says you could tell she was going to be wild, even from the beginning.

In high school Karen had skinny legs, freckled from the sun: lean, long calves, soft thighs. She had a narrow stomach; she wore her bikini Gidget-style, three inches below her belly button, two triangles on the top. She bleached her hair with lemon juice. She ironed it until it was smooth as thread on a loom. She had a beautiful body. She liked to be with boys and they liked to be with her. She had lots of boyfriends: Pat, the son of an ex-governor, John Pritchard, the Dawson brothers. Margaret might date one brother and she the other. She liked to dance. Once her best friend, Connie, took her to a party at a Punahou P.E. teacher's house. The men gave the girls beer; everyone smoked grass.

When she was fifteen Karen made a decision. She said she looked at the world around her and decided she didn't like what she saw. She was reading Ginsberg, Huxley, Dostoyevsky, Camus. *The Joyous Cosmology*. *This Is It*. Then and there she decided to drop out. *Fifteen! I was fifteen!* It was a conscious decision, a conscious feeling. *Karen. My thoughts.*

"At least I can look back and say that. At least I can look back and say, 'There. That's when it started. That was my choice.'"

Just before her eighteenth year, sometime in the spring of 1968, my mother called her mother and told her she was pregnant. Karen was on Maui, where she'd run off to. She'd been gone for a few days. What was she was thinking she'd find there? The islands of Hawaii aren't far enough away to be truly distant. It was a runaway, but a pathetic sort of escape, this trip to Maui. She called her mother—she was frightened—and said, "I'm pregnant." Gamma told her to come home, and my mother did. She visited a doctor in Honolulu to see if she could get an abortion. He put his fingers inside her vagina and asked her if it felt good.

Decisions were swiftly made. Karen would stay with a Mrs. Rasmussen, an older woman who could look after her in San Francisco. The baby would be given to a good family. They would tell her teachers at Punahou that she was going to art school.

In San Francisco my mother would memorize the address and know it thirty years later as 2020 Judah Street, where she lived with Mrs. Rasmussen and learned to make a pie. Judah Street veers close to Golden

Gate Park. Mom took walks by herself there, a pregnant girl with a pixie haircut, down the dark chutes of cypress, witnessing 1968, all the while getting bigger. Once a man exposed himself to her: a man in a long tan coat, a regular flasher.

After the birth the nurses made a mistake. They let Karen hold the baby for a while. She tried to nurse her daughter, though her milk hadn't come in. "Can I name her?" my mother asked. The doctors said she could. Karen would never forget this. She called it bonding. Then the lawyer arrived, and the forms. She named the baby Elsie, after Gamma E., the grandmother she felt especially loved by. She said she didn't know she was old enough to keep her.

She was young—just eighteen. It was the Summer of Love. Forgive her.

Gamma took Mom to a restaurant across the street from the hospital. They ate fish and chips. Then she and Aunt Eleanor and Aunt Isabel took Karen to the Tahoe house to recover. The four women hiked there, under the bright blue sky and the faraway California sun. Isabel wore a dress and stockings and carried a basket. When they got to a lake Eleanor stripped to her bathing suit and dove in. Karen's milk came in after that.

Punahou never let my mother back in. Instead she enrolled at Hawaii School for Girls, down the street from a beach called Sans Souci, at the edge of Waikiki. She worked on her ceramics. She told me Jimi Hendrix tried to pick her up while she was walking to the beach one day. Then she met my father, who remembers her uniform. They had parties where he and his friends and she and her friends would be naked. "We were all so innocent," she would say. And in her high school yearbook—the pixie cut, the hopeful face—she'd say that she would like to go to Greece someday and that she liked psychology.

I was born in September of 1970 in a plantation town called Waialua on the north shore of Oahu. My birth happened at an awkward time for my mother and father. I've asked Mom about it only once. She said I was conceived under a mirrored ceiling at Michael Butler's house in L.A.

Michael Butler produced *Hair*. My father was his assistant, which I think involved scoring drugs. Dad says that he had dinner with Tina Turner and that Barbra Streisand is very beautiful because of her large nose, and that if you saw Charles Manson at a party, like my father had, you could tell he would do what he did.

"Kirk dropped me off at the hospital and then picked me up again when it was over. I went back to our little house after that. He'd been partying with a bunch of his buddies and there were bongs and beer cans lying all over the house."

My father does not disagree. His best friend from Santa Monica, Jim Carter, told him it would take hours. Anyway, he had to get the money together to pay the bill.

This doesn't paint a very responsible portrait of my father—missing my birth, twenty-three, high. It could be, of course, that my mother is lying. Even after all these years she's angry with him for leaving us "with nothing, with forty dollars."

I make my father argue back: *But I was just a kid! A punk surfer from Santa Monica. Owned a vegetarian restaurant, for chrissakes. The Summerhouse, man. Employed your whole fucking family.*

Margaret cooked, Gail waited on tables, Brew washed dishes.

The Summerhouse. It's got hazy sunbeams around it, like in a Warren Beatty movie. Auntie Margaret makes tahini avocado sandwiches and sings. Dad walks into a back office where one of his partners was supposed to have been paying the bills. All he sees are piles of paper, unopened envelopes, invoices on the floor, and there in the middle, his partner and a little mountain of cocaine.

"What was I going to do?" Dad strokes his mustache. "The sixties were crazy. It's like a friend of mine from back then told me: If you remember them—"

"But I was born in 1970," I say.

"You get the point."

The fact that all of this begins under a mirror is a good indication of how the rest of it will proceed.

Kirk Smith was a surfer boy from Santa Monica, Pacific Palisades to be exact. His father, Eldon, was the son of a Wisconsin Welsh pastor. Eldon contracted polio as a child and walked for the rest of his life with a cane, but that didn't stop him from trudging uphill both ways in the snow in order to wait tables and put himself through medical school. He was a doctor in Burma, India, and China during World War II, then he moved out to California and became an anesthesiologist to the stars.

When I was much older, I asked my father to tell me stories about that time and he did. He told me about Eldon, from Wausau, Wisconsin, and his mother, Patricia, from Ludington, Michigan, and the boat that steamed across Lake Michigan between them. Eldon collected guns and played bagpipe music, and each year took his two sons and two daughters to dude ranches. Patricia was depressed, having given up her own career as a doctor to raise children. Once she had been in love with a man back in Ludington. She had even married him. Her father, an Irish attorney named Turk, made her get the marriage annulled.

Dad's stories are the stories of someone who had the first television on his block. *Howdy Doody, The Patty Duke Show.* They are designed as stories; they are tied to American events. He once stole a gullwing Mercedes from a neighbor's garage. He signed his father's name to a prescription of LSD before it was illegal and distributed it in his school. He hired grannies and grandpas to drive marijuana-filled station wagons up from Mexico. His father was at the hospital the night Marilyn Monroe died. "The place was crawling with Feds," Dad tells me, cutting his eyes.

They lived in a fabulous Spanish mansion. The living room was huge and had vaulted ceilings. They would sit down to dinner and afterward his mother would ring a little bell and Jesse, their maid, would clear the dishes.

"The kids I grew up with all went crazy," my father tells me.

In 1962 the script had not yet been written. Granddad plays bagpipe music; cleans guns. Patricia rings her little bell. Kirk spends his California school days stoked in a leather jacket, spinning bottle caps, watching eight-millimeter surf movies in the Pali High auditorium. The Smiths take their first trip to Hawaii.

★   ★   ★

They went to Waikiki. The first time my father walked along the beach at Queen's Surf he thought, *I've been here before.* One of Cook's men, or a castaway. Then the family got back to California, and a Porsche my father had elected not to ride in sailed off the Pacific Coast Highway on its way to Mexico. Everyone in the car died. Dad shows me a book: *What Really Happened to the Class of '65,* about Pali High. *He's dead, she's dead. Suicide. She's dead.*

Jim Carter suggested they go back to the promised land. Kirk agreed. J.C. left for Honolulu to find a house. My father finished school, then followed. On the flight he got bumped to first class. The stewardesses fussed over him, got him drunk. J.C. found free lodging down the road from Sans Souci in exchange for a little work. The store up the block accepted their IDs. Days J.C. and Kirkaby surfed, nights they wandered down to Queen's and listened to the trios play.

No one missed them in California so they stayed. My father would say he had the feeling of coming home.

The first time my father saw my mother, she was in her girls' school uniform—baby blue skirt grazing downy knees, white middy—walking toward Sans Souci from Hawaii School for Girls. Mom was eighteen and had already had a baby, Kirk was twenty-one. The second time was when she showed up at a party he threw at his apartment. She got under the covers with him in the morning, leaving her uniform crumpled on the floor.

She was Gamma and Gampa's flower of the islands. He was a "coast *haole*"—white person—a kind of pest, like cutworm or cane borers.

They dated for a year. When Karen turned nineteen my father took her to his childhood pediatrician in L.A., a Dr. Small. "Kirk," Dr. Small said. "There's good news and there's bad news."

His mother tried to talk him out of it. J.C. tried to talk him out of it. "Come with me to Kauai," J.C. said on the way to the church. "Come surfing."

My father declined. He would do the right thing. Karen got married in a nightgown. I have a copy of the picture. A few years ago she laminated it at Kinko's. She has short hair and a long, pretty face. Her lips are wide, her light eyes curious. She's wearing a pikake head lei; a ribbon encircles her neck. She carries a bouquet of roses and daisies.

"People made fun of me because I got married in a nightgown," she once told me. "I didn't know. I liked it."

The thought of my mother laminating a photocopy of a picture I did not see until I was nearly thirty makes me sad. Her eyes, loose and gentle, make me sadder.

The ceremony was at St. Andrew's Cathedral, the reception, at my grandmother's house in Kahala. Gamma served tea sandwiches and Champagne. The whole affair was over in a few hours.

They moved out to Waialua Plantation, out past Wahiawā, almost to Hale'iwa—what they call country to Honolulu's city. When my mother was a girl, all the way out to country—twenty, thirty miles—cane fields unrolled, each field with its straight-line road etched in red from highway to mountain. The fields did not stop until they reached those mountains, and though what was past them looked mysterious from afar, it always turned out to be the same imported scrub you see anywhere in Hawaii: guava, lantana, kiawe if there were cattle around. At the ends of a few of the roads were the estates of the big sugar planters, where as a child my mother went to parties with her parents. The Dillinghams at Mokulē'ia, the Browns (their estate was in the middle of a cane field), all with their rows of royal palms. The adults got drunk, the kids played in the pool. Everyone went home sunburned.

On some plantations Japanese workers were allowed only so far up the manager's road. Plantation police carried guns and bullwhips. But I was born at the tail end of sugar, when workers were starting to move to jobs at hotels, and there was no one to fill the plantation houses, which were small like Monopoly houses, and which clustered in camps (Filipino camp, Korean camp, Japanese camp) like Monopoly houses, too.

Karen and Kirk lived in dairy camp, where identical two-bedroom cottages squatted in rows on wide grassy alleys, and there was enough room in the backyard for a garden. Waialua was pleasant. Dogs and chickens ran around loose; mango and lychee trees gave fruit and shade. The rent was eighty bucks a month. The roof was corrugated tin. Water dripped down the grooves in the metal and ringed the house in red mud.

"It was a hippie house," my mother once told me. "We painted it different colors, and I fixed it up. I worked on my house. I built things. Did yard work, stayed home. I didn't do drugs. The day before you were born I mowed the lawn."

She laughed when she told me this. I laughed, too. For some reason, this seems to be just the thing to do the day before having a baby. Wash the dishes, do the laundry, mow the lawn.

I liked to sit outside on the porch steps with the shoes. As in Japan, in Hawaii we take off our shoes before we enter the house, and so at the Waialua house—it's evening, the porch light shines—I sit on the lanai and play with the shoes. The adults are in their early twenties. They smoke pot, drink beer, make jokes.

"What's this?" Margaret asks me, pointing to a slipper.

"Shoe! Shoe!"

My mother argues: "Your first word was sky." Or maybe she says, "Your first word was mommy." In any case, sky and mommy both mean mommy.

She left their VW bus in the middle of the highway. It had run out of gas, or broken down—my father was never good at taking care of cars—so she left it there in the road for someone else to deal with. Dad calls it my mother's plantation mentality, though she never actually grew up on the plantation.

So traffic backs up across the Haleiwa Bridge. A cop calls in a license plate. At dairy camp maybe a phone rings off and on for a day.

"Where's the car?" my father asks.

"Squeaky's borrowing it," or, "It's at the shop," or, "What?"

I know my mother. My mother lies. My father says, half gently, half seriously, that, no, she does not lie, she just convinces herself that what she says is the truth.

We moved around a lot after that.

"Your father didn't like to see me breast-feed."

This is her explanation of why he left. It's a strange one, and it makes me feel uncomfortable. I have spent twenty-five years making sure I could determine my life separately from the fortunes of my mother; to be drawn up so close to her, even in memory, makes me feel woozy.

He went to the Big Island. He said he'd send for us when he had a job. After a while Mom followed him. He told her he didn't want to be married anymore. She went back to Honolulu and moved in with a friend.

I have only one picture of my parents and me together. It is at my college graduation. I am standing between them. Mom has just gotten out of rehab. Her hair is blow-dried and styled like Gamma's, in voluminous blond waves. She's wearing a cross around her neck. My father is smiling. Both of them look happy. I am nervous in the middle.

An astrologer once explained it to me: Daughter of Saturn and Uranus, clashed. The energy that created the sixties. Your sun sign overshadowed. A child of baby boomers. Not like the first boom, which created everything, but the first of the little booms, where everything starts to disappear.

The Blue Lagoon

December 2000   Iceland

CHRISTMAS 2000, I WENT TO PARIS WITH DEBBIE. WE climbed the Eiffel Tower and shopped at Fauchon. She bought me perfume and paid for my hotel room. We spoke English in French accents and opened presents together on Christmas Eve. That night my mother wrote me an e-mail saying how Terry had broken up with her and she wanted to die. It was unpunctuated and written entirely in capital letters. I sat at the hotel's computer and tried to write her back, but the keyboard was different, and everything came out wrong. So I called her.

"You just want her money. You've always liked her better."

"No, Mom. No. I love you."

"No one loves me."

"I do, Mom. I do."

I stopped in Iceland on my way back. I stayed for four days. I watched Euro MTV and ate fish paste for breakfast. In the afternoon, right before the sun set at two, I walked to the neighborhood hot pot— pools heated geothermally—a few blocks away. I sat in the water and watched pink Icelanders walk around, steaming. No one goes to Iceland for Christmas. I was alone and on the opposite side of the world from where I came from.

I wished for a boyfriend.

He came from the mist, a philosopher from Pittsburgh. He was perfect. Two years together and we spent half of it apart.

This was both our faults.

Coming to See About You

✼

1977   Lihue, Kauai

I WAS SEVEN WHEN I FOUND OUT MY MOTHER HAD FOR-mally abandoned me. The moment, of course, is fixed: the hinge from which swings the rest. Hitherto, I was one person; afterward, an-other—the person I am now. What happened was simple, if colorful. My mother was a heroin addict, her second husband, a South African surfboard shaper named Neil Daniels. We lived at Pipeline on Oahu's north shore. The year was 1977. The soundtrack was *Rumours* or Rod Stewart. Joints were passed around in crab claws. Hepatitis and scabies were passed around, too. There were guns and drugs and surfers and we knew an unusual number of Peruvians. My mother, though married—she says it was to get Neil a green card—wanted to take me to Texas with her boyfriend, a marine named Owen. She told Gamma about her plan, who told my father. Though my grandmother says she made my father promise to call my mother before he did anything, my father did not call my mother. Instead, he came to get me one afternoon while she was at the store. He flew me to Kauai, where he was living with his new wife, Debbie. He sued for custody; Karen didn't show up to court. I never lived with her again.

I never said good-bye. One minute I was sitting under a plumeria tree making mud cakes with Seabring Paty; the next I was on a plane with my father. He ordered a juice; I started crying. I did not stop for a long time.

After the separation I hung on to an idea of the living Karen—what child does not cling to the fantasy of reconciliation?—but my real mother would fade eventually, and memory would take over. A Karen ghost, pretty and laughing, brown-haired, blue-eyed, sitting in the sun.

Memories were what would orient me. I had never had memories before. I had just lived: here or there with my mother, and this or that man, in this or that place.

On days my mother and I didn't have anything else to do—most days before 1977 were like that—we went to the Pacific Club down the Pali from Nuuanu. Gampa Brewster was a member.

The Pacific Club had a small pool in back, and tables around which aluminum chairs clustered unevenly, as if no one could be bothered to push them in when they left. Mom sat in her chaise in a bikini and got herself warm. We knew the waitresses by name. We ordered Cokes on Gampa Brewster's tab and I practiced my flips.

One day I cracked my chin on the side of the pool, split it to the bone. I was taken to the hospital, where they wanted to sew me up. I screamed. There wouldn't be any needles, I made my mother promise. They took her to the side.

Adults think children can't hear but they can.

"We can use a straitjacket," the doctor said, and the nurse appeared with one in her hands. "Or we could use a butterfly bandage. There will be a scar."

Here was a moment when she could have failed me and she didn't.

"Yeah," Mom said. "A butterfly bandage. Let's do that."

On other days, Mom, a boyfriend named Eric, and I walked a few hundred yards through the kiawe forest in Waianae to a wooden catchment tank to swim. Eventually someone would chase us out, but until they did, we climbed the twenty feet up to the opening and swam in the rainwater. Mom and Eric hooked their arms around the rim, as if it were a hot tub. Eric's blond mustache dripped; he looked like the Marlboro Man. I dove under and swam between them.

Down further makai Auntie Margaret lived in her tepee, among trees strung with tarps, like sails stilled by the forest. A dilapidated house hid somewhere farther back, and people sat in folding chairs and hammocks, playing ukulele or smoking joints. Margaret walked through the green woods naked except for her slippers.

I played with a white tomcat, Hulk, who hunted mongooses during the day. I offered him tuna out of a can. He came close; I pulled it away.

A man near the house watched me.

"No tease the cat," he said.

I did, and Hulk bit my arm.

Someone scooped me up. Too late. At the hospital I repeated what I had heard: "Butterfly bandage?"

I have a scar where Hulk bit me. Two fine white lines, tiny incisions exactly an inch apart. They've grown with me all these years.

There was a party for my mother's marriage to Neil Daniels at a hotel, the 'Ilikai, where Elvis used to stay. I once met a man who had been a room service waiter at the Ilikai. He said Elvis ordered a whole cart of breakfast every day: a few plates for himself, one for Priscilla.

Someone brought me to the party, Gampa Brewster perhaps. We were late. Mom touched my head and gave me a hug. She wore a pikake lei and a cream dress with an embroidered yoke. She smelled like perfume and smoke.

We moved to the north shore then. Neil Daniels lived in an A-frame set up ten feet from the water to accommodate winter waves. Inside, I opened doors that shouldn't have been opened. Behind this one—*oops!* Mom hunched over a table doing lines. Behind another, her and Neil having sex. Her legs were wrapped around his back and she wore one of his collared shirts. I watched them until she told me to close the door.

"Little girl, you have to knock." Neil said *hef* and *nook*.

We left eventually. She told me she hated Neil Daniels, that he was a bastard. She used that word often, *bastard*. It was a favorite, even though as applied to Neil it meant nothing.

I like it as dramatic as it sounds: *hostage*. Mom and me blindfolded, gagged with dirty white sheets. My hands are tied behind my back. I wriggle and chew, kick against the chair. I am seven, but I am tough! Mom's head droops. The wooden walls of the A-frame are brown and sunlit, like forest moss. I am able to wriggle free from my bonds because I am so small. Who would suspect me, looking as much as I do like a hippie Shirley Temple?

I am Kikaida, I am Momotaro the Peach Boy. I am Cinderella and Checkers and Pogo and the cast of *The Lost World,* all the kids on *Sesame Street,* Spider-Man, Robin Hood, Skipper, Baby Alive, Mr. Magoo. I am blind and I can still get us out of this mess. I am Samantha the Witch and Tabitha and Jeannie and the Superfriends. I am all these things and I free my mother, and we walk down the road, past the pole houses. The sun is just setting, and the edges of the road are turning into sand, and we are free.

I know the real story now. Neil owed some money, maybe to the *hui.* One day someone came over and wouldn't let my mother and me leave until the whole thing could be worked out. I was six or seven. After that we left Neil's for good and moved to Renee Paty's, down at Chun's Reef. My father told me about it many years later. "You don't remember that?" I didn't. "Neil was into some bad business and you and your mother got held hostage until he could work it out."

All I remember is that one day Neil hit her and she hit him back. Then we split. Mom's face was bloody and she sobbed. *Fucker. Fuck him!* Blood and mucus leaked from her nose. We had no cash. We waited for a bus; the driver let us on. We sat in the very last seats. People came by and asked, "Are you okay, lady? Are you okay?" She said yes to everyone.

The north shore breezed by. Ironwood trees arced dusty green and feathery into the road. We opened a window and I made myself invisible.

* * *

A few months later I was on Kauai, my scabies gone. I was walking through the parking lot of the Wilcox School cafeteria, reading a letter from my mother. She had sent me an album, pictures she had saved from my childhood. There was a photograph of my father, and one of me on a horse, and one in a canoe, and a few at G.G. and Gampa's in Waimea. My favorite was of my mother and me in the water. She's holding me. Her dark blue eyes are alight, the water around us is sun-dappled. I am looking down, happily oblivious to her, concerned only with what was moving under me: the water, my hand splashing.

The ocean was a constant. The ocean didn't go anywhere. It surrounded one completely, as a home might have for another girl.

Nine Lives

✹

August 1998   Honolulu

WE WERE EATING FRIED RICE AT DANNY'S CAFÉ, A FEW blocks from my father's house in Kaimukī. We were talking about Europe. I was old to have just had a European adventure: twenty-seven already. Friends from college went at seventeen. But Europe seemed a long way from Hawaii, and anyway, going to New Hampshire for college was a little like going abroad.

My mother and I sat by the window. Sun spilled over us. She was warm, and laughed.

"Dutch are really neat, really open-minded," I said.

"Oh yeah, I knew a Dutch guy. Dutch guys are kind of far-out, aren't they? This guy wanted to marry me."

"Oh really?" I said, though I wanted to tell *my* Dutch-guy story: the one about Maarten, and the steak and strawberries and sitting on his patio a few hours before the sun went down in Amsterdam and how he had taken me to the bus in his small car, which looked like a bug.

"Mmm-hmm." Mom scraped her teeth on her lips. Then she smiled. "This Dutch guy, he was from The Hague. He wanted to marry me. Simone set me up with him."

In the one picture I had seen of Simone, she hung over a small wading pool in which her son played. They were in Texas, where my mother moved after I left her. Live oaks twisted in the background. Simone was an elfin blonde, with fringy bangs and pointed teeth and a pointed chin. She wore a bikini and she was tan. When she leaned over the pool, smiling, her breasts fell between her arms.

"Was Simone a prostitute?"

Mom ate another bite of her fried rice and laughed. "Oh yeah, bigtime. She made big bucks. It was, you know, a *paid* date. But he wanted to take me back to The Hague, take Layla, too, and marry me. And he was serious." She nodded. "He wrote me letters and everything."

"I guess Dutch people are really open-minded."

I didn't know what else to say.

"I should have been paid for all that. It's the only thing I've ever been good at."

She laughed and looked up to the ceiling. "The only thing."

The waiter came around to give us more coffee and my mother said, "No, thanks," and I said, "That's not true, Mom."

Really I did not think it was.

Probably we were always waiting for her to fall. I was.

Here is how my sisters and I found out my mother had relapsed: it was night, summer, 1998, the same summer of lunch at my grandmother's house and Margaret's fistula. I was back in Honolulu for a few months and had agreed to sleep at Mom's, though I didn't have a room. I always liked to have a room; thus, I never slept at Mom's. This night was the exception. She begged, and I felt guilty.

I often felt guilty about not sleeping at Mom's, especially as it pertained to my sisters. Layla and Lauren had no choice about where to sleep, because Mom was the only family they had. Layla's father, Neil, was back in South Africa; Lauren's dad was in Houston. Once Lauren's father asked her: *How do I know you're really mine?* Together, my sisters had seen their fathers maybe ten times. This wasn't totally their fathers' fault. Karen had left both men even before their daughters were born.

Layla, twenty, picked me up from my father's house in Kaimuki.

When she arrived she was barefoot and wearing pajamas. She hunched—she looked harried—as did I. She was going to school down the road at a community college. She was trying to get her associate's degree. Layla is shy. Mom took her every year to fill out her financial aid forms. "Why don't you write your dad?" I asked. "Maybe he'll send you money." My sister just shrugged.

We are both dark-haired, light-eyed, large-chested, from Gamma, tending to plump. We both hunch. We look harried. But we are gentle. Layla is very gentle, more than I. My sweetness can be thin, like a candy coating.

Straight to Mrs. Delacruz's in Mom's uninsured station wagon. The lights of Honolulu floated by, gold against black. The air was warm. Layla tapped the accelerator. I sang along with the radio. If Lauren had been in the car she would have been singing, too. We get it from Auntie Margaret, Mom says. All of us talented like that.

Up at Mrs. Delacruz's Lauren stayed in bed till eleven. The house was dark, tucked into the bottom of Punchbowl, but it was cheap and Mom had chosen it so that Lauren could be close to school, though proximity wasn't seeming to help. Lauren slept in; Mom slept in. A few weeks before, I had awoken my mother at one in the afternoon.

"I think Lauren is smoking pot," she had whispered.

Lauren drew pot leaves in the journal I bought her for her sixteenth birthday. She listened to Bob Marley and drew pot leaves.

"Lauren *is* smoking pot."

"She likes it," Mom had said. "She says it makes it easier for her to have fun at parties."

There were good things about having a cool mom: birth control at sixteen, sips of wine coolers, *It's okay if you don't have a license, you can still drive.* Talking about Lauren smoking pot was not one of them.

At Mrs. Delacruz's Van Morrison was playing; Mom was drinking Chimay and erratically swing-dancing in front of the stereo. She wasn't supposed to be drinking Chimay, but, as Karen liked to point out, her problem was never alcohol.

"Tara!" She giggled. "Come dance!"

Lauren, loosely arranged on the floor next to her, snorted. She had lately been into cross-country, training by strapping rock-filled plastic bags around her ankles and running up Punchbowl. Mom wouldn't buy her weights, Lauren said, though perhaps this was less cruel than practical. Our mother might have been able to afford them then—she was still working—but she knew her youngest daughter. Lauren is a bit distractible.

Now, she was on the floor, groaning, wrapping and unwrapping damp industrial paper towels around her thighs. Her blond hair fell over her shoulders. She smelled like Tiger Balm.

I sat down on a futon to watch her. "Rub my back," Layla said, and positioned herself in front of me.

Mom stopped dancing. "Lauren looks just like me when I was her age," she said, looking down at us.

It was true—the lithe thighs, the surfer-girl shoulders—but something worried me about this statement. Lauren, too. She rolled her eyes: *I'm not you.* It also worried me that my mother was wearing Lauren's pink spaghetti-strap minidress. But I was used to that. Mom was almost fifty and could still get a date.

"I'm going to take the cats to the humane society tomorrow," she cried, and twirled, and tipped her head back to the Chimay.

"What?" I said to Lauren.

"Cat shit," she whispered.

Lauren was talking about the strays, brought down a few days before by Mom's upstairs neighbors. Layla and Lauren had named them immediately, like they always did with the animals Mom brought home: Cassius, India, Rain, Sunny.

"No!" Layla cried. "Sunny! Tara, remember Sunny?"

I remembered Sunny.

Layla and Lauren had their own dog in Waimea, on Kauai, when Mom moved there in the mid-1990s, trying to start Exotic Weddings of Kauai. She had it all figured out: Japanese tourists would get married at the Waimea Foreign Church, where Gampa Faye and Maggie Lindsay and Aunt Isabel were buried. Then they'd have a *lū'au* at the Cottages.

She even had cards made. She wanted to start a mango festival, too, and a clothing company: Guava Toes, for the guava mush that squeezed between your toes when you were up in Kokee hiking. They were good ideas, but she ended up falling in love with a married plant geneticist—Monsanto had come in after the plantations—so she spent a lot of time making him mango cheesecake and listening to him play love songs on his guitar.

Karen worked in the fields, inseminating corn. When the geneticist left, she moved over to Vern Watanabe's failing lumber business. Vern had a crush on with Mom and died of a heart attack right after she loaned him five thousand dollars. She never recovered the money, but every time she went to Kauai after that, Junko Watanabe, Vern's mother, loaned Mom Vern's old Nissan to use. All Mom had to do was bring sweet *mochi* for Junko's altar and mangoes from Waimea if they were in season.

Sunny had been a happy little poi dog, tan, with floppy ears. Layla loved him, like she loved all animals. Then he disappeared. Maybe he ate a *bufo*—one of the toads brought in by the plantations to control pests. In any case, Sunny went off to die. Layla could never find him again.

"He needed to go to the vet." Layla frowned. "He ate a bufo and needed to go to the vet and Mom wouldn't go. And now Sunny's *dead*."

All those lost animal souls, floating around my mother like a halo.

Karen shrugged. "Look. You want to know what I did today? I woke up, went for a swim, and I cleaned up cat shit."

Lauren laughed. I laughed.

"Don't laugh! That was my day!" But she was laughing, too.

"Lauren was sleeping in it!" Layla giggled. "Lauren, tell!"

The night before, Lauren awoke once or twice, smelling cat shit. She fell back asleep. When she rose at eleven it was smeared all over her.

"Lauren, Lauren, didn't you notice it? Didn't it bother you?" I said.

Lauren shrugged. Very little here bothered anyone.

"See?" Mom nodded, scratching her arms. "The cats shit all over Lauren. That's why I'm taking them in."

She stood up and danced again, to "Brown-Eyed Girl." Karen has blue eyes. Dark blue, like the ocean where the reef ends and the island falls away.

"Mom, you're a good dancer!"

"Duh!"

Layla reached her arms out. "Give me some love, Mom. Give me some love."

Mom shimmied away. Layla took the Chimay out of her mother's hands.

"Hey!"

Take the bottle away, she'll grab it back. Take the house and she'll find another one. "I'm a survivor," she says, "I always have been."

"Yeah, but it takes its toll on you, Mom."

"What's that supposed to mean?"

"Why don't you dance, Layla?"

"Yeah. With sexy Mom and her *Chimay*?"

My sister was being saucy but moved toward Mom anyway. She never got there. "Layla, give me a cigarette," Mom drawled, and headed toward the door.

Layla passed her one. "Where are you going?"

"Nowhere. Upstairs."

"Right." Lauren called from the floor. She was picking at her navel ring. When she spoke it was to her stomach. "You're going out to talk to your crackhead friends."

Mom scowled. "You know what, Lauren? You're a bitch."

"So? I got it from you."

Layla handed Mom the lighter. Lauren stared at our mother as if she didn't know her. Mom stepped into the night and the screen door banged behind her.

Karen was a junkie when Layla was born, in 1978. My sister arrived two months premature, induced, someone told me, as a result of Mom hot-tubbing in Tahoe with Neil. A relative took me to Kapiʻolani Hospital to see my new sister but I was too young to go in, so I looked at Layla through the glass in the preemie ward. Tubes coiled; her plastic crib curved like a spaceship. Then someone escorted me out. Layla never got to breast-feed after that.

Five years later, Lauren was born in Monterey, where Mom moved after Texas. Margaret had just had her first bout with lupus, and her younger sister went to take care of her. When it came time to deliver, Mom had a C-section, then it got infected. I was visiting that summer, my thirteenth. Paint it in hospital hues: Layla, Mom, and I alone in a seafoam room. Will Stewart, Lauren's father, had sent balloons and they hovered above the chalk-colored cot. Mom was too sick to name the baby, so I did: Lauren Elizabeth. I got the name from a booklet I found in the lobby. I thought it sounded preppy. Daniels, after Layla's father. Technically they were still married.

Lauren was skinny when she was born, and big-eyed. She looked like a little old man.

Back in Monterey, Mom and Patti, a friend of Margaret's, staked out parking lots and stole old ladies' handbags. They cruised for heroin afterward. Layla says now that she knew what they were doing, even at five. She told them so. "I know what that is," my sister said, pointing to folded paper squares. Mom denied it.

"You." Karen says to me now. "You didn't go through anything. When I think about what I did to Layla. God. Three little crack prostitute babysitters for three days. And poor Beatrice."

Beatrice was Will Stewart's childhood nanny. He was from an old Houston family, with real Southern names like Mimi and Lucinda. Mom and he had met at a strip club there—a "boobie bar," Will called it—after she moved to Texas with Owen. Will was straight and twenty-three; Mom was thirty. The night they met they realized they were both related to William Brewster, from the *Mayflower.*

Will wanted to look like Luke on *General Hospital.* Mom had a thing for curly-haired men.

Every time she was fucked up she'd leave Layla with Beatrice. Beatrice would call: "Will, I got Layla over here, and I got to go to church."

"I can't do anything, Beatrice."

"Will, I got to go to church."

Layla doesn't mind. Her memories are patchwork. All the times they ran away from restaurants. That grocery store where Mom made Layla steal the steaks.

They moved back to Honolulu around 1983. Layla was forgotten at an airport (she spent the night at a stewardess's); there was the brief stint with the guy who had a glass eye; Mom's friend Franklin wrote *I love Karen* twenty times underneath the Kahala freeway overpass. ("Don't eat ice cream," Franklin told Layla. "It's got bacon fat in it. Same as eating a pound of bacon fat.") In 1984 they moved in with Bobby the Vietnam vet.

I had started high school by then. I lived with my father and Debbie on the Big Island. Freshman spring Bobby bought me my prom dress: hot pink brocade, with a sweetheart bodice. I didn't know what to say except thanks.

Layla says the most scared she's ever been was the day she and Mom and Lauren were on the bus, crossing over the Pali up by Polihiwahiwa, green vines dangling and all those waterfalls. Mom's head was down and she was puking into a red jacket. My sister didn't know for sure it was heroin, because she was only seven or eight, Lauren a toddler. They had left Bobby's and were sleeping in the back of Uncle Brew's truck, pillows and bedclothes spread out as if at the drive-in.

They stepped off the bus. A car stopped and a stranger asked them if they needed a ride. Mom and the man smoked a joint. Then he took them all home.

Soon after, Karen got busted for forging the checks of a lady whose house she cleaned. Gamma bailed her out. Mom could either go to jail or rehab. Rehab was a place called Women's Way, run by the Salvation Army. The building was up in Mānoa, next to the Wai'oli Tea Room. Hawaiian girls had been sent there in the old days to be trained in the art of serving: tea, curried chicken salad, almond cookies. A Wilcox had donated the land. The dormitory and playground were surrounded by a chain-link fence. Anyway, it was better than jail.

It stormed the night my sisters got to Women's Way. Mom's car broke down in the parking lot as soon as she pulled in. This was Lauren's first memory: the storm, the car. Layla told her about counting the seconds between the lightning bolt and the thunder that followed it. "The fewer the seconds," Layla said, "the closer the storm."

Women's Way smelled like a hospital—ammonia and bodies—and looked like one, too. Metal countertops lined the kitchen; green industrial carpet trailed the halls. To the right was the living room, two rooms to the left, the dining room with a cafeteria table. Sleeping rooms occupied each end of the building: bunks for kids, cots for moms. In the social workers' offices, desks sat primly beside stacks of addiction literature and baskets of teddy bears and anatomically correct dolls.

They escaped after a few weeks. Just left one night on the bus, hauling their clothes in garbage bags. I don't know where they went, probably Brew's truck again. A few weeks later they returned, this time for good.

Women's Way: It was where four-year-old Lauren kissed her first boy, Kaleo, also four. On the paved terrace behind the chain-link fence softened by white ginger, my youngest sister rode a bike for the first time. My sisters got rattails at Women's Way. It was where they did their homework, where they got their clothes (donations), their food (also donations), and other things, like compassion and humor and strength. It was where Layla and Lauren grew up, where they first remember being children.

Women's Way lasted two years, after which Mom graduated into the transition house down the hill. She went to meetings and met with her sponsor: Alcoholics Anonymous and Narcotics Anonymous and Codependents Anonymous and Adult Children of Alcoholics and Alanon. She'd served time in rehab and was off drugs. She had a brief affair with Claudia, the piano instructor she met in AA. Claudia wore pleated plants and her business card featured a single red rose against piano keys. The kids figured it was so Mom would have a place to stay when she left rehab.

In front of the transition house, in the middle of the grass, sat a filled-up pool; probably it had been for the Waioli Tea Room girls. The oblong ring of cement was still there, and next to it, the turquoise diving board. When my mother and sisters left Women's Way in 1986 for the last time, sometime during my junior year in high school, they took the bus. The last thing Lauren saw was my mother's old car, still parked next to the filled-up pool, still broken from the first time she came.

"Lauren, are they really crackheads?"

She shrugged. "Crackheads, junkies. Whatever."

I didn't think they looked like crackheads. They looked like old hippies, edge people, post-Californians. Hawaii got a lot of them. One had a long face and a goatee and pants that hung loose around his waist, showing too much of his abdomen. He had come into the house earlier that night with the kitten that was brother to our kittens. He said, "Karen, do you mind if I use the phone?" and my mother said, "Sure." Mom always says sure to people who need to use the phone, or crash at her place for a while, or use her food stamp card. When the skinny hippie left, he left the kitten, too. "God, these cats!" Mom sighed, but she didn't take the kitty back.

"I found a syringe on the lanai," Lauren said suddenly. "I found a syringe and then I heard fighting and a lady came down to the door looking for Mom. Her lip was split and bloody and her eye was swollen and she was pounding on the door. She said Mom was supposed to give her something, and I said, 'She isn't here and you're going to have to leave.'"

Lauren's voice was husky and she didn't even smoke.

"She said, 'Please help me,' and I said, 'No, you have to leave.'"

My sister looked at her thigh, wiped her hand across her nose.

"What?" I said. Layla repeated me: "What?"

"She's using again. I know it."

"What are we going to do?" Layla said.

I shrugged. Being the eldest made me anxious. "I don't know. Talk to her?"

Layla shook her head. "Right."

Mom descended the stairs at midnight, falling on her ass walking down. Back in the house she lay on her bed, shoes still on. "I'm loaded." She sighed. "*Load-ed.*"

She eyed us. "It's just from the booze, you know. The Xanax and the booze."

None of us said a word.

"At least it's legal," she mumbled, and kicked the door closed.

My sisters would say it started years ago, when Mom left Stan for the male nurse, Terry. Stan's furniture all matched. Lauren and Layla each had her own room. Stan owned a fishing boat and a big TV and a truck. He had a mustache and curly black hair. He was like a father to my sisters; they loved him. Then Mom stole some money from Stan right in front of his son and when Stan confronted her she denied it, so that was the end of Stan.

I say it was earlier, when Mom left the program, and her little house in Kuliʻouʻou, for Stan. She had a Chinese landlady there, an angel with the Angel Network. The Chinese lady had leprosy once and didn't have a nose, so I guess she was sympathetic to folks like my mother and gave her a house for free. Mom strung lacy scarves over the louvered windows and put all of her pictures and candles and hippie knickknacks out. Sometimes she painted and made crazy baskets with leaves and fungi and vines she found hiking.

They say in the program that you never mature beyond the day you first got high. Mom started at fifteen, with the usual suspects; progressed to heroin in her mid-twenties; got clean at thirty-four; and relapsed at forty-eight. Toward the end of those years she dabbled once in a while—Terry and she got stoned a few times—but for the most part she was clean.

After the night at Mrs. Delacruz's something changed. Mom didn't go swimming anymore. She lay in bed most days and watched American Movie Channel. Terry the male nurse with a double master's in public health and social work didn't care when she had breast cancer or hepatitis C. She tore down his precious *liliko'i* vine in vengeance and poured M&M's down his gas tank and looked for him at Anna Bananas, where they used to go for a beer in the afternoon. ("Terry is an alcoholic. An *al-co-hol-ic*. Did you know that?") She wailed outside his apartment off the Ala Wai until he called the cops and slapped a restraining order on her.

"Intervention?" she spit when we tried one. "I know interventions. I'm a *counselor.*"

Mrs. Delacruz kicked her out. So she moved in with spacey Marc, whom she met at a bar. They were "just friends." Then she did crack with Ted from Guam, her younger man, and got pneumonia. Then she met Ron. Then she disappeared.

"Something's always fucked up," I told her once, and she shot back, "You don't know. You've been gone. Why don't you stay with me once in a while? Then you'd know."

I did stay with her a few times, though the night at Mrs. Delacruz's was one of the last. She gave me a nightie to sleep in, served breakfast on a tray in the morning: papaya with lime, Cream of Wheat, coffee milk. A pink plumeria flower floated in a jelly jar. She stroked my hair, asked me if I wanted to take a shower. I couldn't wait to leave.

I wish I could go back there now and change that.

II

CONTACT

"In the reign of Kamehameha,
from the time I was born until I was nine
years old, the pestilence visited the
Hawaiian islands, and the majority of people
from Hawai'i to Ni'ihau died."

DAVID MALO, "On the Decrease of
Population in the Hawaiian Islands," 1839

Tara and Kirk, 1976

Once Upon a Time

✄

1854   Lihue, Kauai

T HE DREAM OF TRANSFORMATION IS SOMETHING ONE
gives up slowly, if at all. Think of Rumpelstiltskin and that poor
besmirched girl, sitting in her cell spinning all that straw. Or the tears
that Rapunzel shed to give a blind prince sight. A stepmother takes an
apple, turns it into poison. The ordinary—straw, tear, apple—made
magical. Hold your breath, something might happen.

My great-great-grandfather drained a swamp and spun into money
a particularly carbohydrate-rich member of the grass family, *Saccharum
officinarum,* first cultivated in New Guinea and brought to the islands by
migrating Polynesians sometime in the first century A.D. Green gold,
planters called it. The Hawaiians called it *kō.*

Hawaii itself, a land that could cure what ailed you. Great-great-
great-uncle Knudsen was sick when he came. He had malaria—the Chagres River Fever, they called it then, after the Chagres River in Panama,
infamous for its poisonous air. Valdemar Knudsen had gone to Norway
to see his dying father, his pockets lined with gold dust, so the story
goes. Going back to California across the isthmus, he fell sick. The band
of Irishmen he was traveling with left him for dead, so a kind Indian
woman nursed him back to health by feeding him goat's milk. Back in

California, the wet climate of the Sacramento Valley did not agree with him, so he decided to venture further south: Chile, where land grants were being given. He was about to get on the boat when he heard the harping of the captain's wife. Unable to bear the thought of a six-week journey in her company, he walked down the San Francisco quay and chose a ship bound for the Sandwich Islands instead.

Major epidemics—illnesses brought by those same ships—had swept through the islands only a few years before. In the winter of 1849, measles, dysentery, and influenza killed ten thousand people. The year 1853 saw smallpox take six thousand in a summer. Most who died were Hawaiian. Typhus, tuberculosis, and cholera cut the native population by a third in only a decade. Missionary churches emptied, labor became dear, and land, the commodity most desired—previously only legally owned by Hawaiians—was traded, bought, given, willed, sold, and leased with unprecedented alacrity.*

So here was the situation that greeted Valdemar Knudsen in the mid-1850s. After working in Lihue and finding that its wet climate aggravated his fever, he investigated an opportunity to lease from the crown fifty thousand acres of pasture, swamp, and mountain land on Kauai's dry west side. His annual rental would be fifteen hundred dollars, renewable every twenty years. Alexander Liholiho, King Kamehameha IV, executed the deal.

Mistrustful of Americans after a train ride across the States in which his valet, a haole, was allowed to travel in first class while his brother and he were forced to travel in the colored car, Liholiho liked Norwegian

---

*In 1848, under increasing pressure by foreigners eager to own land, the Hawaiian monarchy under Kamehameha III decreed what was known as the *Mahele,* or Division. Before the haoles arrived, no one in Hawaii really owned land. Commoners worked it, lesser chiefs and *konohiki* administered it, *ali'i,* royalty, ruled it, but the idea of private ownership had not existed. The Mahele of 1848 transformed Hawaii's land tenure system to a capitalist one in two years. Hawaii's four million acres were divided thus: one-third to the Hawaiian crown, one-third to the chiefs, and one-third to the people, through hereditary claims known as *kuleana.* Those who did not apply for their kuleana in a timely manner lost their claim. A newspaper article of the day outlined the choice: "Either . . . secure your lands, work them and be happy, or . . . sit still, sell them and then die. Which one do you choose?" Of four million acres, only thirty thousand went to native tenants.

Knudsen and made him *konohiki*. From the Waimea River to the first valleys of the Napali coast, Knudsen would govern more than one hundred square miles, almost a fifth of the island of Kauai, receiving taxes in the old manner from his four-hundred-odd tenants—in work or food. His marriage in 1867 to Annie Sinclair, a Scotswoman twenty years his junior, helped solidify his claim; in 1863 her family had purchased the nearby island of Ni'ihau outright for ten thousand dollars in gold coin.

Knudsen's son Eric, in a book called *Kanuka of Kauai* (Kanuka was Knudsen in Hawaiian), would call him the Viking who became a king.

Paradises changed people, made them better than they were before: richer, more powerful. Regular people became royalty.

Mōkoi Street

⚔

1977 Lihue, Kauai

So we arrive on Mokoi Street, on Kauai, an unremarkable lane distinguished chiefly because it was where some of the haoles from Lihue Plantation lived in the old days. They were brought over by Hans Isenberg: Germans, like him, several hundred of them, managers and overseers, called *luna*. They built houses that reminded them of where they were from. Dad and Debbie's house, for example, with peaked roofs and fireplaces. They beat the men sometimes—contract Chinese, five years in hock to the plantation, a few Hawaiians. Sometimes the Chinese and Hawaiians beat them back, with hoes and cane knives. They'd go to Lihue jail then, presided over by Sheriff Sam Wilcox, missionary descendant.

In 1893, when the monarchy was overthrown by American businessmen and sugar planters, Isenberg was in Bremen. American law would not allow contract labor, he knew, so he wrote to his associates in Honolulu. Put Princess Ka'iulani, niece of Queen Lili'uokalani, daughter of a Scotchman named Cleghorn, on the throne, he wrote. Give her an American adviser. That way contract labor, the back upon which sugar profits were made, could be saved.

No such thing would happen. Liliuokalani would be jailed in her own palace for eight months by the rebels; contract labor would end, though a dollar-a-day wage would not take hold until the twenties; and Princess Kaiulani would die of tuberculosis seven months after annexation, at twenty-three, alone, in Scotland.

Kaiulani: a favorite of Robert Louis Stevenson. *Light of heart and bright of face: The daughter of a double race.* We had a picture of her at Mokoi Street, black and white, in a bubble of blown glass. My stepmother told me that the princess would look at me whichever direction I walked. Try it, Debbie said, and I did. Her sad eyes looked out at me everywhere.

I was standing at the sink. I had just washed the dishes. Above the sink a large window opened. I was a girl waiting for her father.

I looked at the dust on the panes, and then past them, at the dust on the screen and the small flies trapped in the mesh, the opposite of stars, and then at the brown empty carport and smudged driveway, which, on Mokoi Street, where I lived that first year with Dad and Debbie, was always gray and green. Further off, like an ornament, hung a diamond patch of sky.

A hatchback VW creaked into the carport; an emergency brake cranked. My father walked toward the kitchen, past the maids' quarters off the carport, where our tennis pro lived. Not everyone in Hawaii had their own tennis pro, I realized, but Debbie and Dad worked in the hotels, and when you worked in the hotels you had things like tennis pros. He rented a room from us. He had a bouquet of curly brown hair. I remember him wearing, unsurprisingly, a terry-cloth headband and tennis shorts.

Kirk was back from Honolulu, from court. Custody, I knew. Perhaps a custody battle. Karen, crying, her lips swollen, her long nose pink and flaring, pleads with the judge: *Your honor, he stole her. He stole her while I was at the store.*

The screen door opened. I saw a plush forearm first. My father has the air of a woodsman—short, blunt, thick-calved, mustached—in a flowered aloha shirt. Above his nape his dark hair had been mussed from the plane seat, showing his curls. He needed a haircut, he'd say. Curls needed cutting. In a photo album sandwiched between *Surfing* and *The History of Walt Disney*—Kirk Smith was a Santa Monica boy nursed on Mickey (Dora and Mouse)—there was a picture, just one, in which my father had long curly woman's hair, hippie hair.

But that was before, when he owned a vegetarian restaurant and produced rock concerts in Diamond Head Crater and did LSD and was charmed by my mom.

My father looked tired and a little restless. His hazel eyes, heavy-lidded, fixed on me for a moment, then slid to the fridge. The usual quarry: Budweiser in a can, pull tab.

I wondered who would speak first.

I did: "What happened?"

Dad swigged. I watched his Adam's apple bob.

"Your mother didn't show up."

I must have looked surprised.

"What did you expect?"

He isn't cruel, just practical. "What did you expect?" was probably meant simply, like a question, as in, "What did you want to happen?"

"I don't know."

Perhaps I thought I would be going back.

He wiped his mustache of foam. Our Lab, Kona, barked, and my father cocked his head to hear him. I turned the water off, or ran my hands under the stream, or whatever.

"Now, Tara—"

"Kirk—"

Debbie was there, too. She wore her thick black curly hair loose. She had a pretty oval face, tiny white teeth, thin lips—so thin she wouldn't wear lipstick, said it looked like she'd been sucking on a Popsicle. She tapped her unpolished fingernails on the yellow Formica of the breakfast nook; now smoking a Benson & Hedges; now flicking her slim white fingers against her nose, a nervous habit. Her breasts, bigger than my mother's, nudged the table. They were encased in a maroon T-shirt that read KIAHUNA, the condominium hotel where she worked. Debbie had been a waitress, now she was a manager. She wore shorts. Her thighs flattened against the bench; her shapely calves drooped; her long toes arched. Two of them she used to scratch the other foot's ankle. She was a young woman still, only twenty-three. Her age was betrayed in small gestures, like this one.

"Hush," she said to my father.

"Well? What am I supposed to say? She didn't show up. That's the truth."

My father had talked to me about truth—during father-daughter walks around the cane haul roads with Kona. Truth was what you told if you wanted someone to believe you next time.

And Debbie had talked to me about "breakfast nook." The breakfast nook was where she had installed me to do my homework, copy out my Roman numerals. Debbie had taught me these words: Formica (she didn't like Formica, or canned vegetables, something about how they reminded her of the fifties and her mother, the beloved big-bosomed Southern California smoker, Grandma B.); vagina (Mom called it "dido," but at Dad and Debbie's we weren't ever to call it "dido," always vagina); fiancée; *beige* (rhymes with hedge); burgundy; condominium; breakfast nook. One had to sit in the breakfast nook for hours copying one's Roman numerals. I had gotten an N on Roman numerals at Wilcox Elementary. Nonsatisfactory. I didn't understand Roman numerals, their strange logic. Soon I would come to love Roman numerals, as I would come to love C for Commendable, and my stepmother.

I dried my hands, looked at the brown and silver harlequin wallpaper above the stove. I must have been crying.

"Now, dear," my father said softly.

Frustrated desire has the effect of hopscotching to another object, submerging, or evaporating, like dew in the morning. I used to cry and cry for my mother to come to my crib, so much that I'd throw up all my milk. I always managed to fall asleep after that.

Debbie, however, was unimpressed by tears. Some months or years or maybe just a few minutes after this moment, my father drinking his Bud, Debbie at the breakfast nook, she would issue the edict: "Crying might work with your father, but not with me."

So let it come up to your throat, let it sit there like a tumor. The window is there, and the sky, and the sink.

Dust in the air sparkled. My vision wasn't sparkling on its own. Dust inhabited the air and sparkled in the sun. This was the age when I realized certain things about the limits of my own powers. I used to think I could climb the walls, like Spider-Man. After Mokoi Street, I no longer thought I could.

For Debbie's birthday that first year I asked her what she wanted. We were leaving the Kauai Surf. I was about to close the door of the Ghia. I looked down at the pavement under the car before closing the door, as I always did. I wanted to see what was disappearing.

"How about you call me Mommy?"

I must have looked strange because then she added, "Just for today."

Monkeypod trees made a green tent for the Kauai Surf parking lot, kept the rental cars cool. They shed brown seedpods the shape of skinny babies, to be cracked by car wheels and slippers and golf carts and helicopter legs. (There is a heliport at the Kauai Surf. Jack Harter starts his tours of the Garden Island there.) The seeds smell yeasty, like brown, if brown were a smell. A bit sweet, a bit dirty.

I shook my head. "I can't."

Debbie looked ahead and set her mouth. She started the car. She wrapped her arm around the back of my seat and pulled out. Sun shifted through green, all that was substantial shimmered.

We didn't talk on the way back, but she would forgive me eventually. And I, her. She saved me, after all. When I came from my mother's I had scraggly blond hair, a rat's nest. I had the clothes on my back. I had scabies. We cured the scabies; I got my hair cut. It grew back brown. I cleaned up little by little. Habits encouraged by my mother—eating cookies before dinner, talking back, staying up late—gradually were reformed. Debbie was good for me. On the Big Island, at age three, I had shown my stepmother how to roll a dollar bill into a little straw for cocaine. Now I even took my naps when I was told.

Debbie taught me to say please and thank you, to put my napkin in

my lap at dinner, to hold my iced-tea glass with my pinky aloft, like a
lady. I took a nap every afternoon. Otherwise I would be cranky. I made
iced tea for her from the Lipton jar. I made the salad and washed the
dishes. I cleaned the dog's pen.

"No slippers to school. No sleeveless outfits. No shorts."

"But everyone wears shorts to school."

"No buts."

Julia Wilcox would remember me as the brown-haired girl who
wore dresses. Until then I had always been a blonde.

At Dad and Debbie's this is what we liked: Scrabble, fondue, Chardon-
nay, sourdough bread, San Francisco, Triscuits, Camembert cheese, and
sarcasm. My father liked hot dogs topped with Hormel chili; Debbie
liked *Cosmopolitan* magazine and iced tea stirred by her stepdaughter.
She didn't like messy hair or fussing, she didn't like ribbons or frills or
barrettes or earrings on young girls. She thought my mother was a fruit-
cake and her family assorted tropical nuts. She did, however, like me.

Dad wore his aloha shirts untucked and only liked pullovers. He had
short hair, balding at the top. When he was thinking or reading or
watching TV, he touched the spot. He claimed it was from balancing a
surfboard on his head. It was why he'd come to Hawaii in the first place:
sometimes in California you'd have to walk a mile to get a break.

They weren't strangers. I had been with them before, on the Big Island, when I was three. Mom had gone to California with a boyfriend
and I was sent to live with Debbie and Dad in a big plantation house in
Hilo, with a green lawn and a wide roof that curved like a temple's.
They were scenic months: we saw the last eruption of Halemaʻumaʻu in
1974—someone hoisted me above the railing to look at the lava shooting into the sky, pooling at the bottom of the crater. I visited Grandma
Betty and Debbie's stepfather, Grandpa Norm, at Hōnaunau, near the
coffee plantations. Norman owned a charter fishing boat. Sometimes
we'd take it out and see a whale.

I lived with them at Poʻipū, also on Kauai, with Auntie Laura, Debbie's
little sister, the summer Dad's mom shot herself in the kitchen of her house

in L.A. My father's younger brother, still in high school, found her, blood all over the linoleum.

I had called her Tutu, Hawaiian for grandmother.

But I was a tourist daughter then. This time I was meant to stay.

I went to school. With Karen, school had been more like a goal than something you did every day. For Debbie, school was a strangely fixed event. She drove me to Wilcox Elementary in her lemon yellow Karmann Ghia. (Major shame. Locals had Tercels.) After school she picked me up and drove me to Kiahuna in Poipu or to the Kauai Surf. Every day.

Debbie was good at working. Her office was beige. She drank Tab.

The drive to Kiahuna was south and west, on Kauai's one belt road. I had always known this road: down the hill at the mill in Lihue, the manure stink of it. Up past Grove Farm, the Wilcoxes' plantation. Sugar straight on out, flat and waving green. The big brown Wilcox house, Kilohana. Mount Wai'ale'ale past it, crowned in clouds, the Wettest Spot on Earth. Puhi, Puhi camp, Puhi store on the left, a line of luna houses in front like a set of false teeth. Past C. Brewer (they made the fertilizer and the pesticides), POIPU 6 MILES. From there out, sugar. Sugar, sugar, sugar. The Wilcoxes owned it.

Then the road split. West, the direction we never took, except for cookouts at Polihale, were Kalāheo, Hanapepe, Waimea, Kekaha, Mana, where my mother's family was from. Everywhere you could see the blue ocean.

Debbie asked me how school was.

"Fine."

"And your teachers?" She was sincerely interested. She turned to me, touched my thigh.

"Fine!" I shouted because the top was down. I didn't want to answer any more questions, but I wanted to appear friendly, bright, so I said it louder, brighter. We were still nervous with each other.

"I'm fine!"

"Just fine?"

I nodded, cleared the hair from my face.

This was the part I liked, the hill Debbie took faster. The yellow line at the center of the road wobbled; our yellow car dripped into it.

I remembered something: My mother drove with one hand on the wheel, one foot on the dash, looking at herself in the side-view mirror, picking at her teeth.

Debbie reached over, chucked me under the chin. "We have to do something about that hair."

It had not been fine. Walking in halfway through the school year with the wrong clothes—new Garanimals from Woolworth's, there hadn't been time to pack a bag—I looked like the teacher's pet I would become.

Wilcox Elementary consisted of long concrete boxes laid like strips of something on a conveyor belt, one after another on a roughly square piece of land in the center of Lihue. Though it sat on a plateau several hundred feet above the ocean, it was as if the town existed at the bottom of a bowl. I remember it as a depression, its one-story buildings edged in red dirt.

Elsie Wilcox gave the money for the school, Mabel and G.N. Wilcox for the hospital. Down on Rice Street was the courthouse, the public library, the Lihue Museum, where pictures of the Rices and Wilcoxes, Sloggetts, Alexanders, Isenbergs, Robinsons, even the Fayes—all plantation people—hung.

Between each of the boxes was a grassy courtyard. If I stood in the courtyard I could see the sun. If there wasn't enough time to get to the playground, I could remain there, trading snacks at recess, playing Chinese jump rope or lemon twist, or Chinese jacks on the sidewalk, in the shade.

We were the usual complement of Hawaii kids: Filipinos, Hawaiians, Japanese, Chinese, Portuguese, Koreans, a few Samoans, some haoles. Mostly we were *hapa,* mixed. We wore cheap clothes and *rubbah slippahs,* jeans, shorts, T-shirts. There were the predictably popular girls: Jocelyn Kawamoto, with her long black perfect Japanese hair (also Josselyn Kawakami, but she was plainer). Nina Madeiros was brown-eyed, part Hawaiian, part Portuguese. A few haole girls: Emily and Dee Dee Padgett's father owned an ATV. They lived over by Grove Farm in an

A-frame and had horses. Emily and Dee Dee's mom was a Wilcox. Charity Cruz lived in Ulumahi and had long blond hair, even though she was Portuguese. Edwina Loro, Filipino, painted her fingernails magenta and wore glasses. There was a boy named Jesus, which confused me, and another named Blaine.

People probably spoke to me. I walked between the long buildings looking straight ahead, or up at the sky.

We were the sons and daughters of plantation people, cops, nurses, and construction workers; hotel maids and yardmen; dentists and lawyers and teachers. Dad and Debbie worked in the hotels so I was a super haole. I spoke haole English at home, not just in class. I had a weird car. All day long my parents spoke to tourists:

How are you, Mr. Jones?

Well, thanks, Mr. Smith, I am just fine, and you?

Would you like some milk, Mr. Jones?

Why, yes, I would like some milk, Mr. Smith, to go with my sausage and eggs here for breakfast.

Some of us were poor, some middle-class, some rich. You wouldn't know it. Land—'aina—was more important than money anyway. Kama'aina, we memorized, child of the land; kua'aina, backbone of the land; hoa'aina, friend of the land; maka'ainana, eyes of the land; malihini, newcomer.

She hadn't forgotten about me, the other mother. She sent word through Uncle Brew. He came to Kauai that first year to give me a present. We rode around the wide quiet streets of Lihue: red dirt lining the curbs, storefronts sagging. Lihue had been the center of the plantation. There had been a movie theater once, a company store, and a dance hall. Now the theater was a roller rink with a lit floor and a disco ball. Not quite dead, but getting there. The Kress would close down in a few years, then the Woolworth's, then the Liberty House. In the 1980s a bypass from the airport would be constructed. Wal-Mart would open on the way out of town.

The present Brew brought was wrapped in a Foodland bag and dressed in yarn. It was from my mother. I read the card. She was still on the north shore of Oahu, an island away. She was waiting to see me, soon, soon, since she was having a hard time and was going to the mainland for a while but would be back, and we'd be together again. She and I and the baby she was having, Neil Daniels's, a girl. She underlined the words *a family*.

The baby she was having?

Brew tried to explain. He smoothed back a tassel of blond bang and sighed.

"She's going to Texas. With Owen."

Owen. I remembered Owen. Owen lived out near Pearl Harbor on the ugly side of Oahu. He had pale skin and curly black hair. When we lived at Neil's, Mom and I used to sneak over to Owen's condo in the afternoons, eat his Pringles and watch HBO.

Once I saw a bungee cord snaking across the well of the backseat of Owen's car. I knew what it was for. I stretched it, shot it like a sling. Mom sat up front, her feet on the dash, oblivious.

"I know." I nodded, even though I didn't. Really I just liked the feeling the words gave me.

Brew took me to Pizza Hut. Pizza Hut sucked. Pizza Hut was dumb. I hated Pizza Hut. Debbie had forbidden me to say I hate anything.

Back at Mokoi Street, I looked at my mother's handwriting: half cursive, half print. *Tara Bray Smith, c/o.* In care of, as if I didn't actually live with Dad and Debbie, as if I were just visiting. I opened the package: Joan Baez's *Diamonds and Rust,* an album we listened to at Pipeline. On the cover Joan Baez was laughing—hand up to her dark fine hair, chin tilted, thin legs folded beneath her. She looked like my mother, just coming out of a migraine, spaced out and a little fogged, but happy.

I had a record player in a white plastic carrying case and a few albums: *Grease, Snow White.* I liked "Someday My Prince Will Come" and "Whistle While You Work." One my mother, the other my step-mother. Mom would come to claim me, kiss me, and I would awake from my sleep in my glass coffin. But I could whistle while I worked, too. The forest animals would love me.

H-1

⚐

August 2002　Honolulu

I FLEW A LOT AS A KID, BACK AND FORTH BETWEEN THE islands, after I left my mother. Dad would get the nicest lady he saw sitting at the gate—a tutu type—and ask her to accompany me. Once aloft, I liked the way you could remove yourself, looking down. All the fields stretched out like tiny manicured lawns, palm trees were no bigger than toothpicks.

I memorized the spiel. *There are eight islands in the main Hawaiian chain.* Pause, click, resume. *O-ah-hoo, the Gathering Place, is home to Wai-kee-kee and Ho-no-loo-loo, the state's capital. From Mow-ee, the Valley Isle, one can see three of Ha-vy-ee's smaller islands: La-nah-ee, the Pineapple Isle; Mo-lo-kah-ee, the Friendly Isle; and uninhabited Kah-ho-o-la-vay, used for United States military training.* Pause. *Ha-vy-ee, dubbed the Orchid Isle for its exotic blossoms*—breathe, pause, click—*is also called the Big Island, as Ha-vy-ee is larger than all seven of the other islands combined. Kow-ah-ee, or the Garden Isle, named so because of its verdant valleys and lush foil-age, is neighbor to Nee-ee-how, the Forbidden Isle. Owned by the Robinson family, and home to pureblooded native Hawaiians, access to Nee-ee-how is strictly forbidden to outsiders.* Pause, breathe, resume. *Now sit back, relax, and enjoy the short flight to Lee-hoo-ee Airport on the island of Kow-*

ah-ee. Complementary soft drinks, tropical juices, and spirits for a nominal charge will be served shortly. And once again, mahalo for flying Hawaiian Airlines.

This was the official story of Hawaii. Various words happened: *kapu* (taboo), *ahupua'a* (pie-shaped land division stretching from the mountains to the sea), *mana, ali'i.* Cook came, Man Who Was Taken for a God. Then he was killed for not being one. King Kamehameha united the islands. Missionaries came to do good, ended up doing well. Sugarcane, pineapples, immigrants, melting pot. Pearl Harbor. Hooray, the fiftieth state. Michener, Waikiki.

This was the official story of my mother's family: We had money once, and Japanese servants. It all went downhill when Mom started doing drugs. Still, children should be seen and not heard and always write thank-you notes.

I didn't have an official story, but I wanted one.

I read books, histories, novels, anything that would help me understand my mother: why she was the way she was; what happened to her; what happened to her family. Many of them were written by haoles, versions of *vini, vidi, vici.* The old ones are filled with breathy awe: The flowers! The laughing natives! The mysterious Asiatics! *Poi!*

Once we came by boat, later by plane. Even after fifteen years I still dream of flying over Hawaii. I'm soaring around, looking down at the ocean and the folded green valleys. I'm trying to find one valley, a magic valley, its walls so steep you can get there only by sea or by air. Usually I crash, but once I walked right into that valley. Everything was strange and twilit. A river ran through its center. On its banks, pink mollusks nested in the grass.

There are valleys on Kauai so isolated that an entire species would have evolved only there, on that one island, in that one valley, on one single ledge. Their whole lives played out on that tiniest stage. It is heartwrenching: a true home.

Now I am on United or Northwest or American. Perhaps not every tourist who visits Hawaii is fat, but I can only look at the ones who are. I myself am a tourist, in mainland garb: black shirt, dark jeans.

We prepare to land. The flight attendants roll their carts down the carpeted aisle.

Mom used to pick me up from the airport in whatever jalopy she could beg or borrow, a plumeria lei that Lauren had picked from a neighbor's yard in one hand, McDonald's in the other. It was something she liked to do, pick me up from the airport, as if she were trying to make up for all the years she couldn't. She would smile, a french fry in her mouth, and hug me and touch my hair. I'd have gotten fatter or paler but she'd still say, "Hi, honey! You look beautiful!" Then she'd take us to the beach: Sans Souci or Kahala or Makapuu to bodysurf.

But that was years ago—ten, at least—when I was in college and Mom had just gotten out of rehab and had short hair and a job.

Today my father picks me up. He waits with his hands clasped in front of him, head down, at the baggage claim. Honolulu smells like the day I left fifteen years ago: tarmac and plumeria flowers.

I always see my father before he sees me. He's heavier now, but his hair hangs on and his mustache is still full.

"Hey, babe."

"Hi, Dad."

"You're pale!"

"Yeah."

"I'll get the car."

I stand at the baggage claim and watch the biggest bags I have ever seen cycle past me. Tourists always bring far more than they need. The small Japanese lady next to me is not a tourist. I can tell: her hair is home-permed. Japanese ladies from Japan never have home perms. This one's forms a fuzzy reddish halo around her head. Also, her blue aloha shirt, silhouettes of all the islands, darker blue Bermuda shorts, and yet another shade of blue ankle socks under black *tabi* are faded. Japanese tourists go all out: brand-new Chanel, Burberry. This lady's spotted with moles—mainland Japanese are milk-pale—and looks soft and weather-worn.

A few weary Polynesians—more likely Samoan than Hawaiian—wear signs that say ALOHA MR. AND MRS. and hold plumeria or Vanda orchid lei. They are called greeters by the hotel industry, the only industry besides the military that matters here anymore.

Honolulu floats by same as it always does. I am surprised by how drab the city looks driving home from the airport; how depressed someone from somewhere cold and landlocked might feel arriving here midafternoon to see the scabs of freeway, warehouse, gas station, slapdash hotel, stucco house, pavement stretch unbroken, like the freeway itself, from here to Diamond Head. Anyway, Diamond Head is just a little hillock of dusty green in the distance; turquoise Waikiki is nowhere to be seen. Where are the crystal clear waters? The sugar white sands? The smiling natives?

I know all the exits on the freeway and why they are named what they are named. This is one thing about an island: the past is right there on a green and white freeway sign. This is another thing about an island: time seems to pass more slowly. Thus, conversation with my father goes like this:

Me: "How are you?"

Him: "Copacetic."

Me: "How's work?"

Him, looking dark, growling: "Bill got a new Jag. Fucking idiots."

Then we're quiet.

Him: "How are you? How is [whatever is happening in my life at the time]?"

Me: "Fine."

I always say fine. And I am. I'm in graduate school. I'm a writer. I have friends. The boyfriend—that's harder. When there's so much to tend to in Hawaii, a certain distance is required. I have never gotten comfortable with the idea of needing someone. Addiction, need, want: they're related. And Karen needed for both of us. My mother kept things together while my sisters were young. Mouths to feed gave her purpose. Who needed her now? Ron?

It was exactly the opposite for me. I had worked very hard to erase need from my life.

Exits flash by overhead. PUNAHOU ("New Spring"). Where Gamma went to school, where Mom went to school, where I went to school—

though only my senior year, the year my mother had left. WILDER. Mom used to wash his great-great-granddaughter's laundry, back when I was five, up on Tantalus. Her name was Kinau. We lived in her washhouse.

Dad pats my knee. "You want to get some shave ice?"

We are already pulling off, onto King. (There were six kings, all told: Kamehameha I through V, and Kalākaua. Only Kamehameha I, uniter of all the islands, reached sixty.)

The shave-ice store is part of a convenience store, but there are hysterical signs telling you it's not. TWO SEPARATE BUSINESSES!!! ORDER FROM THIS WINDOW FOR SHAVE ICE!!! WELCOME TO NUMBER ONE SHAVE ICE STORE, PLEASE DO NOT ORDER INSIDE. ONLY ORDER HERE FOR DELICIOUS SHAVE ICE IN NATURAL FLAVORS. The store is suspiciously bare of goods; therefore I think it's a front for drugs and porn. My father orders something simple: raspberry. Mine is wildly tropical: passionfruit-guava-coconut. I am too glad to be home.

We don't talk much. My father and I have a comfortable relationship, but he's a reserved man. He knows why I am quiet. It must be confusing for him. By thirty my father had been married twice. His mother was dead. He had a daughter and a serious job. I am almost thirty-two, have no job, and am still hung up on my mom.

We get back in the car and drive to Kaimuki. Everything is so pleasant in Honolulu. The sun shines; the shave ice is sweet and cold. There's a rainbow above Manoa Valley, where the university is. UH's mascot is a rainbow: hence the Rainbow Warriors, or the 'Bows, or the UH Rainbows. They're not even self-conscious about it. There's a divorcée haole Republican lady running for governor. Her opponent is also a woman: first-generation Japanese-American. Our congressman, a true believer named Neil Abercrombie, still has a ponytail. We're a wing-nut state, someone once told me. I don't know what wing nut means, but it seems right.

My dad has lived on Ocean View Drive in Kaimuki with his girl-friend, Deirdre, for almost fifteen years. When people see "Ocean View Drive" on my driver's license, a rainbow arcing over the picture, big blue letters spelling HAWAII, they laugh.

During World War II, Diamond Head Crater down the street housed long-range artillery. Now it's a popular day hike for tourists. Lava-rock checkpoints and bunkers where I kissed boys and smoked joints in high school crumble at its base. Leʻāhi, the old military hospital, houses the state's last Hansen's disease patients. It's all real: the lepers and the checkpoints and the artillery, but no one cares about this where I live now. No one even knows about this.

Tomorrow or another day I'll go looking for my mom.

Iron Was Their
Principal Object

✄

January 18, 1778   Waimea, Kauai

BEFORE EVERYONE FOUND EVERYTHING, CARTOGRA-
phers and explorers used to call the blank spaces on the map
"sleeping beauties." Wild animals slunk around the edges, serpents and
gorgons and other scaly beasts with an Oriental cast. Until 1521, when
Magellan sailed from South America to the Philippines, the whole Pacific was like that: a vast and mysterious sleeping beauty untrammeled by
the geometer's line. Of course, this only applied to Europeans. Polynesians had been navigating the ocean they called *kai,* sea, for more than a
thousand years, using only currents, wind, sun and moon, birds, stars.
The wake of the island of Hawaii is said to be five thousand miles long,
enough for someone in the South Seas to see it and know there was land
north.

The earliest Hawaiians came in colonizing visits from their ancestral
home in Kahiki (Marquesas or Tahiti, two thousand miles away) as early
as the first century A.D. They sailed twin-hulled voyaging canoes that
held a hundred people. Not knowing where they would land, or what
that land would offer, they brought with them the necessities of life: *kalo*
(taro), ground to a paste and mixed with water to make poi; *kukui* (can-

dlenut), its oil burned for light; *'ulu* (breadfruit), a starchy relative of the fig, whose sap made glue for birdcatching and whose wood made a light surfboard known as *alaia*. *Kō* (sugarcane), used for medicine, as well as to pacify babies, thatch houses, and sweeten pudding; dogs, pigs, chickens, bamboo, gourds, *milo* wood for bowls, *hau* for canoe building, *kapa* (paper mulberry) for cloth, the *tī* plant for cordage, bananas, sweet potatoes, coconuts, the mountain apple, arrowroot, and rats.

Twenty-four species in all, not including humans.

For millions of years the islands waited, collecting one species every twenty thousand years or so until the coming of man, which brought several. All of them had time to grow and change, and they transformed into creatures that needed little in the way of protection; there wasn't much competition for anything in Hawaii. Birds that had made their way to the islands on the wing lost their ability to fly; nothing on land was poisonous; there were no mosquitoes, snakes, scorpions, spiders, no venomous creatures of any kind. Even the rose lost its thorns.★

To a modern mind, it is almost a ridiculous picture—something out of those magazines Jehovah's Witnesses leave at the door. We don't believe in paradise because paradise is inviolate, and nothing on earth, since the age of the ship and the airplane, is inviolate. Everything fell apart a long time ago.

The first Hawaiians settled in places that offered access to both the sea and inland sources of water, food, and wood: valleys mostly, like Waimea, on Kauai, which by A.D. 610 was completely irrigated—wetland kalo is a thirsty crop—with ditches and dams, featuring a kind of cut-and-dressed stonework not found anywhere else in the Pacific. They were industrious and took their laws seriously—intricate and interlocking laws, called *kapu,* which governed everything from who could eat bananas (men), to who could prepare food (men), to where to fish (chiefs up to the reef, commoners further out), to when to plant. They lived eight or more to a house, converging in great numbers on the

---

★Of Hawaii's precontact species, 99.4 percent were not found anywhere else in the world, the highest known percentage of endemism anywhere.

windward side of each island, where kalo grew abundantly, though they also cultivated in places where there was little or no water, as in Mana and Kekaha, where kalo was grown on floating rafts.

Their chiefs, alii, were believed to be descended from gods, Wākea (Father Sky) and Papa (Mother Earth). Ancestors were worshiped in the form of 'aumākua—totemic gods. Aumakua resided in everything: in the wind and the ocean, in the sharks that patrolled the channels and fed at the mouths of the rivers, in streams, in the 'alalā, the black raven, known to hang about the houses, a sign of good luck. Early Hawaiians had no writing, instead passing down their stories, genealogies, and physical knowledge in mele (song) and oli (chant).

Once Europeans got involved, with their pānānā (compass) and their palapala (paper), lines started to be drawn, divisions made. At the end of the eighteenth century, nearly the whole of the Pacific was methodically mapped and plotted by a day laborer's son named James Cook, in a boat called a collier, used to ply coal along the coasts of Mother England, the kind of boat Cook learned to sail as a lad. Back and forth, Cook laced up the Pacific on three separate voyages in two boats over twelve years. His aim was to find the Northwest Passage, which would link Europe with the Orient by way of a fabled North American inland sea. On his last voyage, heading to Alaska around Christmas 1777, Cook and his second in command, Charles Clerke, charted a group of islands he would name after his patron, John Montagu, the earl of Sandwich. The Sandwich Islands, they would be called, and then, once Americans got involved, Hawaii.

Cook and Clerke anchored at Waimea, on Kauai. Though foreigners were equally mistrusted and welcomed throughout the insular islands of the Pacific—strangers always brought something, be it a gift or sickness or war—Hawaiians on this day balanced suspicion with need. They wanted iron. Each village had a bit, washed up in driftwood from faraway continents or shipwrecked vessels. A few sixpenny nails bought several pigs. Cook and his crew, having just come from the South Pacific, spoke enough Tahitian to transact business, which was brisk, even under the spell of mutual discovery.

The HMS *Resolution,* Cook's ship, spent a total of three days off Kauai, taking water and provisions. The *Discovery* was detained longer by a storm. The boats met on nearby Niihau a few weeks later, gathered yams for their journey to Alaska, and were under sail by February 2, Cook believing that he had tarried too long. Though it was his express desire not to spread "the Venereal distemper" among "these innocent People"—going so far as to forbid intercourse with native women—an overnight stay on Niihau undermined his plans. "Thus the very thing happened," Cook would note in his journal, "that I had above all others wished to prevent."

Within a few decades, Hawaiians died of smallpox, influenza, syphilis, bronchitis, whooping cough, tuberculosis, and "convulsions." They had, according to a French doctor who visited a few years later, on the first European ship after Cook, "buboes, and scars which result from their suppurating, warts, spreading ulcers with caries of the bones, nodes, exostoses, fistula, tumors of the lachrymal and salival ducts, scrofulous swellings, inveterate opthalmiae, ichorous ulcerations of the tunica conjunctiva, atrophy of the eyes, blindness, inflamed prurient herpetic eruptions, indolent swellings of the extremities, and among children, scald head, or a malignant tinea, from which exudes a fetid and acrid matter."

Before contact with Europeans, Hawaiians were a singularly healthy people, with a lower infant mortality rate than their European counterparts, and a longer life expectancy. They were clean, and they knew how to set broken bones without infection. They were doubly blessed with rich soil in the mountains and plentiful fish from the sea, and in many areas of Hawaii, a seemingly inexhaustible supply of fresh water.

It was this fresh water that would eventually allow large-scale sugar cultivation, and, before the diseases, it was this fresh water that would cause the death of the first Hawaiian by a foreigner's hand. During Cook's short anchorage off Waimea, Lieutenant Williamson was sent ashore to fill the ships' casks. A Hawaiian chief and his retinue greeted Williamson's boat, the chief immediately making for its iron hook. It was unclear whether the man was trying to help Williamson land or steal the boat's anchor. The lieutenant, thinking the man's intentions to be the latter, shot him dead.

A year later, on a return trip to the islands—again for wood and watering, this time to Kealakekua Bay, on the island of Hawaii—Cook and several of his marines died in another scuffle over a boat, most likely killed by spears fashioned from the hammered-out nails they themselves had traded. Captain Clerke ordered the entire village burned in retaliation. More than twenty Hawaiians were killed, priests' quarters and homes gutted, and two Hawaiians were decapitated, their heads stuck on pikes on the deck of the *Resolution*. Careful not to be taken for cannibals, the sailors threw the bodies overboard in full sight of Hawaiians, who jeered from the shore. Kamehameha himself, who was said to have met Cook during his stay, bore scars on his face from the battle. The two sides were reconciled a few days later.

Samuel Kamakau, a Hawaiian historian, wrote in the 1860s that the Hawaiians called the foreigners *haole,* "without breath," because they wondered if they were alive. *Hā* means "spirit, breath, life"; as in, *Hā ke akua i ka lewa,* God breathed into the open space. *'Ole* means "not, without, lacking; to deny; zero, nothing, nought, negative; nothingness, nobody; im-, in-, un-."

Hawaii was one of the last places on earth to be settled, and one of the last settled places to be "discovered," January 18, 1778, nearly three years after the outbreak of the Revolutionary War. Laws by which all things were ordered broke down forty years after Cook arrived. Kapu was abolished, and Hawaiians learned the new rules to keep up. Apt students, they dressed in the latest fashions from Lākana (London) or Pokekona (Boston) and worshiped a Christian god. With the help of New England missionaries, they devised an alphabet and learned to read. They ordained a king, Kamehameha, like Keoki (George) from Beretania, whose dynasty would last almost a hundred years. They drafted a constitution, opened schools and hospitals, and traveled the world: Hawaiians were considered excellent seamen. Almost seventy years later, King Kalakaua would be the first monarch in the history of the world to circumnavigate the globe, a case of the student being faster than his teacher.

Slowly a population that had created one of the most complex civilizations in the Pacific, with divisions of labor more precise than in Europe at the time, that had traveled over countless miles of open ocean a thousand years before Columbus crossed the Atlantic, shrank. An estimated four hundred thousand *kanaka maoli* lived in Hawaii at contact. By 1890, a little more than a century later, forty thousand remained.★

It was called the "Great Dying," and it lasted through most of the nineteenth century, the Hawaiian population thereafter declining at a rate of about 2 percent a year.

★The number is contested: the first count, four hundred thousand, was based on visual estimates by one of Cook's officers. Some historians have put the number as high as eight hundred thousand to a million, others as low as two hundred thousand.

The Manager's House

✄

Christmas 1978   Waimea, Kauai

ON THE BICENTENNIAL OF CAPTAIN COOK'S FIRST LAND-
ing in the Hawaiian Islands, my grandmother took me up to the
old Waimea town hall on the hill, where I could see the sky through
cracks in the slatted walls. A gray-haired man sat at a table behind a stack
of slim books. Gamma called him a cousin, related to us by marriage
through the Robinsons. His name was Mr. Gay. She bought me his book
while she chatted. I waited and smiled, a polite child. It was called *Tales
of Yesteryear.* I read it twice before I left Waimea.

I was visiting my great-grandparents, G.G. and Gampa, at the plantation for a week over the holidays. Mom, Gamma, Margaret, and Brew
were there, too. At the end of the week, my father and stepmother
would pick me up and drive me down the palm-lined lane, down the
black highway, back to Lihue on the other side of the island. My mother
would leave to go to Texas. I wouldn't see her for a while.

Tales of Yesteryear kept me company. I liked the story about the shark-
headed hunchback, a demigod who devoured his Makaweli neighbors
when they came back from fishing in the afternoon. And the story of
the ghost paniolo riding their phantom horses to Kokee. Or Kā'ala and
Kā'ai'ali'i: Kaala's father imprisoned her in a sea cave to keep her away

from her lover, Kaaialii. Eventually she died from the damp cold, and from the tiny sharp bites of eels and crabs, and from the loneliness.

Or the story of how Kauai got its name:

Papa birthed a daughter by Wakea. The child was beautiful, and her father bore her on his shoulders, to better show her off. It was the only way the little girl allowed herself to be held. Soon people knew her as the one who rode astride her father's shoulders. They called her Kaua'i, "Straddling the Neck." The gods Kū and Lono saw Kaua'i and marveled. She was so lovely they turned her into an island, the better for her to be admired. And Kauai was of course the most beautiful of all the islands, just as she had been as a girl.

Kow-ah-ee. Stewardesses pronounced it this way, so it had to be right. At the manager's house we always called it *Kow-eye.*

Kow-eye was lilikoi chiffon pie from Hanamā'ulu Café, prune juice in the fridge, sand in the sheets. G.G.'s pink marble egg filled with Almond Roca. Gampa's feather hatband. Crabgrass, salt air, the lily pond at the front steps, the big banyan spraddling the lawn. Green Garden, the restaurant where an auntie spilled the drink she'd hidden in her purse all over the hostess. My great-grandmother's row of shortie muumuus and high-heeled shoes. Grapefruit and melba toast, the camp houses, the sewing room, the starfruit tree, the sugarcane patch at the front door.

Kow-ah-ee implied something older and secret, something not me. It wasn't clear whether I belonged on *Kow-ah-ee.* On *Kow-eye,* at least, I knew my place.

Nap hour at the manager's house was from three to four in the afternoon, ending exactly one hour before cocktails, which were at five. During cocktail hour, the Fayes sat in twin armchairs across from the television, Gampa on the right, G.G. on the left. I served them drinks and peanuts on a small lacquered tray. During nap hour, however, I was expected to rest.

I was the only child to nap at the manager's house; now my mother was having a baby: a girl, I hoped. Neil Daniels would be her father, so

she would be my half sister, but Mom said we didn't have to tell anybody about that. Mom wasn't living with Neil anymore. She was living
with Renee Paty at Chun's Reef. During the week I spent with Mom
over Christmas, I thought many times about the baby. She was like a
fish: slick blue, faceless.

During nap hour, I was always awake. Strawberries dotted the wallpaper. I counted them when I should have been sleeping. I counted
everything: green glass fishing floats that hung from the ceiling of the
Outrigger at the Kauai Surf. The steps down to the lagoons, the mile
markers to Kiahuna. Counting things helped me know where I was.
Now I was at Gampa and G.G.'s house in Waimea, in the sewing room,
where there were 122 strawberries on the top row of the wallpaper. Sun
congealed the air and for one slow hour I lay still under a pink coverlet
and counted. If Gamma poked her head in to check whether I was
sleeping, I closed my eyes. The door shut and I counted until five, when
my mother came to release me.

"Good morning!" she said, even though it was afternoon.

I mussed my hair, rubbed my eyes. I walked half-lidded out to the
living room.

Cocktails, dinner, a walk on the beach, maybe a bonfire ensued.
Then bed. The walls of the sewing room narrowed. It was dark and
cool; the waves rolled in, bufos croaked. I couldn't see the strawberries
but I knew that on the top row there were 122. My mother lay on her
side, facing me, a sheet loose over her stomach. She made circles on my
back, or she drew pictures: letters, a house, a palm tree, the sun. I fit beside her, in the crook of her arm, my face close to her breast. She
smelled like coconut oil and bikini, faded beach towel, cigarettes, going
in only up to there and then diving in, swimming out, coming back
tired.

She sang a song:

Sidle, sidle, sidle
Goes the little crab.

> How I often wonder.
> How I'm often sad.

I never knew any other verses. The ending seemed so final, I was always happy with just the one, repeated until I fell asleep.

In the morning the sewing room rose up so white it hurt to open my eyes. It was late: the birds *kookakoo*ed like they did in the middle of the day, and I was alone. Today was Christmas Eve, tomorrow Christmas, and I would leave.

Down the hall, past the black-and-white pictures, past G.G. and Gampa's room facing the lawn, past the living room, in the kitchen my mother and great-grandmother stood behind a counter. Mom wore a green flowered apron and stirred a pot on the stove. G.G.'s head bowed.

"Look, honey!" Mom beamed. "I'm making rice pudding! G.G. and I are making rice pudding! Maybe you'll get the almond!"

G.G. looked up from whatever she was doing and blinked under a cap of white hair. She was almost eighty and elaborately wrinkled. Fuchsia lipstick licked the seams around her mouth. Whiskers sprouted from her chin. Her blue eyes bulged.

"Would you like a doughnut, dear?"

I weighed my options. Breakfast at the manager's house was always the same: poached eggs on melba toast, half a grapefruit, powdered milk, oatmeal, and, like a kind of dessert, a frozen sugar doughnut. I had to eat all of the eggs, even the yolks I despised because they tasted like mucus, in order to get the doughnut. G.G. called me spoiled if I didn't clean my plate. If I licked my plate, maybe I'd get two doughnuts, as well as a "Good night!" "Fulla beans!" or "What a gal!"

"Dear?"

"A doughnut, honey." My mother raised her eyebrows.

"Uh-huh."

G.G. pursed her lips. "Uh-huh?"

"I mean yes."

"Yes what?"

Just then Mrs. Tavares walked in. Mrs. Tavares was G.G.'s maid. She wore cat's-eye glasses and had obsidian hair and a faint mustache. She smelled like Pine-Sol and Rose Milk. Thank god for Mrs. Tavares.

"Rude," G.G. said, shaking her head vigorously and tipping the point of her knife to me. "Rude, rude. This girl is rude."

Mrs. Tavares kept her eyes on the sink. "Well, Mrs. Faye."

"Mm-hmph!" G.G. sniffed.

And we had been so happy the night before, talking about the abortion. *Peter and I were in Europe,* G.G. had whispered, and clicked her tiny nails on the breakfast table. *There was a doctor on the ship.* Mom nodded and looked down at her coffee cup. Geckos chirped. G.G.'s nails clicked.

When there are stories to tell you forget little pitchers have big ears.

The morning sun spilled into the kitchen, making the table bright, but it was a tight kind of brightness, as if everything had just been scrubbed. I thought of a story my mother had told me once: "G.G. is mean," she said. "I broke my arm when I was a little girl and she didn't believe me." At the center of the breakfast table, which doubled for bridge, a candelabra of guava fruit and leaves spread. Guava jam glowed pink, margarine shone yellow, the bowl of sugar cubes, very white.

I snuck one while I waited for my eggs.

"How does this taste, G.G.?"

Mom blew on a wooden spoon, holding it to G.G.'s lips as if she were feeding a baby.

G.G. winced. "Needs more sugar."

"More sugar?"

"Yep. More sugar."

During nap hour the day before, I heard Mom thanking G.G. for letting us sleep in the sewing room. Then I heard her asking for two hundred dollars. Auntie Margaret had to sleep upstairs, where floors creaked. There was no wallpaper up there, just avocado green paint and a few windows facing the sea.

I could smell my doughnut in the oven when Gamma walked in, her gold bracelets clinking. She wore a sleeping kimono and her blond hair swirled around pink curlers.

Mom smiled but her eyes stayed flat. "Good morning, Mom."

Gamma smiled back. "Good morning, Karen."

Gamma stood behind my mother. One hand rested on the counter next to the stove while the other fingered the curlers. "Not too much sugar, Karen, or it will burn."

I wanted my doughnut.

"Can I have—"

Gamma took the spoon from my mother's hand; Mom stared into the pot. My great-grandmother wiped the counter and Mom walked out. She opened the sliding glass door of the kitchen and headed toward the ocean.

This is what it feels like to wait for your mother: the pain starts low in the stomach, maybe a little more on the right. Not pain exactly, more like melting. Take a breath. The hands sweat and tremble. This is maybe the worst, the way the hands betray you.

She was probably swimming; maybe she was taking a walk. She was just angry. When she was angry she'd leave for a while but she'd always come back.

Hadn't she come back this time? She brought gifts: a Holly Hobby bonnet and Chinese pajamas with matching pink satin shoes in cellophane. They were supposed to be my Christmas presents, but when she picked me up from Dad and Debbie's, Mom said, "Why not open them now?" The wrapping paper whirled around the car and Mom tickled me. Some of it flew out the window. We didn't go back to pick it up.

I could have gone to swim with her but I was afraid. Hammerheads— ugly creatures, plugs for heads—washed up on the beach at the manager's house, rotted there. Still, I could do it. I could be brave like that.

When you're eight years old and bored or waiting on a plantation, this is what you can do: read, suck sugarcane, take a walk down the beach to look for kukui nut shells and driftwood shaped like animals. There's a dilapidated dollhouse in one of the shacks by the starfruit tree; you can investigate that. The banyan tree is like a castle, its roots carving rooms that open to the sky. Gampa might take you on a walk to feed sugar cubes to the horses; G.G. might let you try on her shoes. You can swim or walk or make a cocktail. Or you can open a coconut.

Not yet knowing the delights of the cocktail, I opened a coconut. This is not as difficult as it sounds. Uncle Brew showed me how. Drive the sharp end of the pick into the ground. The flat end sticks up like a knife. Hold the coconut and slam it into the blade, making parallel cuts all the way around the husk. Place the coconut between your feet and start to pull back the hull. This is dirty business. A little brown sphere, like a doll's head, is there at the center. Clean off the remaining strands of husk, a pale browny peach like hair. A nail and a hammer can be found in the garage, next to the machetes, the lawnmower, the rakes. There are three eyes on the coconut; tap the juice here. A few sips—bland and refreshing if green, soapy if mature—are enough. Emptied of juice, the coconut is now ready to crack open. The smooth concrete of the carport is perfect for this. Balance the coconut here, bringing the hammer down upon its face. The bursting will yield a pleasant crack, bright and hollow, not unlike how I imagined the cracking of a skull.

The enjoyment does not last much longer than the eating; then you have to find something else to do.

Where was I? What was this place? It seemed to correspond not at all with the other lives I'd lived—Dad and Debbie's house in Lihue, my old life with my mother. This was called a plantation, though I never connected the dusty weeds of the land around the manager's house with the sugar that grew as far as I could see. That was sugar; this was the house where old people related to me lived. Sugar seemed to have an existence of its own, vaguely connected to the mills that chugged and the cane fires that burned at night, but really as much a part of the land as the ocean or the mountains.

I missed my mother. It was hard to see her so briefly. There wasn't time or space or privacy for anything. But how could I say that? Things were as they were and would not change. A kind of sac enclosed the manager's house. Smells were pleasant and astringent, the air tangy with salt. The grass was short and well tended. It grew and was cut back by yardmen. Everything got blown out with the wind: a perpetual state of remembering and forgetting. If each of us could remember and forget what had gone on before, then everything would continue as normal.

Christmas Eve at the manager's house meant rice pudding with cinnamon. This was a Norwegian tradition. Inside the pudding hid an almond. The person who got the almond was the winner, and received a silver dollar—to be traded for a paper one if the winner could find someone who actually had money in her wallet. Children only won once. Otherwise they became spoiled. The adults drank aquavit. Then everyone went to bed.

"Hansi," G.G. crooned. "Hansi!"

My great-grandmother's voice came from somewhere beneath the dining-room table. She was calling her dog, also under the table. Her blue shortie muumuu rode up her legs, showing a taupe slip and a spiderweb of veins. Getting old was scary.

"Hansi!"

We had just finished Christmas Eve dinner. I had helped myself to three servings of Gamma's marshmallow yams and then accidentally dropped my napkin. Hansi, G.G.'s dachshund, got it. There had been another Hansi before this one, but it had died a few years before—choked on a napkin. There would be another Hansi after this one, and another. Five in all, not counting Gampa, whose name was Hans.

I thought Hansi was a mean little dog.

"Can someone help me?"

G.G.'s white head stilled somewhere near my ankles, but my thoughts were only of pudding. I hoped I'd get the almond. She didn't mean me, anyway. Children should be seen and not heard, and there was no one else in the dining room. So I started playing with my silverware.

The knife was the good guy, the spoon was the pretty lady, and the fork was the bad guy. The knife and spoon were getting a divorce. The fork was trying to have an affair with the spoon.

Gampa went under the table. "Hansi. Hansi boy." The heels of my great-grandfather's shoes shone black; his ankles above his socks were pale and mole-spattered.

"Ah!" Gampa cried.

"Peter!" G.G. exclaimed.

Gampa emerged, cradling his hand. He stood at the head of the table; his shoulders hunched. A strand of spit at the corner of his lips wobbled.

Gamma walked out of the kitchen, holding a tray of coffee.

"Dad!" she cried. "What happened?"

"Hansi got Tara's napkin and Dad got bitten." G.G. frowned. "Little dog."

She meant Hansi, but she was looking at me. Gamma set the tray down, strode to her father's side. The swinging door pushed open. My mother stood in the doorway with the rice pudding. In her hands the glass bowls sparkled.

"What's going on?"

"Tara dropped her napkin," Gamma said. "And Hansi ate it."

My mother looked sad. She faced me, her chin doubling slightly over her freckled chest. She set down the rice pudding, then brushed the hair away from my face.

"That's okay, honey."

"I didn't mean to."

"No, no."

Gamma sighed. "Anyway, it's late."

Mom looked up but didn't say anything.

She held my hand while we walked past the Christmas tree, past the television, past the old framed pictures into the sewing room. It was only when I lay down that I realized I had forgotten to let go of the silverware.

★　　★　　★

Everything was fresh again in the morning. A gracious smile curved on G.G.'s lips. Margaret passed eggnog, Gamma laughed at the piles of wrapping paper, her good teeth shining. On Christmas morning a certain festive messiness was encouraged. Paper and ribbons and discarded gift tags—*Read the card first, Tara!* and *What do you say?*—could accumulate and not be cleared away. I played the elf in a red Santa cap, delivering presents to the adults who sat with tumblers in their hands, placid in their chairs. Lawrence Welk caroled. Gampa's hand—it had only required a Band-Aid, after all—outspread on his knee. G.G. knitted. Mom lay on her side next to me on the white carpet. I had even gotten to eat an Almond Roca.

My mother was lying down. I wanted to get on top of her and hold her there.

I opened my second present. Mom's chin rested in her palms. Gamma had wanted to wait, but Mom had snuck the gift to me and now the adults hushed, watching bemusedly. I was, after all, the only child.

To Tara, xoxo Mommy.

"I gave her her presents already on the way out." Mom stroked my back but looked at Gamma. "This is just a little something extra."

I slit the tape. I untied the ribbon. Even though it was okay to rip on Christmas, I didn't want to. I wanted everything to go very slowly. An old Liberty House box, white with pink and gold stripes, showed inside.

It felt like clothes. I tried to undo the box with my nails but it tore a little anyway.

"What is it, dear?" G.G. leaned forward in her chair. She wore the same pink lipstick she had worn the day before. I could see her bra strap.

"Go ahead and rip it, Tara!" Gamma laughed. "Rip it!"

I ripped. Under a layer of tissue paper there was a silky nightgown like the kind Mom wore, satin buttons lining the front. I held it to my chest; it felt smooth.

"That's my wedding dress from when I got married to your father." My mother smiled. "Remember, Mom?"

"Oh, Karen." Gamma laughed. "That will be much too big."

"No, it's not. It's not too big."

I was being fresh.

I slid the nightgown over my head. My arms found their holes and the hem fell to the ground.

"See? I can use it for dress-up."

"But you have it on backwards, dear," G.G. laughed, pointing a knitting needle. I looked down. I did. I tried to pull the nightgown off but it got stuck so I yanked it down again. The doorbell rang. It was noon on Christmas Day and that's when my mother promised to let me go.

"Next time," Mom said, forcing a smile.

I took off the nightgown. Mom folded it like they did at the store so that the buttons faced up and put it back in the Liberty House box. I heard voices in the hall. Margaret went to greet Dad and Debbie; Gamma started packing up my presents.

We said good-bye in the sewing room. She started crying, as did I, though part of me didn't want to. There were things I didn't understand, decisions adults made that did not concern me. Really it was for the best.

The red dirt road leading to and from the manager's house was lined with coconut trees as straight and tall as telephone poles. When you entered the lane, it was customary to honk in greeting. This was so the Fayes could straighten up or set out snacks or fix a drink if you were expected. Upon leaving the manager's house, you did not honk, you waved. This was obviously more polite. In good weather the Fayes would gather on the front steps near the lily pond and wave back at you until you turned right onto the highway. Then they stopped because they couldn't see you anymore.

CHAMP

September 8, 2001 Honolulu

THE LAST DAY I SAW MY MOTHER, IN EARLY SEPTEMBER 2001, we shared a coffee in the morning at a little Vietnamese place called Ba-Le on Fort Street. I was alone. Layla was in class. It was right after Lauren had moved to the mainland and I had come home for a few weeks. Mom was living with Marc in an apartment on Queen Street, taking care of an old man who lived in the building. I was worried. Downtown isn't a good place for an ex–drug addict. And she didn't have any money. But Marc was helping her, she said; she had a psychiatrist friend who would loan her a thousand dollars if she needed it; and Miss Cleo, the television psychic, said that soon she would come into a lot of cash.

At Ba-Le Mom was late and carrying a paper.

"Sorry, honey," she said, smiling. She had recently dyed her hair red and it made her look pale. She had lost weight. And she had a cough.

"I had to help Marc with something." She cleared her throat. "So . . . sorry."

My mother is always apologizing and I am always wanting her to.

"That's okay," I lied.

We got coffee. She took me on a little tour of Chinatown. We

105

bought a pack of cigarettes and a Coke at a pantry down Fort Street Mall. It was my first time hanging out downtown and I didn't like it. Fort Street was full of hollow-eyed bums. Though it was a sunny day, the wind that blew past the old brick buildings and down the narrow alleys felt dark.

She walked me up Maunakea Street past the lei stands and karaoke bars and then back down again as if I were blindfolded and she wanted to confuse me. Finally she took me to the methadone clinic, CHAMP, Comprehensive Health and Attitude Management Program. CHAMP was where she went to get her doses.

A woman in a bandanna stood in the lobby. Mom said hello to her and to the mustached, toothless check-in man behind the laminate counter. We walked down a white hall; small rooms opened on either side. It felt both medical and illegal. In a back office a vaguely familiar blonde sat behind a cluttered desk.

"Remember Paula, from Women's Way?" Mom asked.

Sort of. Not really.

"Hello." Paula had a feline brow, tawny hair, and what sounded like a German accent.

"Paula's one of my counselors!" Mom shimmered. "Paula's son is a big football player at UH."

"Yes," said Paula. "I'm very proud."

My mother bobbed her head and smiled. Down the hall she was less charitable: "Paula used to be a hooker. Can you believe it? I'm here and she's there, sitting behind that desk? I got *out,* man. I got *out.*"

It was a strange interpretation of what was happening, since Mom was ostensibly still hooked on drugs.

In another office, a heavyset, handsome black man spilling gold earrings and a gold chain sat behind a desk. His hands rested in front of him, his legs set apart slightly in a way that suggested someone taking his ease. Mom flirted in a daughterly way. "*Hiiii, Raaaay,*" she teased. "Tara, this is Ray. Ray, this is Tara. She's the one I told you about who lives in New York. My eldest."

I shook Ray's hand. "Nice to meet you."

Mom batted her eyelashes. "Ray, tell her how good I am doing."

He smiled. "Well, all right."

Ray wore an aloha shirt. He had slick black hair and soft eyes and he was looking at my mother in a way that made me think he really wanted her to make it. So I sat down in one of the chairs across from his desk. There were two, as in the principal's office. Mom walked into the hallway and started to close the door. "I'll be right back." She winked before she left. "You guys talk."

Ray started up, a bit uncomfortable, but polite. "So. Your mother tells me you're a writer. You live in New York."

"Yeah. Just visiting."

"Good for you. Creative pursuits. Myself, I used to be a singer." Ray stretched his palms in front of him, looked at his fingernails. "But that was a long time ago." He curled his hands back into his lap.

He'd been a musician in New York City, he said, where he was from. We talked about that for a while, how he wanted to get back into creative pursuits one day. Then we talked about New York, and his troubles there, and I looked at the framed pictures crowded with smiling people on the wall beside his desk. Silver script inscribed *Aloha* and *Mahalo Ray*.

Ray did not look overworked but I imagined he was. His life had to be real small, he said, so that he didn't get back into it.

"What?" I knew what he was talking about, but methadone clinics make you bold.

"You know. The life."

It. The life.

We were quiet. I fixed my eyes on the wall behind him. It was made of glass bricks, popular building material in Honolulu during the sixties. Dirt streaked where the rain had come down. What was outside blurred.

"How did she get addicted to methadone?" I asked. "Was it from heroin or was it just from the methadone?"

It must have sounded sudden because Ray's eyes widened. He leaned back in his chair.

"Well, now that's confidential."

Why methadone versus heroin was so important to me, I don't

know. I had just learned that she was a meth head a few months earlier. That's what she called them: meth heads. She told me on the phone. I was on my bed in New York, by a window. It was late, as it always is when I talk to my mother. Her voice was quiet, so I knew she was telling the truth. "I've been using methadone," she said. "I'm a meth head." Then she laughed because it was such a silly thing to say.

"I know," I said too quickly. "Layla told me."

I have a habit of stamping on things before they flower, in expectation of the failure to bloom.

"It's a bad, bad drug," my mother said balefully. "God, it's awful."

"Yeah. Anyway."

It's the needles. I hate thinking of her shooting up. I've never done methadone or heroin or morphine or opium. First of all, the needles scare me, but since I could smoke it, snort it, or swallow it, I think it's the size of the monkey that gets me. Mom was clean for fifteen years when she picked up again.

"So?"

"You'll have to ask your mother about that," Ray said finally, chin down. He joined his fingertips in front of his chest, palms apart. *Here is the steeple, here is the door. Here are the people, come back for more.*

I didn't know what to say. I crossed my legs and uncrossed them. Ray swiveled in his chair. I wanted to leave. I felt embarrassed for asking, breaking "confidentiality." You can't break rules with program people. They're so fucking inflexible, really. They make you feel guilty for just wanting to know the truth.

Mom walked in smiling and we split. "Bye, Ray," she called back. I told him again it was nice to meet him. She waved to the people in the rooms along the toothpaste-colored hall. I looked ahead. Outside it was sunny: a bland, perfect Hawaiian sunny. All the meters stood in rows, like little soldiers.

In the parking lot she looked through her purse. She reapplied her lipstick and folded her hair onto her head. "Well?" she chirped, though her eyes shifted. "What now?"

I shrugged. "You could have told me where we were going."

She put her lipstick back into her purse and rubbed her lips together.

"It's not that I didn't want you to take me there." Though I didn't, it was depressing and staffed by ex-hookers and people with no teeth. "It's just that you surprised me. I don't like being surprised."

My mother eyed me. "I'm sorry, honey. I just wanted to share. I wanted to let you know about my life."

I should have asked her then—methadone or heroin?—but I was too busy getting pissed at her for taking me there in the first place.

The Cape

1978 *Lihue, Kauai*

ON THE HILL THAT I CLIMBED TO MY FATHER'S OFFICE at the Kauai Surf there were often one or two Filipino men cutting back the hedges. They smiled at me. I smiled back. They tipped their hat at me. I said hi. It was like a little game. Smile, smile back, tip hat, "Hi," clip-clip, smile again.

My father and stepmother had a Filipino yardman and a Filipina housekeeper named Adaluz. The Kauai Surf had many Filipino yardmen and Adaluz cleaned the Surf's rooms. That's where I stopped thinking about it and looked at the ocean lapping at the beach. Another sunny day in *Hawai'i nei.*

Picture from the sky a well-tended plot of land, a thousand or so acres in all, including the beach and the shallows, jungles, palm trees, golf course, condominiums, honeycombed hotel, lagoons, and tennis courts. There you have the Kauai Surf, my Kauai Surf, where my father worked as food and beverage manager (think napkin folds, pineapple boats, a deluge of drink umbrellas, teriyaki steaks for a thousand), then resident manager (he who goes up to the room after someone has offed himself) for three or so years during the late seventies, when I was still a kid.

We lived a few miles from the hotel. It's where I went when I was bored or hungry, or on weekends, or when Dad and Debbie were at work. I visited my father in his office, which was beige like Debbie's, and on the ground floor, over by the torch ginger and the public bathrooms. I felt strange walking into my father's office, as if I were a guest—albeit, a very small one.

"Tara!" my father said, and smiled. "What's going on?"

I hardly knew my father at all, though I had a crush on him like I had a crush on Burt Reynolds, whom he resembled.

"Nothing. Fishing."

"Mmm. Tilapia. You can share it with the yardmen."

I laughed. His secretary, Marilyn, laughed, too. She was an indeterminate light-skinned hapa—usually hapas and Portuguese and Japanese got the office jobs, Filipinos cleaned and did yardwork. Hawaiians worked at the beach or at the activities desk. Haoles bossed everybody around in bad pidgin but pretended like they didn't. I was old enough to notice this about Hawaii.

When my father was nervous he moved around. He was nervous now. "I'll be done in forty-five minutes," he said, bouncing away from me.

"Just give me forty-five minutes, dear."

I wasn't sure what I'd do now; I had come to my father's office to extract a few dollars from him for Ms. Pac-Man. There were video game machines near the ice-cream parlor, and usually I'd spend the end of the day there, trying to improve my game so that I could at least compete against Dee Dee Padgett. Now I felt I shouldn't ask. I made a pyramid of paper clips, spun the little gymnast on his metal bars. I leaned on one hip then the other. Marilyn started typing.

"I'll meet you back here then?"

"Yup. Back here. Forty-five minutes."

I waved. "Bye, Marilyn."

Marilyn rested her right hand on the typewriter's space bar and fluttered the other at me. Her nails were enviably long—I bit my own.

"Good-bye, dear."

The last thing I heard was her typing, and it sounded nice and crisp to me, and I wished that I could stay in the office and curl up on the brown carpet and fall asleep to that sound, like rain on a tin roof.

Late-afternoon sun illuminates each blade of grass, the air smells of flowers and the sea. Who created this paradise? A man named Dudley did. The Kauai Surf was one of the first modern hotels built by Inter-Island Resorts, Inc., a company run by Dudley Childs. Dudley had three daughters: Flight Attendant Cheri, Twist-A-Bead Pam, and Her Condo Fell Off the Side of a Cliff During a Waterspout Jill. Flight Attendant Cheri and Twist-A-Bead Pam were friends of Debbie's in high school on the Big Island. It's how Debbie met my father—she and Cheri cocktailed at the Surf in Kona; my father was the headwaiter, on the lam from my crazy mother and me. Debbie was eighteen, her first summer after high school. My father was twenty-four and already had a kid. He liked Debbie, Debbie liked me. College seemed far away, I suppose, and rather cold.

That's the story I heard. Not heard, but pieced together. Debbie and Dad didn't talk to me about adult matters—money and divorces and cocktail waitresses and how Jill crossed police lines when her condo fell off the side of a cliff so that she could get her you-know-what. Stories were being told all the time, though; you just had to keep your mouth shut and listen to them.

Here is how you fish: Get a bamboo pole from the activities desk. Darlene's mom is there, a scarlet hibiscus flower tucked behind her ear. And Uncle Thom, who has a mustache like my father and whom I suspect of having an affair with Debbie because they spend so much time together until she tells me Thom is gay. I'm not exactly sure what "gay" means, though I know it prevents the suspected affair. Tutu is at the activities desk, too—not my tutu, who killed herself; the hotel's tutu. Tutu has a smoker's voice and her coiffed reddish brown hair is pulled into a tight bun. A froth of waxy tropicals erupts at her nape. Tutu strings lei with tourists, gives hula lessons, talks story with nosy haole kids who mispronounce everything. Everyone's grandmother, Tutu smiles, forgives.

Get the bread from the Snack Bar Lady. The Snack Bar Lady is black-haired, genial, and grayed by successive Pall Malls smoked out back by the generators. She saves Love's bread for me, hands me tabs to sign. "Tie-ra! Hello! How is your daddy? French fries for you today?"

I love tabs. At eight I've developed a signature.

Take the french fries, the moldy Love's, the bamboo fishing pole to the lagoons. These were once actual fishponds, but that was a long time ago, when people actually lived here, not just visited. Sit against a co-conut palm. Ball the bread onto the hook. Not too big: tilapia are small and flat like disks of metal. Sink the line, catch the fish. Tilapia offer no resistance. Pull them up—there is no reel—dig the hooks out of their mouths. Throw them back again.

Often I caught the same fish over and over, its mouth torn and bleeding, bearing an older hook, rusted, which I had failed to take out on some other fishing day when, feeling lazy, I bit the line instead. I always tossed them back. The lagoon smelled like thrown-back fish, the bottom of things.

Sometimes I got phone calls from my mother, from Texas. "You should be with me instead of waiting for your father or *Debbie* to get out of work." Always the sneering *Debbie,* as if my mother were talking about an eighth-grade girl rival. "I like it this way," I told my mother, and I did. All the food at the Surf was free—teriyaki steak, banana cream pie, chocolate éclairs, coconut pudding—all the hedges kempt. Towels washed, toilets cleaned. Flowers, all kinds of flowers, all in bloom. Nothing died at a hotel; or if it did, it was cleaned up. I didn't know anyone so it didn't matter if anyone left. People were leaving all the time, in fact, and new ones appeared to take their place. Japanese tourists wanted to take their pictures with me. Maids patted my head and snuck me turndown mints meant for the hotel's numberless pillows. The wind came through the lobby and swept everything out. Everyone was always smiling.

But I was sick of fishing alone.

So get dressed up—something rayon, orchid-printed, spaghetti-strapped. Walk though the darkened lobby; the elevator is bronze-paneled. At the top, right beside PH, a button reads THE CAPE: the fanciest restaurant on Kauai. An actual feather cape hangs in the lobby, encased in a glass frame. Thousands of yellow feathers—each one plucked from under the wing of a black 'ō'ō bird, now extinct.

The cape has mana—personal power, spiritual power—power that makes enemies crumble and commoners fall to their faces. A feather cape has so much mana that it was the one thing Hawaiians wouldn't trade for iron when the haoles came. So latter-day explorers like Dudley fished them out of burial caves, along with poi pounders and spears and kapa cloth, back when you could do that kind of thing.

At the Cape I watched the lavash pass. I watched the ramekins of herb butter. I watched the escargot and the cherries jubilee and the *crêpes flambées* and the filet and the chicken cordon bleu and the prime rib and the Cabernet and the sommelier and the rose sellers and the Shirley Temples. I watched my father's hairy chest and Debbie's feather-chokered cleavage rise, fall, rise, fall. I watched the waiters bow and the chef walk to our table, hands clasped behind his back. *How is everything this evening, sir?*

Excellent. My father answers in his hot-dog-selling voice. Kirk Smith was an actor before he worked in the hotels. He said that the girls were better looking in the drama department, and easier. He played Robert Louis Stevenson, a surfer-hippie on *Hawaii Five-0*, and he hawked Miko hot dogs on TV.

I watched the sunset. It sank in front of me while I buttered my lavash, behind Kalapakī Bay and Mount Hā'upu. Pink and orange and purple and red, awash in gray. The Cape, of course, had smoked its windows. The Cape was classy.

"Your daughter is so good." This could be anyone: Debbie's Okie grandmother, visiting from Youngstown, Arizona; a Surf manager from another island; the German, Fritz, who pioneered the in-room safe.

"Such good manners."

"Really, no, she's a very good girl."

The kind look, the tug on the cheek.

"So anyway, Dudley—"

Our dinner companions were invariably burnt, their gold chains glinting. I was invariably bored. Contrary to my pert looks, the hotel business bored me. And that's all anyone ever talked about at the Cape: hotels. So during the lull between lavash and appetizer I walked to the smoked windows, looked around.

Ten stories below, tourists packed up their beach totes. Some folded their towels, some didn't. Percy, the beloved beachboy, would send his bronzed minions to pick them up.

The tourists looked tired. The sun had rendered them frizzy and crisped. A woman shook out her towel, dusting the man next to her. He awoke, rubbed his eyes, inspected his roasted stomach. There would be white seams where his fat gathered.

The day was over. Tab with lemon turned to Mai Tais. A few cigarettes, then dinner: casual tonight, buffet, the Outrigger. A canoe hung from the ceiling. Then sticky sex, then a call for air-conditioning. The bufos sung at night and they were loud, not relaxing at all. Finally, sleep. The sleep of the tourist, sunburned and profound.

The woman hugged her beach towel. The man looked after her. I put my fingers to the glass. Here was my life now, and it was small, like the people below me, and it was bounded, like the hotel was, and it was safe, like how they felt.

"Come here, honey." Debbie pointed to my escargot. I had ordered it for the butter and the garlic, but the snails weren't bad, either.

"Tara likes escargot."

"My goodness!"

"Once, Debbie, remember when we were at the Maui Surf and—"

"She was impressed by the double sheeting!"

"Oh ho ho."

"Aha!"

"*Very* sophisticated."

"Yes, but she still likes the mints at turndown."

"Oh!"

Who knows what we talked about then: occupancy, capacity, conventions, sex, who was a cokehead, who was fucking which security guard or tennis pro, what Dudley was doing, how many twist-a-beads Pam had sold. We ate. I talked about school when asked (fine); I performed skits when asked. I ordered filet for my entrée and chocolate mousse for dessert. I chewed with my mouth closed, as Debbie instructed. I became sleepy at the point where my father sniffed his Grand Marnier. I didn't say it; Debbie knew I was tired when my elbows crept onto the tablecloth—"Off, young lady!"—and my head sagged. It was time to go under the table.

Debbie was warm, her breasts soft and broad. "You want to go under the table?"

I nodded.

"She's a good girl."

I looked at the calves of the adults, their shoes—Famolares, Bass Sunjuns—the illicit wads of gum. I listened to their boozy conversation, wondered if anything would happen like it did on TV: a long-nailed finger tracing a crease from knee to crotch. *Crotch:* another word I learned from Debbie.

Nothing like that ever happened. After a while the conversation became truly dull and was muffled by the dark air, the velvet, the smoked glass above me. Then I slept for real, the sleep of the child under the table, cool and warm both, dark, surrounded by bodies. You wouldn't think it, but I felt loved there.

Down in Chinatown

✄

August 2002 Honolulu

WHY DO I DO THIS ALONE? IT'S MY SECOND OR THIRD day back and I'm heading to Fort Street by myself. I've made a few calls. No one's heard from Karen in three months—not Gamma or Margaret or Layla or Ray. Gail said that a guy she knew from AA told her that Mom was a psych aide at Queen's Hospital. It seemed unlikely, but I checked anyway. Nothing. I have called too many unfamiliar numbers in my life asking for Karen.

I feel weightless, and it is not unpleasant. I call my boyfriend. There are no hysterics, no tearful I miss yous. He knows why I am home; I know why I am home. We do not press. What's the use? He has his studies; I have my missing mother. The distance feels comfortably familiar. It feels like love.

I call my sister. I tell her I'm going downtown but I don't invite her along. Layla's in school, and I'm used to this.

I do my research. It is what I am best at: books, reading, paper, writing things on paper. Treatment options are good in Honolulu, though Mom's demographic is hard to match. The Consuelo Foundation sounds like it could be for women and it is: Filipina women. A lot of them want you with kids, or beaten up. Women's Way, for instance, but she's already been there. The Housing and Community Development Corporation sounds to me like a trade zone. The River of Life Mission says they take anyone, but Jesus Christ dominates the last page of their Web site, and that worries me. Karen has undergone conversion several times; she even became a Mormon for a while. She likes having coffee with people, and the religious are particularly good for housing.

Then there are the programs she's been through—Salvation Army—and the ones she's worked at—Hina Mauka—while she was trying to pass her CSAC, the state drug-counseling certification. This is the life of the addict, as far as I can tell. Either you are one or you're helping one, or you toggle between the two.

There's Sand Island, the treatment center off Nimitz Highway. Built on a spit of land near Honolulu Harbor, Sand Island was used by the monarchy for quarantine during the dying decades. Seventy-five years later, Japanese-Americans waited there to be shipped to California for internment. Homeless Hawaiians constructed shanties on Sand Island during the 1970s; when the city tore those down in 1980, the island was made into a park. Now it houses a rehab facility. Sand Island doesn't cost anything, which is important. It helped my friend Melissa's mom, too, and she was a rich Honolulu caterer.

I call a help line downtown. An outreach counselor with a scratchy voice asks me: "What is your intention in finding your mother?"

It sounds like a script. "I want to help her?"

She's quiet, then she asks me my name.

"Tara."

"Tara—" she repeats. "You know, sometimes it's family that they are running away from. Sometimes the family is a part of the problem."

She clears her throat.

"But listen. Give me your number and I'll call you if I hear anything."

I decide she doesn't know what she's talking about. I never hear from her again.

Finally, I call the Institute for Human Services: IHS, also known as the Peanut Butter Ministry. It's the only emergency shelter on the island.

They've helped thousands of men, women, and children find permanent or temporary housing, says their Web site. They sound swamped. There's only one intake woman. *Oh yeah, you're looking for your homeless mother? Get in line.*

That's not what they say, but that's how I feel. I go to IHS one morning soon after I'm back. It's just a few blocks from 'A'ala Park downtown, where dozens of bums lie on their faces surrounded by their shit in garbage bags and shopping carts and backpacks. A favorite homeless accessory, the backpack.

There are six thousand official homeless in Hawaii. They live in parks, on beaches, in abandoned cane fields, in bus shelters, and at the airport. Some have tents, bikes, hibachi stoves. On Oahu almost half are native Hawaiian, and in the state, nearly a third, second only to haole. Recently Health and Human Services found a psych patient from New York with a one-way flight to paradise. The practice is called Greyhounding, though the metaphor isn't applicable.

In the 1870s every Hawaiian citizen paid a two-dollar-a-year education tax, and all boys and girls went to school. Isabella Bird, the English travel writer, supposed that there was not a better-educated country in the world. The mission school on Maui, Lahaina Luna, got a printing press before San Francisco, and Iolani Palace, the former residence of the monarchy, was wired for electricity before the White House.

Today, though Honolulu is consistently ranked as one the healthiest cities in the nation to live in, it is also one of the most expensive, with median home prices near four hundred thousand dollars. The state has the greatest incidence of crystal meth abuse in the nation, and when I was in high school in the late eighties, boasted the country's highest teenage pregnancy rate. In 2002 Hawaii had the most cars stolen, and it is the state with the highest per capita enrollment in private schools.

At the Peanut Butter Ministry I stand behind a yellow line painted on the cracked sidewalk and wait to be called while the receptionist, indistinct behind bulletproof glass, shuffles forms.

"What's her name, dear?"

"Karen. Karen Morgan. Or try Brody."

She looks at me kindly, nods. I return to the yellow line. She calls up on a PA to the second floor.

"Karen Morgan or Brody?"

More forms. A few minutes later, still behind the yellow line.

"Tara?"

I walk up.

"Uh-uh, honey. Nothing."

I am half depressed, half exhilarated. One day my mother is sleeping under cardboard, the next she's gone. Really, really gone.

I try to reconstruct her day. I have to imagine because I don't actually know what my mother does every day. I haven't spent more than a few weeks with her since I was thirteen. She's mysterious, it's true, but after she relapsed I stopped asking. There were hints of a life when she was living with Marc on Queen Street—the methadone clinic, the old man—but now she's homeless, so things must have changed. I even go to the university. My great-great-grandfather's papers are there, in folders labeled by plantation: KEKAHA, WAIMEA, MANA. Letters to Knudsen in Norwegian; managers' logs of what was bought (fertilizer, machinery, soap, rice, beer, horses) and who was hired (Foss, Madeira, Kaluna, Kaiwa, Nishimoto, Yashida, Rodriguez, Revera, Li Hing, Chung Poi). None of it has to do with Mom, really—it's all from a long time ago, everyone is dead—but the lists and letters and names comfort me. Real people make messes.

And I like this part, the looking: the days spent alone, the what-ifness of it all. What I'll do when I find her—and I will find her, we're on an island—is hazier.

So: Karen wakes up, has coffee at Ba-Le. She eats, perhaps a croissant or a sweet bean bun. She bums a smoke. She reads the paper. She is a good reader. She's quick and opinionated and looks for basic human motivation in all situations. She uncovers all manner of fakery and do-goodery and secret hatred and hidden pride. Usually she can read a situation pretty well, except when she's high; then she gets dumb.

At nine she gets her dose at the methadone clinic. She goes into a lit-

tle room and they give her a few pills. It takes about fifteen minutes,
what with the check-in and saying hi. Afterward she's dull and quiet and
her pupils are little pinpricks of black against the same old blue. Then
she starts to scratch. She scratches and scratches. Opiates make you itchy.
Lauren told me that. Last time we talked she told me someone had offered her methadone at a party in Houston. "Watch out," he warned
her. "It makes you itchy."

"Did you try it?" I asked.

"Are you kidding? I went to the bathroom and threw up just thinking about it. Mom used to scratch, you know, at Mrs. Delacruz's."

I didn't. There is a lot my sisters know about our mother that I don't.

She showers at a health club. She goes to an AA meeting at noon.
She sleeps afterward. It will be two in the afternoon and she'll already
have had a full day.

It's a small life, just like Ray said.

I call the methadone clinic. Ray remembers me. "Your mom hasn't been
around," he says, which should be good news but in this case isn't. If
she's not taking methadone I don't know what she's doing.

He allows that I should check Fort Street, where she hangs out.

"The worst thing that could happen is that she would be embarrassed in front of her peers."

Briefly I think of my mother's peers: Ron, whom I've never met,
Marc, and a girl named Joanna, whom Layla went to high school with.
Layla knew Joanna really well; they were best friends until Joanna ran off
to San Francisco with her boyfriend and became a junkie. Now Joanna
is back in Honolulu, sort of puffy, her tattoos less sexy, more tragic.
Layla sometimes sees her on benches around downtown.

Joanna used to see Mom more than Layla did.

"But go with your gut," Ray says. "Still."

Ray isn't talking about my instinct. He is talking about my actual
gut. It's scary in Chinatown.

So I do. I go downtown. You can find anything in Chinatown:
muumuus, rubbah slippahs, roast duck, phone cards to Cambodia, booze,

phô, plate lunch, dirty magazines, matching tourist togs, luggage, pa-
payas, pineapples, *pakalana*, pakalolo, a T-shirt that says NO HAWAIIANS
NO ALOHA, one that says GOT SPAM? Old men squatting, old women
hawking bean sprouts, silk orchids, cell phones, dazed and moist tourists
still with their airport lei on. *The beach is dat way, brah!* Drugs. You can
find drugs in Chinatown.

At the close of the nineteenth century opium was so popular on the
plantations that there were underground tunnels leading out of the bars
along Hotel Street so that suppliers could meet the dealers and from
there move out to the country, twenty miles or so, to where the fields
were. Back then Hawaii was T'an Heung Shan—"Fragrant Sandalwood
Hills"—after the native wood Chinese used to line their chests and burn
on their altars.*

The first ship of two hundred coolies, commissioned in 1850 by the
Royal Hawaiian Agricultural Society, sank. After this inauspicious start,
almost fifty thousand Chinese came to the islands to cut cane, in several
labor infusions, from 1852 to 1900, before Hawaii became a territory and
the United States's Chinese Exclusion Act became the law. They made
three dollars a month for five years, minus expenses for passage and clothes,
and moved as quickly as they could off the plantations when their con-
tracts expired. They brought with them pidgin, also rice, *hasu* (lotus
root), noodles, kumquats, jasmine, leprosy (so it was thought), and opium:
for personal use, for trade, *fo make bettah* the long days *hāpai kō* (haul
cane). It was better than swipe, homemade beer made from mashes of
fruit and fermented in big barrels under the single men's barracks. Unlike
in the Caribbean, in missionary-influenced Hawaii very little of the sugarcane got turned into rum. First of all, distilleries were illegal, and even
if they weren't, it was against the law to sell alcohol to Hawaiians.

They had developed a taste for opium, too. One cowboy named

---

*In the early 1800s, sandalwood was the only thing American merchant ships could find to
trade for the masses of silks, wood, tea, and porcelain from China. So Hawaiian callusbacks,
named because of the amount of wood they hauled—140 pounds per man per day—left
their taro patches and fishponds to cut sandalwood. To stave off more cutting, the callusbacks
pulled out any saplings they saw by their roots until there was no more sandalwood to trade.

Lono at Lihue Plantation liked it so much he kept his stash under his horse's tail, training the animal to be ornery around anyone but him. The camp cook might bring it in envelopes at the top of the lunch pails to the fields; pensioners procured their supply from village stores, carrying it home in clamshells. Addicts requested their wages every week.

Though opium was technically illegal, one of the last monarchs of Hawaii, Kalakaua, sold licenses for the drug, thereby collecting de facto taxes on the trade. It was the 1880s, large-scale sugar cultivation had not yet begun, sandalwood was nearly extinct, and whaling had long been in decline. The discovery of petroleum in 1859 and the American Civil War grounded the industry almost completely. Most of the large parcels of crown land had been leased; the monarchy was broke. Haole nobles who wanted to curb Kalakaua's power used moral outrage at the Opium Bill to force through what would become known as the Bayonet Constitution. Its laws, among others: representation in the house of nobles was restricted to men of property, almost all haole, and the ratification in 1887 of a previous concession of the reciprocity treaty of 1878 gave the United States exclusive naval rights to Pearl Harbor, the subsequent and obviously intended effect being to weaken the Hawaiian vote and allow a foothold for Yankee imperialism. Haoles took over the country six years later.

In short, opium signaled the end of a kingdom. But then I'm looking for answers.

I was scared of my mother when she had her head on. She could see through people and tell you what they wanted; she really could. She could see the devil in the self-righteous and the saint in the schizophrenic and she'd tell you so. I always wondered why she'd stare so much when I was little. She'd look out and fix her eyes and be gone. When she was high she was passive, spacey, gullible, fake dead. Not much trouble to anyone but herself.

Every square-jawed face I see is Ron, every skinny woman with long dyed hair—she never would have cut her hair—is Karen.

On Hotel Street I pass an ancient shriveled Casanova, blind in one

eye, wearing a pink aloha shirt. He walks into Esquire Risqué, where assorted folks looking for a good time in a dark place at noon walk in and
out, eventually spilling onto the sidewalk, dazed or intent, depending on
what they did or didn't get inside. Across the street an old girl about the
same age, wearing a wide-collared polyester shirt, a ruffled hoopskirt,
and an actual bonnet, rolls a smart red suitcase behind her.

Mom wouldn't be alone. She works best in small groups where she
can be mother, sexpot, sister, confessor, counselor, little girl. So I look
at them: up and down Fort Street, past the high-rises and low tiled roofs
from the territorial days, past the old American Factors building where
Gampa used to work. I'm wearing black—an unfortunate choice in August—my hair is short. A man sails by on a bike.

"What are you doing, lady? Sightseeing?"

In a way, I am. I gawk. Some of the men have longish hair, like I remember Ron having in pictures, so I look twice. On a bench a gaunt
woman and a squat man lean into each other. They laugh. They seem
to be enjoying themselves. Or they look spaced-out, or angry. Mostly
everyone looks very earnest. It's a full-time job keeping oneself alive on
the street: clothed, fed, washed. Two are discussing a meal ticket; three
others argue about something that occurred the night before. They hang
out on pedestrian Fort Street because that's where their peers are. I
wouldn't want to do anything to embarrass her in front of her peers.

I notice a short blonde. She is plump, awkwardly assembled. Her eyes
flicker, she waves her arms up and down as if she's dancing or trying to
fly. She's dressed in two shades of blue: light blue top, dark blue pants.
Like a big baby bluebird, flapping. She's everywhere: at the top of the
mall, where it's seedier, then at the bottom, near the big buildings,
where the downtown workforce in alohawear sits outside eating *bento,*
smoking cigarettes. She walks into the John Something home. I follow
her to the door.

A bald man leans against a wall. He holds the door open for her. I
walk on by.

I'm so depressed I stop at a restaurant called Indigo for a drink. It's an
Asian-fusion place tucked into a building facing a corner park. A sign

advertises their new OPIUM DEN & CHAMPAGNE BAR. I order a gin and pineapple. Layla turned me on to gin and pineapple. Even though pineapples are practically the state fruit, there are only a few fields left in Hawaii. Dole moved most of its operations to Costa Rica.

I wish my sisters were here. I was wrong thinking I could do this alone.

In the women's bathroom there's a trapdoor. I've heard it leads to one of the underground passages. Cebu, the big den was called.

The alcohol helps. I pay the tab; walk up to Sun Yat-sen Mall on either side of Nuuanu Stream. It's sunny, midday. Everything has been made fuzzy by the sun and the gin. Tables hunch under concrete gazebos. Old men play cards and mah-jongg. There's activity: skinny toughs lean on bikes, watch the various games, but it smells like piss. And all along the river, bums and tramps huddle. A few are obviously worse off than the others: they are simply passed out, surrounded by stuff. I don't get close enough to see their faces.

This is Iwilei, "The Collarbone," a triangle of land between the Nuuanu Stream, Chinatown, and Honolulu Harbor, one of those places, like the red-light district in Amsterdam, or the Bowery in New York, famous for its drugs and prostitutes and blowsy squalor. Until Iwilei got cleaned out by the territorial government in the early 1900s, nearly three hundred whores worked here, ages twelve to twenty-nine. Pimps boasted girls of every stripe.

There are still prostitutes in Iwilei, but mostly they drift around Nuuanu Avenue just past the stream. Johns come up in cars now, but it's still a hasty act. I watch a few of them. Their studiously lazy dealers—they're not old enough to be pimps—sit under trees near the cardplayers and watch, too.

And only a quarter-mile down King, the old mission houses and Kawaiaha'o Church stand. Honolulu's dirt is kept small and deep, as in a little boy's pocket, right here in Chinatown.

Two women could be my mother: one has red hair, one is a platinum blonde. They wear tight jeans, high heels, slut tops. The ginger one is pretty, freckly. The blonde is skinny, how I picture my mother to

be now, but I don't think it's her. I look at the woman's shoes: cheap
black platforms. Mom always had nice shoes. I look at her ass: low,
heart-shaped. Mom's is more of a bubble. Anyway, she wouldn't be
walking alone.

I end up in Triangle Park, across from the methadone clinic. This is
where she said she was sleeping last time we spoke and where Layla saw
her in May. Layla was on the bus, riding to her job as a waitress at the
Spaghetti Factory. A guy in a wheelchair had to get out. He was taking
forever. Two tourists from England were sitting in front of her. "Hey,
look at those people!" one remarked to the other. "Are they sleeping in
the park?" And there was Mom, on her back, smiling. Ron was on his
side, looking down at her.

Layla sucked in her breath. "How bad is that?"

"Bad."

"I freaked out. I wasn't going to get off because I was already late for
work."

I remember Layla when she was a little girl: her rattail and her fun-
nily spaced teeth and how she loved to be tickled.

"Is it a real park?"

"No. It's by the bus stop. More like a beautifying thing they do. Trees
and some grass? It's so depressing. To actually see her sleeping in the
park, and she was like five pounds. I was like, 'Oh my god.' I couldn't
get off."

"Did you cry?" Layla doesn't always cry, even when she's sad.

"I waited till I got to work, then I cried."

"That's good." I didn't know what else to say.

I ask a guy who's cleaning up. "Have you seen a woman who sleeps
here? Red-brown hair? Five-ten?" I realize I've made her taller than she
is. Nor do I know the color of her hair now; it was auburn that last day
at CHAMP. Then, for no apparent reason, though I also shared the information with a man who sold me cigarettes, I offer the following:
"She's my mother. She's homeless."

The man shakes his head. "Plenty people up here at night."

We don't have much more to say.

"Hard, yeah?" He's looking at me. He's Hawaiian. It's his job to clean up after vagrants like my mother.

It begins to rain: scattered showers. The joke about the weather in Hawaii is that it's always partly sunny, partly cloudy. The weather girls have to learn how to say the same thing seven different ways.

Maybe she is working at Queen's, like that guy from AA said. He came to Gail's one day in July looking for Mom. He asked for her address. Gail didn't have it. She and my mother don't talk anymore. Mom claims Gail is trying to steal her daughters away from her, and Gail claims Mom actually did steal a bunch of antique coins once when she house-sat a few years ago. I try to stay out of it.

Last week the same guy from AA was found in his car parked up in Nuuanu, OD'd. Gail heard about it from a friend in the program. She tries to reassure me. "I'm sure it's not about your mom."

"No, probably not."

On January 20, 1900, the territorial government burned Chinatown, all forty acres of it, after the bubonic plague came in on one of the boats, killing seventy-one people. It was the first official act of the brand-new territorial government, since the decision to burn was made on December 30, 1899, two days before the Organic Act went into effect, making Hawaii, along with Cuba, the Philippines, Wake Island, and Puerto Rico, territories of the United States.

It wasn't a particularly targeted decision; all across the world, burning was considered the best way to eradicate disease. But after a headline in the *Advertiser* read, "MRS. BOARDMAN'S LIFE GOES OUT—ONE HAWAIIAN ALSO DIES," the decision to burn was made. (Lorrin A. Thurston, the *Advertiser*'s publisher and one of the key men in the monarchy's overthrow, considered it the white man's burden to clean up Honolulu.) Because of leprosy, Chinatown was an easy scapegoat. Families lived together in close quarters, and most of the prostitution, gambling, drinking, and drugging went on here, not to mention shopping, eating, writing of newspapers, and general working-class life.

It's pleasant in Triangle Park, as mini parks go. There are benches and planters, and the grass is green. I try to picture my mother sleeping here, under cardboard, with a man I've never met, but I don't want to. All I can see is Layla on the bus, on her way to the Spaghetti Factory. She wears her uniform: black pants, aloha shirt, black shoes. Her hair is in a bun. She sees our mother in the grass and then she bows her head. Her eyes are soft; her lips sealed. She waits until she gets off the bus, then she starts to cry.

I can't find my mother today so I'm going home.

Morgan's Corner

THIS IS THE LAST TIME I SAW HER: AFTER WE STOOD IN the parking lot of the methadone clinic that day a year ago, we decided to go to Jackass Ginger. We were already in the car by that point, everyone and their towels. Mom, the intensifying redhead. Mom's new boyfriend, Ted, who stayed with her occasionally on Queen Street. Ted was thirty-five or so, curly blond hair, big teeth. He had last been in the service in Guam. He was jumpy and overfriendly and he gave me the creeps. *"Thirty-five,"* she mouthed. "Your mom's still got it."

I smiled. Wasn't she supposed to hit menopause one of these days?

Mom always suggested Jackass Ginger, just above downtown, further up the Nuuanu Stream. You could get there fast and there was no sand or salt to wash off, nothing sticky. You were in the concrete alleys of Honolulu one minute and five minutes later you were in a jungle, sliding down a rock slide into an inky green mountain pool.

Jackass Ginger, Morgan's Corner. A tunnel underneath the Old Pali Road connected them.

Mom moved around a lot as an adult: the north shore with my father; Manoa after Dad left us; Tantalus with Kinau Wilder; Waianae with Eric; Gamma's in Kahala with me; Pipeline with Neil Daniels; Orange, Texas, with Owen ("The only thing tropical is the name"); Houston with Lauren's dad; Monterey with Margaret; Bobby's house; Brew's truck; Women's Way; the transition house; Kaimuki; Kuliouou; Stan's; Waimea for Exotic Weddings of Kauai; Manoa again; Mrs. Delacruz's on Punchbowl; Marc's on Queen Street; Anita's; Triangle Park.

But these weren't her real homes. Her real home was where she grew up, Morgan's Corner up the Nuuanu Stream, in a house called Polihiwahiwa. At Morgan's Corner on the Old Pali Road, where the mountains start to rise and shadows deepen and the stream climbs the cliffs that form a wall between the island's leeward and windward sides, you could go back in time. Jackass Ginger was a paradise. Sweet Nuuanu Stream, not yet sullied by runoff, gurgled over smooth stones; white and yellow ginger lined the banks. You could swim or slide down the rock slide or hike further up to the waterfall.

Lately, though, Jackass Ginger felt dirtier. The water smelled like iron and Honolulu was in a drought. Plus the lepto. Leptospirosis: parasites from animal urine. Jackass Ginger just wasn't what it used to be.

"So why's it called Jackass Ginger?" Ted asked. He smiled too much and too widely. I could see his gums when he spoke.

"I don't know." Mom shrugged. "Ginger? Lots of ginger? My mother had the lei for her wedding picked here." She was looking out the window of the car, up at the trees, banyans and stray royal palms and monstera, someone's houseplant that had escaped a century ago. *None of these plants were here back then.* I was always having thoughts like this. *Nothing is the way it used to be and nothing will ever be that way again.*

"By Chinese women," Mom added.

I had seen pictures of my grandmother's wedding. She looked like Carole Lombard. She was glamorous and beautiful and her bridesmaids held long ginger lei in their hands, all strung by Chinese women with delicate fingers. I had bought it all, Chinese women and everything.

"My poor dad." Mom shook her head and scowled. "He got screwed."

* * *

Brewster Morgan was a handsome man, with bright blue eyes and an oval face. He was kind and funny, and when he took me to lunch at the Pacific Club he ordered plantation iced tea for both of us and told me stories about the war. He's dead now. His second wife had been rather protective, so the kids and Gamma didn't see him until he was in the morgue. Gamma cried; Mom, Margaret, and Gail cried. "Get him on his good side," Gamma said, and someone took a picture.

Mom loved her father but they never really had a relationship. That's why she thought she was a sucker for unavailable men. "It's because of Dad," she'd say. "Mom divorcing Dad when I was young, and him marrying *Frances*. Yuck. Anyway, that's why I was so codependent with Terry. Because he looked like Dad."

She bit her lip.

"Bald."

Brewster Morgan's father, James Albert Morgan, had come to Hawaii by way of Massachusetts, Cuba, the Philippines, and Pennsylvania. He attended Little Blue School, Allen's English and Classical, Cambridge Latin, and Exeter. After that he went to Cuba and the Philippines for the Spanish-American War, where, according to a biography, "with troops chasing Aguinaldo through the jungles he gained his most adventurous and valuable experiences." He returned to study medicine in Philadelphia, met Elsie Johnson, an artist, and moved to Hawaii. He spoke several languages, including Spanish and a few Filipino dialects. He worked at Queen's Hospital in its earliest days; took offices on Young Street and studied the ailments of the ear, nose, and throat particular to Hawaii. His subjects included gonorrheal infection of the eyes; a case in which a wooden toothpick was recovered from the sinus; marked edema of the nasal, pharyngeal, and laryngeal tissues due to an "extreme idiosyncrasy" to English walnuts; disciform keratitis, which seemed to affect men working in cane fields; rat-bite fever; and last, a story that I remember very clearly, as it was one of the few my mother told me about the Morgan side: A centipede had moved into a cane worker's ear and lodged there, eventually reproducing. The eggs gestated and burst; Dr. Morgan was called to the camp to tend to the woman, but her fever was too high, and she died.

Advantages allowed to haoles in the early territorial days gave Dr. Morgan a certain position in Honolulu. He kept a boat in the Ala Wai Harbor; he built a villa in Nuuanu and gave it a name, choosing for a spot a shady glen where the Pali Road swung out toward the Nuuanu Stream. Banyan tendrils spilled onto the pavement there, monstera crept, and it was dusk at every hour of the day.

The bend grew to be dangerous when sightseers crowded the Pali, and the spot where the road switched back became even more so, for a canopy of trees shrouded the already somber spot. It came to be known as Morgan's Corner because old Dr. Morgan—always the first to an accident—tended to the dying or the maimed, called an ambulance, or let the injured use his phone.

In 1948 Morgan's Corner earned its name. That year, James Majors and John Palakiko escaped from Oahu prison. Later they would say they were looking for something to eat. They ended up near Morgan's Corner, just down from Polihiwahiwa. Theresa Wilder lived in a house near there, alone. The two men bound and gagged the old woman; she was found dead in a chair. Majors and Palakiko were picked up a few days later. They were tried and convicted, and sentenced to hang. At the last moment, just as they were being handcuffed for their walk to the gallows, the governor stayed the execution. Many felt that if the men had been haole they wouldn't have been sentenced to die. They would have been the last people executed in the state of Hawaii.

After Theresa Wilder's murder, a mythology of Morgan's Corner sprang up, tales populated by ghosts and kidnappers and stranded couples and murderers with hooks for arms. Dr. Morgan killed his wife, it was told, by strangling her with a monstera vine. Mom had even wanted to start a series of books for teenagers called *Morgan's Corner.* The main characters would be girls like my younger sisters or the Morgan kids when they were young. They would be smart and gutsy, and they would solve mysteries, and they would romp around the rain forest like my mother did when she was growing up there. They would always solve the puzzle, these smart and gutsy girls; they would always survive the tale. Morgan's Corner would not be the fixed place of childhood that it is, gone now save the apocryphal stories whispered at summer camp, but a place that could be imagined and reimagined forever.

"Jack London wrote a story about it," I said. We were on the trail down to the stream. Mom had already taken off her shoes and stripped to her bathing suit. I tried to picture what she looked like when she lived here: bucktoothed, knock-kneed.

"He wrote 'To Build a Fire' in Honolulu, you know."

I had been to private school. I had read "To Build a Fire."

"Oh." Ted and Karen bobbed their heads in unison. "My daughter is so smart, isn't she?" Mom stopped on the trail to squeeze my hand.

I knew I was bragging. No one really cared about why Jackass Ginger was called Jackass Ginger. (For a donkey that was tethered there in the early 1900s, and for the ginger that borders the stream.) Mostly Ted and Karen seemed nervous.

We walked the fifty yards or so through hanging vines and down the boulder-strewn river. Ted, from the uglier parts of California and then Guam, for god's sake, looked thrilled.

"Jeez, Karen, you grew up here? *Paradise,* man. *Paradise.*"

Mom tossed her head. I shuddered. This? This was nothing. Jackass Ginger wasn't anything like it was before.

Still, we swam, we slid. I took pictures with a disposable camera. I thought my mother looked like a beautiful water-wood nymph. Hawaiians sang that love was cool, like a mountain pool, not hot, because everything is hot in Hawaii, and here in the green pockets where time stopped were places one could imagine lovers entwined on smooth black stones, tinkling murmurs of Hawaiian, that most lilting language of love. Kahu'ailanawai, "Place of Tranquil Water," the name of this spot before the ginger and the donkey arrived.

I was deeply in love with my mother, in the way that someone is in love with something she really doesn't know and can never have.

After fifteen minutes Karen looked at her watch. She carried the face of one in her purse, its straps lost somewhere. When she needed to check the time she dug into her bag and pulled out a pair of glasses missing earpieces and held them to her eyes. Then she fished out the watch with no straps.

"Well! We'd better get back," I said, though it was my mother checking the time.

"What?" She looked confused.

"We'd better get back. Your old man."

My mother was always taking care of old men and old women, and because of bad episodes in the past, I worried that she would steal from them and be arrested and thrown in jail.

I figured she stole anyway. Otherwise where did all the knickknacks she gave my sisters and me come from? Two squares of moth-eaten Chinese embroidered silk, blue. A coral bracelet with the hinges broken. An ivory brooch shaped like a rose. Auntie Mig's diploma from the Sorbonne. A pro-annexation book: *The Hawaiian Revolution,* signed to Hans. A filigreed silver spoon, MADE IN NORWAY stamped on the back.

"Oh. Right," she said. "I guess we'd better get back."

"Hey, ladies!" Ted called out from under the waterfall. He was grinning. His hands rested on his ringleted head in the manner of an actor in a shampoo commercial.

She gestured to her bare wrist. Ted nodded, dove under. I idly wished he would stay there.

"Yup, better head back," he said when he emerged.

"Well, okay." My mother ran her hands over her eyes to clear them, then looked at me. "Don't you want to go in again, honey?"

"No." I was cold.

When I was a kid I spent whole days at Jackass Ginger. In and out, warm yourself on the rocks, get in again. Jackass Ginger meant wet dark greenery and cool brown water. And Hare Krishnas with Monchhichi hair. Auntie Margaret, naked on a rock.

My mother dropped a cigarette on the way back. A butt, not even smoking. It rolled down the path and under a boulder. I reached down to get it.

"Litterbug." I couldn't help it.

She looked down the path at me. "I'm worried about you."

I stiffened, notched my chin up. "Yeah, well, I'm worried about you."

Ahead of us, Ted laughed. "Pretty good. Pretty good. Now I see the resemblance."

We were quiet in the car until Polihiwa Street.

"Polihiwa! That's where we grew up!"

Mom pointed at a green street sign and a bank of grass. The owners had subdivided the land after Gamma E. died in the eighties. Now all you could see were a few tidy ranch-styles.

"Wow," Ted simpered.

You couldn't see anything, and anyway Polihiwa was soft and tasteful, not a "wow" kind of place.

"Slow down, Tara!"

I slowed down.

"Morgan's Corner! This is Morgan's Corner!"

"Gosh, Karen, I didn't even know this was up here."

"Morgan's Corner, Ted. Don't you know about Morgan's Corner?"

Only people who grew up in Hawaii knew about Morgan's Corner. The hairpin turn. Old Dr. Morgan, his wife hanging from a vine.

"Morgan's Corner was the famous place where my grandfather lived. Dr. Albert Morgan," she recited. "He was on the *Mayflower.* Tara, did you know that?"

"You mean his ancestor was on the *Mayflower.*"

She ignored me.

Jackass Ginger. Morgan's Corner. They used to work like magic.

Karen shook a lighter up and down. It flickered in the wind. "Tara, tell us what you are going to do when you go back."

"I don't know. Find a job."

The year before I had been fired for the first time. I was an administrative assistant for a trade association. I did a lot of filing. I typed e-mails for my boss. I went to Disney World for a convention. Mostly, though, I called in sick. When I wasn't calling in sick, I came in late. My boss, a grandfather type, said I did not seem happy. I wept in his office. I begged him not to fire me. He was a nice man, and it seemed depressing to be fired by someone who looked like a grandfather.

I didn't want to find a job. I wanted to think about Morgan's Corner and other lost things. Morgan's Corner was the perfect place where my mother grew up, nestling in Gamma E.'s very white, bony, Episcopalian bosom. Now Gamma E. was buried under a gardenia bush. "You should see what the new owners have done," Margaret sniffed. "Ruined Gamma E.'s table. Ruined her chairs. She carved all of them herself, you know."

Down the Pali Highway, past CHAMP. We'd been there only a few hours earlier, but it felt like a long time ago. I deposited Ted and Karen on Queen Street. "Thanks," they said. Mom waved brightly, then shifted her bag onto her shoulder. She moved closer to Ted.

"Call me." I was leaving in a few days.

She blew me a kiss. "I will."

Back in Kaimuki my father asked me, "How's your mom?"

"Fine."

Sometimes I said, "Fucked-up." Or, "I don't know." But this time I said fine because I so wanted it to be fine, and though I didn't like Ted, really she seemed okay.

"Where'd you go?"

"Just Jackass Ginger."

My father was sitting in his armchair in front of the TV. He scratched his stomach, shook out his paper. "I wouldn't go there if you paid me. It's a running sewer. It's got lepto, you know."

I bristled. "It was still nice."

Ted ended up stealing a thousand dollars from my mother. They were doing crack together, it turned out. Also, Gail had hired Ted to cut some branches off her banyan tree—he cut the shit out of it, she told me—and afterward he stole fifty dollars off her daughter's desk. For a while Gail blamed it on Mom, but Mom denied it. "That wasn't me!" Mom said. "That was that creep, Ted." But on account of the coins and Margaret's guitar, Gail didn't believe her. Anyway, it was still her responsibility, my aunt pointed out, so Mom wasn't welcome at Gail's house anymore.

I stayed in Honolulu another two days. Mom never called. It was the first time I would be leaving Hawaii without saying good-bye to my mother. I went to her apartment on Queen Street and rang the bell again and again and no one came down.

I left Honolulu at four o'clock on September 10 on a flight bound for New York set to arrive at ten the next morning. The last thing I saw was Pearl Harbor. An hour outside LaGuardia we got rerouted to Detroit. Planes descended all around like locusts—I could see them through the big airport windows. On the bar TV, the only one on, the World Trade Center was falling, over and over.

When I finally got through to Honolulu Mom told me spacily that everything was going to be okay, but that she had to go because she was having a smoothie party with her girlfriend.

"Remember Joanna? Layla's friend?"

"Yeah."

"She's over."

"Oh."

"Hey—do you think it's because they knew a lot of the people in those buildings were Jewish?"

"Huh?"

"Jewish. All the financial institutions."

"No, Mom, I think they were crazy."

"Well, I just thought. Never mind. Just be safe, okay, honey? Why don't you come home?"

A man at a counter across the way from me was fighting with the Northwest Airlines ticket agent, gesturing to his ticket, smoothing his hair back from his face in a particularly aggressive way. The ticket agent repeated, "There are no flights going anywhere, sir. All of the flights in the entire United States have been canceled." He threw up his hands, readjusted his carry-on, and walked away.

"The flights are all grounded, Mom."

"Oh. Right."

I never really arrived in New York after that. I went back of course, but it was by bus. I never really landed.

III

TROUBLE
IN PARADISE

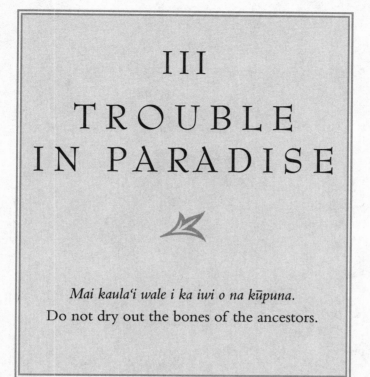

Mai kaulaʻi wale i ka iwi o na kūpuna.
Do not dry out the bones of the ancestors.

Karen, 1970

Sans Souci

September 2002   Honolulu

WE'LL BE DEAD IN A YEAR.
  What?
Dead. You and me. In together, out together.
No, no. I'm going to get well. You'll see.
Mom did it. Mom wants us to die.
No she doesn't. God, Karen. Why do you say stuff like that?
Because it's the truth.

"We'll be dead in a year" is what my mother told Margaret last spring, before she went missing. Today, Margaret reports the prediction to me.

"That's what your mom said. Can you believe it? God. Talk about negative."

We're at Sans Souci, the beach at the base of Diamond Head. Mom calls Sans Souci by its Hawaiian name: Kaimana, "Diamond," what the first sailors here thought they saw sparkling on the crater behind us. (Leahi was in fact speckled with olivine, tiny green volcanic stones, only slightly larger than grains of sand, and worthless.) My father calls it Dig Me Beach, on account of all the leather bags that roast here: overtanned chicks in thongs and bandeau tops; bronze gods with waxed groins and

Speedos. It's a dated, George Hamilton look they're after. Hawaii some-times feels like this, out of time, as if you've walked into an episode of *The Love Boat*.

I am taking Margaret to swim. Wade, really. She hasn't been to the beach in six months owing to an infection in her leg. Four years of dial-ysis has taken its toll. We take a beach chair and set it at the edge of the water. She's changed into a pair of surf shorts and a crinkly spaghetti-strap top like little girls wear. There's still the ubiquitous long cotton shirt over that, on account of the sun and the fistula.

She weighs ninety pounds. Fluid collects around her eyes and down by her ankles. What used to be long, languid brown-black hair is now short, thin, and gray. She looks like a little old girl-man.

"But I want to live! I love life!" She's waving her feet back and forth gently on the water. She looks up every so often at the horizon. Waikiki stretches out to our right, sparkly in the afternoon.

"Anyway she was joking. About being dead, I mean."

I don't know what to say. It's weird, talking about wanting to live. I am only thirty-one, my mother fifty-two, Margaret a year older than that. Too young to be talking about dying. G.G. lived to 101. That's fifty more years. Margaret has just gotten accepted to a special rehab place for people on dialysis. She is sick—she moans when we walk—but she's hanging in there. And we're in *Hawaii*. Palm trees sway overhead. The water, oh, the water is so blue. Who'd want to die here?

"Me, too," I say awkwardly. "I want to, too."

It's been too long. "What? You want to what?"

"Nothing." I rest my hands on Margaret's shoulders, rub them a lit-tle. She mews in response. She says my grandmother won't give her mas-sages. Gamma, for her part, says she's trying to teach Margaret how to be an adult, take care of her own needs.

"That's good." Margaret sighs and pats my hand.

"How do you feel? Are you ready to go?"

"Just about," she nods. "Just about ready."

We fold up the chair, start walking back to the car. About halfway up the beach I turn to my aunt and ask her, straight on, when my mother started using heroin. I've never asked anyone this before.

"Yeah, I know when she first started. It was with Danny Hong. Do you remember Danny Hong?"

I nod. I remember Danny Hong.

Danny Hong lived next door to my mother and me in a dark little apartment off Punahou Street, when I was six, just after we left Gamma's. Stacks of albums leaned against a low table bearing a record player, his speakers, a tuner. Danny Hong's stereo faced his punee where he and my mother reclined and watched me dance. I liked to dance. Danny looked at me. He was the first man who ever looked at me like I was something worth looking at. "She's a good dancer. Wait until she gets older, wow." He had a wide, handsome tan face and longish black hair. He was sexy, my mother was sexy. They were sexy, intertwined on the punee. I danced to "Sexy Sadie." I became sad at "Eleanor Rigby." I played "Let It Be" over and over again until Danny Hong and my mother crept into the even darker back room where Danny Hong's bed was.

"It was with Danny Hong."

"That's who got her into it?"

Margaret nods. "That's who."

A few years after the Danny Hong period I was in San Francisco with my father and Debbie. It was the week of John Lennon's death. People in San Francisco stood around a public square with candles. I cried too much for a little girl who didn't even know John Lennon, so much that my father had to tell me to stop.

"I remember, because she would always come and pick me up at the airport when I got back from the mainland, and one time she wasn't there." Margaret sighs. "Danny Hong. God, he's got Parkinson's now, all sorts of things. Denise, too. Denise is homeless. I saw her on Kapiolani in a doorway with all her stuff."

Denise and Mom go-go danced together. Then Denise had twins with a military guy. Now the girls run an espresso cart.

"Anyway." Margaret shivers a little, readjusts her hat.

For years people have alluded to my mother's problems—God, your mom. How is your mom? Have you heard from your mom?—but nothing was ever specific. Usually when she was high she'd just disappear. I'd ask my mother how it started if I could, but since she's missing I can't. So I ask Margaret instead. She must be sick of answering for my mother's life.

We pass the natatorium, a big outdoor swimming pool with concrete stands climbing up toward the palm trees. It's been fixed up, but only on the outside. It's beautiful: terra-cotta and white stucco, territorial-style. Duke Kahanamoku swam exhibition matches here for tourists, after he'd come back from winning the 1912 Olympics. He was a big star then. Like ukulele music and the hula-hula. Like Hawaii itself.

The natatorium is a seawater pool, separated from the ocean by a rock wall that's deteriorating now, mottled by seaweed. A fence has been installed above the wall so people can't get in from the ocean, but I've done it, climbed right over the fence. The bottom of the pool seemed to float, the water was so clear. Boulders and chunks of broken concrete and seaweed and blue-green water, daubs of reef. I felt like I was doing something terribly bad and special. I felt like Mom.

"So then Danny Hong—" Margaret's panting a little, trying to tell me the story.

I realize I know it already. I thought I didn't, but I do. Back in the late eighties Mom used Danny Hong—he became a lawyer eventually—to win a neck injury settlement from a car accident. She bought a used black IROC with the money.

That's not *the* end, of course.

"You can finish the story later," I say to my aunt. "When we get back to Gamma's."

"Oh. Right."

We walk, Margaret slowly. I hold her hand and she takes little steps. Somewhere before the car I lose the key and we have to stop and search for it. It's just one key, no ring. Margaret sits in her folding chair and waits. She's very patient, I think. "It won't take long," I tell her. I've lost keys before, in this very park, in fact, when I was fifteen and stoned. I found them then, so thirty-one and sober should be easier. You just have to retrace your steps, look at the ground, at the grass. Feel around with your hands. Look for the glint from the metal. Go left, right, left. Don't look up.

Texas

✍

1979 Houston

B Y THE SUMMER OF 1979 I HAD NOT SEEN MY MOTHER for almost two years. I flew from Honolulu to Houston on Braniff Airlines, which would go out of business that summer, making me worry about whether I could use my ticket home. I was an unaccompanied minor, so the stewardesses checked on me and gave me an aisle seat with free headphones and playing cards and sodas anytime I wanted. For a while my companion was a puffy pink lady with a halo of blond hair. "I'm a beauty queen," she told me. "I compete in pageants." She let me fall asleep in her lap. When we changed planes in Denver I waved good-bye but didn't ever get to touch her again.

The flight to Houston got bumpy after a few hours. The captain said it was a Texas roller coaster and everyone around me laughed. The last time I talked to my mother, she had told me about the thunderstorms in Texas. She said there was no rain, just heavy black clouds that settled near the horizon and lightning that spread a yellow web across the sky.

The bumps got worse and the person behind me started throwing up. A croupy baby coughed. I couldn't take it: the coughing and the bumps and the puke. I pushed the call button and got moved up with the stewardesses.

The ceilings at the Houston airport were high; all the windows faced the freeway. Over the PA system they called my mother's name every half hour for four hours. I sat near the windows so I could watch the cars as they drove in. I don't know why I thought I would recognize my mother's car. I had a hard time remembering her face. I counted the times her name was paged, making sure I could see every entrance. I waited, and over and over they called my mother's name.

A stewardess from the plane stayed with me for a while, but then she had to leave and the way she said good-bye sounded sad. I cried when she left because I was still an unaccompanied minor and now I had only the check-in people to look out for me.

When Mom finally arrived she was flanked by a short dirty-blond man who wore tight jeans and a leather jacket. It wasn't Owen and I was confused because that's who Mom said we'd be living with. She introduced him as a friend, then she tried to pick me up, even though I was too big, and she said she was sorry for being late but she thought my plane arrived later than it did and she had to get a babysitter for Layla and there was traffic, and god, she was sorry, and was I okay? I was happy to see her but I cried as soon as she tried to pick me up because I was angry, too. She kissed me on the head. She smelled like perfume, and the pink leather jacket she wore made her look pretty.

The car smelled like cigarettes. Mom's friend rolled down the window. Houston was warm, different from Hawaii warm—hot and moist and heavy. Dead armadillos spiked the highway. We stopped at a house set back behind a spreading tree with a swing. Mom and her friend said they'd be right back and told me to wait in the car. I looked at the house. We were in neither the country nor the city. The house was ramshackle. A buggy porch light shone onto the grass. I pretended to drive by turning the steering wheel. Soon it got so dark that whoever was inside turned on the lights and I could see people moving. I waited until I couldn't see the swing anymore and then I honked the horn. My mother and her friend came out after a while and she said she was sorry it took so long but that now we were going home.

She sat in the backseat. I fell asleep in her lap.

We went to her friend's apartment. He had a swimming pool and a Jacuzzi. It was late and I was sitting in the Jacuzzi with Mom and she had her eyes closed. I hadn't seen her in a long time; I was just getting used to her face again. She said I could stay up as late as I wanted to watch cartoons. I must have asked where Owen was. She tickled my stomach with her toes and put a finger to her lips.

She and the friend started yelling at each other early in the morning. I had already gone to sleep despite my plans, but I awoke when they started fighting and soon my mother came to get me. We gathered our stuff and caught a cab to Owen's. She told me to tiptoe. Before I fell asleep I heard her telling Owen that my flight was late because of all the thunderstorms and he mumbled something and that was it.

Owen's lasted the rest of the summer. *If you like piña coladas, and getting caught in the rain.* It never rains in Texas. Texas is dry and hot, and the only state besides Hawaii that was once its own country. I learned this in Hawaiiana, which I had taken every year by third grade, never with a Hawaiian teacher. There were watercoolers in Texas because the tap water was so bad. Owen's watercooler was in the living room of his duplex, along with a fan and a TV. I had a sticker book I had brought from Hawaii and I spent most days between the TV and the fan, watching soaps, looking at stickers. Sometimes I played at the pool with a little girl I'd met. Every afternoon there was dry thunder and we had to duck for cover in case of lightning. Inside Mom made peanut butter on Saltines.

One day, standing over Layla's crib, she told me I was her favorite. The admission, made in the company of my baby sister, made me uncomfortable. Gray light fell over us, followed by a bit of a breeze. The room smelled like soiled diapers. I didn't like Texas, nor did I like Owen. Owen was moody, and always smoking cigarettes, his mouth grim under a black mustache. Like at Galveston: Mom and I walked around, picking our way across oily sand stuck with feathers and bits of rubbish. Derricks floated on the horizon. Owen sat in the sand, smoking. We went to a water park afterward, which struck me as strange; we were right next to the ocean.

Then one night Mom didn't come home till late. I was up watching a scary movie with Shirley MacLaine. Mom walked in and Owen accused her of fucking a nigger. They stood at the top of a flight of carpeted stairs. He hit her; she hit him back. He hit her again, this time on her mouth. She started bleeding. Then she got Layla from her crib and held her daughter in front of her chest like a shield.

Afterward we sat in the condo office and waited for the cops. Mom was hysterical. I was quiet. I looked at magazines, minded Layla. Then we got driven to a battered women's shelter. It was on a run-down street bordered by an empty lot bounded by a chain-link fence. Broken glass littered the sidewalk. I hated it.

A few days later Owen picked us up. He called me Rugrat and gave me a ten-dollar bill on the ride home. Mom bought me Fashion Plates. Layla didn't get anything special because she was just a baby and didn't have to be bribed.

On the way back to Hawaii I stopped in Casper, Wyoming, to visit Grandma Betty, Debbie's mother, and Grandpa Norm. They bought me roller skates and I planted radishes and watermelons in Grandma Betty's garden. They had a sheepdog named Jason. Before I left I married him. Grandpa Norm officiated; I wore a sheet for a veil. By the time I flew back to Hawaii we had picked the radishes, and even one of the watermelons had ripened.

At home I said I had a great summer, especially in Texas.

Circle Island

August 2002   Honolulu

I DON'T WANT TO GO BACK DOWNTOWN. I MAKE EVERY excuse not to. I ask Layla if she's seen Mom. "No." She makes a face. "I'm not going down there." I avoid that part of Honolulu. Instead, I spend time with my sister at Sans Souci, or Lanikai, or at the movies. I see Gail, my father, Deirdre. I'm without a car, so occasionally when I'm on the bus going down King I look for my mother. I squint at the banyan tree by Star Market under which a gaggle of bums live, or I scan the benches at Sans Souci, but these are passing glances. I'm just going through the motions. I've called the shelters. I've done Chinatown. I've left messages with Ray. My mother will be found only if she wants to be.

There's a bus, #52 Circle Island, that goes all the way around Oahu, through the Wal-Marted suburb of Mililani, past Hickam and Schofield Barracks near Wahiawa, past Waialua, where I was born, over to the north shore: Waimea Bay, Sunset Beach, Pipeline. Then around the east side: Laie, where the Mormons are, Chinaman's Hat, Kaneohe, and back over the Pali. It's only a dollar-fifty and you can ride all day. So that's what I do on a lark. I take the Circle Island around.

Today Oahu is early-September brilliant. Once I get out of Honolulu I realize why people congregated here. It is really the perfect island: the folding cliffs and sandcastle spires of Kauai without all the rain; the beaches of Maui; the weather of the Big Island minus the vog—volcanic fog from twenty-five years of eruption at Kīlauea. Oahu, younger than Kauai but older than the rest, has wide bays and deep harbors and tiny islands that skim the shore. Kualoa, where Chinaman's Hat floats, was supposed to be the seat of Hawaii's highest alii, the place where voyaging canoes bound for Kahiki made preparations for their six-month sail south.

I am lonely. I miss New York. I have to be comforted by the scenery: an island just beginning to be undone, a lovely sight indeed.

Layla and Lauren have spent a lot of time on the bus. They know the drivers: Sansabelt slacks, slicked-back hair, tinted glasses. They know the passengers: old ladies carrying sun umbrellas, old men in collared shirts, students in surf shorts, laughing.

I have spent a lot of time on buses, too. On the mainland it's the cheapest way to get around and I kind of like it. Take an airplane and there are no lines to cross, no mile markers ticking by, no way to sense the passage of time. The destination feels the same as the departure. Take a bus and you feel how long it takes to go from, say, Newark to Chicago, as I once did. My seat partner was a Vietnamese woman named Thu, who was traveling home from grad school. After Indiana we began to chat. "I'm Amerasian," she said, and then she asked me if I could tell. I said no, though she had a cleft in her chin like Kirk Douglas's. Thu said that in Vietnam no one wanted the children from the war. Their mothers took money and comfort from American GIs. They made mistakes.

I got lucky with Thu. Usually they are crazier on the bus. I lived in Portland for a year after college with a boyfriend. We got along fitfully, but I thought he was handsome and funny and he had gone to boarding school and listened to the Grateful Dead and this intrigued me. We fought a few miles past the New Hampshire border about which Tupperware to buy for the road. We might have turned around then, but we were young, so we moved across the country together. When we got to Portland we lived off Burnside Street, where hobos came in off the trains. Our car had died somewhere in Wyoming, and we were too poor to buy another one, so in Portland we took the bus. On the Burnside route I sat next to a woman in a witch's hat; also a man with a paper bag over his head, holes cut out for the eyes.

On DaBus #52 Circle Island, the woman next to me reads *Reader's Digest*. She's pretty, or was once, but there's something wrong with her, a corner turned down on a page somewhere. She's gabbing with the driver—always an ear. Her sister is gay. She has had three abortions and she's Catholic and she once kidnapped her mother and took her to Kauai. I know all of this from sitting next to her on the bus.

And there's that guy in the back, jerking off. And somehow everyone is carrying plastic bags.

Once I heard on the radio a list of odd items found on Honolulu city buses: a glass eye, false teeth, a cane knife, a typewriter, a backpack of turkey tails, five kids.

A man rides to his job in the fields: It is sometime in the early 1970s, before sugar on Oahu died and all the fields turned to suburbs, shopping malls, industrial parks, freeways, movie theaters. The man is brown and leathery; his hands are callused. His fingers curl into his palms and he rests them on his thighs, which show through his cotton pants as thin, muscular. He sits at the edge of the plastic seat. Sometimes he closes his eyes and his face goes slack; the corners of his mouth fall into his chin. He wears rubber slippers and carries a bag with a change of clothes for the afternoon: his razor, his comb. He wakes up just as the driver stops and in his haste he forgets the sack that is farther under the seat, past his bag. In this sack is his knife.

Perhaps he knows right away that he's forgotten it but when he turns around to wave, the bus is speeding down the hill away from him. Black exhaust floats from the tailpipe into the sky. Or maybe he does not realize it until he is some distance down the road. In any case, he never claims the knife. It sits in the lost and found in the Honolulu terminus until one day, after its presence has been duly noted—along with the false teeth, the typewriter, the turkey tails, and the five children—it gets thrown away.

Of course this little story is a fantasy. Sugarcane cutting had been mechanized long before 1970. The only thing you use a cane knife for now is weed whacking in the backyard. And it's the fantasy of a plantation girl, a girl named Tara.

Hawaiian Homes

1980   Lihue, Kauai

MOM CAME HOME FOR A VISIT, WITH LAYLA, TWO YEARS old, so chubby she had creases between the fat on her thighs. Blue almond eyes, wispy blond baby hair. We stayed at Gamma's. I slept with my sister every night until I heard Gamma say that it was unhealthy.

She called me Sister, as my mother instructed.

"This is Sister. Say Sister."

Layla and I stayed in the back room; Mom and Will slept in the bachelor's cottage. Will Stewart was Mom's new friend from Houston. He was nice, and funny. He took pictures of Layla and me leaning on Gamma's plumeria tree: Tara in a dark blue polyester kimono top, Layla baby nude.

"Good, good. Great, great." Will played photographer. I cupped my chin, rested a hand on a hip. Mom had blow-dried my hair and I was wearing makeup: frosted-pink lip gloss, a little mascara, blush. Mom was into blush but lost the brush so used her fingers to wipe it into our cheeks.

My kimono plunged, slit between my ten-year-old breasts. I had nothing to hold it in place. Layla was naked from the waist up, her little belly tight. We wore yellow-and-white plumerias behind our ears. I held a bouquet of pink bougainvillea.

"Yes, yes. That's right." Will moved around me and I tried to look exotic.

Mom liked pictures. She took us to Sears, to photo studios, to friends with cameras. We were foxy, sexy, gorgeous, beautiful—never just pretty. Layla had *gorgeous* eyes. I had a *beautiful* mouth.

"Isn't she a fox?" Mom asked Will. She stood under the lychee tree, next to a pile of leaves. She soaked us in. The look was strange. She was smiling but even at ten I could tell she was angry—not at me, but at something.

She nodded, put her hands on her hips. "My daughters. That's right. My daughters."

Things were looking up. Will had a condo with a pool—and the Galleria was in Houston.

"Remember the Galleria?"

She was applying lipstick in the mirror and I was watching her. Top lip, bottom lip, pucker a few times to rub it in.

"No."

"It's the big mall with the ice-skating rink. Remember? When I took you there? Bought you Fashion Plates?"

She rubbed the lipstick off her teeth.

"Do you still like Baby Alive?"

I got my immunizations late enough to remember them. Mom bought me a Baby Alive afterward. I loved the way its little mouth moved and made mewling sounds. At Pipeline we ran out of the packaged food so I fed my Baby Alive grape jelly. After that we had to throw her out because she rotted inside.

"I'm too old for Baby Alive."

"That's right," she said, nodding. "You are."

Mom was wearing her pink leather jacket and as she spoke she pulled the sleeves down, adjusted her cuffs, fluffed her hair out in back.

"I got this at the Galleria." She turned. "How do I look?"

Will and she were going to Scruples. It was a nightclub in Waikiki, but she told Gamma she was going to the movies.

"Pretty."

"Just pretty?"

She sucked in her cheeks and shook her hair.

"I mean beautiful."

At Fred Lunt's house in Nānākuli, Patrick Cockett played guitar in the open-air living room facing the sea. Patrick Cockett used to play slack key with Auntie Margaret. At Fred's, surfboards leaned against the house; a hose snaked through the grass. Rooms ran all the way down the lanai, like a hotel, and in each room was a bunk bed. Me on the top, Mom and Layla on the bottom. At night she whispered up to me: *Blood is thicker than water.* I told Patrick Cockett I hated my mother and he spanked me.

"You never say you hate your mother. You never say that."

I was ten. I didn't know hate.

Outside, Shorty, skinny, raisin-faced, got more and more tan. I didn't know what Shorty did at Fred Lunt's, but when Mom and I visited she said, "Hi, Shorty! Remember Tara?" and Shorty acted like he remembered me but I could tell he didn't. What did we do at Fred's? Swim, make mud pies at the edge of the beach where the half-flower *naupaka* grew. Back on Kauai, I'd named our new little dog Naupaka because he only had one ear. He had been the runt. He died after a while. Debbie cried. It was sometime after Dad started commuting—he worked on Oahu and came home only on weekends. So now it was just Debbie and me. And Naupaka always had been a little sickly.

Mom pierced my ears on that trip. Sears again, Pearlridge. I chose golden hearts. It hurt and the lady punched them crooked but Mom kissed me and called me a big girl and showed me how to care for the holes with peroxide and twist the studs every day. "Debbie doesn't allow pierced ears," I said too late.

"*I'm* your mother."

The day I was to fly away we went to the state fair out in the country, by Pipeline. The fields smelled sweet like manure. "*Lani* Moo!" Mom said as we passed. "Lani Moo!" After the baby cows and the baby goats and the lambs we ended up at the bins of baby chicks. I adored the baby chicks. I petted them; I petted them. I loved them so much I wanted to squeeze their guts out. Mom bought me two, ten cents each. The man behind the bins put them in a paper bag. I blew on them on the ride to the airport. I named them Robbie and Fluffy. Fluffy because that's what they were and Robbie because I couldn't think of another name.

Debbie frowned and shook her head when she saw the chicks and the pierced ears, but what could she do with what had already been done?

Chickens don't do much except grow up into awkward scraggles of wing and beak. At the Puhi house I kept them in a green laundry hamper in the washroom near the garage. Sometimes I let them peck around in the grass, though I worried that Kona would eat them, so their brief freedom never lasted long. They didn't seem happy in the laundry hamper—it smelled like chicken shit and it was cold—but at least they were safe.

I found Fluffy cold outside his hamper one weekend when Dad was home.

"Maybe he committed suicide." He laughed. It was sort of funny. Then he put his hand on my head and said, "I'm sorry, dear."

I gave Fluffy a proper burial in a shoebox, vaguely sorry that the one with the better name died first. Only Robbie was left, and I didn't play with him anymore. You can't really pet a chicken.

It was my father who suggested what to do with him.

We had gone shell collecting at Secret Beach and were laying out the shells in the garage side by side to dry out their squishy bodies. It stunk for a while, but then you washed out the gunk and had a pretty shell to put on your shelf.

"We'll take him to Chickenland."

I brought a spiral auger up to my nose to smell it. It was brown and white and it smelled like the ocean.

"There's no such thing as Chickenland."

"Uh-huh." He nodded, raising his eyebrows. "Chickenland is where all the chickens retire."

"No, it isn't."

"Yes, it is."

"No, it isn't."

Past Grove Farm's fields, past Lihue, down through Lāwa'i, Waimea way. I looked at the sign at Colonel Mustard's Last Stand: HOT DOGS. The Tourist Trap sold puka shell necklaces and tikis and kapa cloth. I was surprised they were so honest.

"Who would stop there?" I asked Dad. "It says Tourist Trap!"

"Tourists go anywhere you tell them to."

The broad plain of Hanapepe Heights, McBryde Plantation. Port Allen, where the sugar got loaded onto the boats. You could see all the way to Niihau.

On the right and left a sudden development of low-slung concrete-block ranch houses appeared, each with its yard and carport and hedgerow of hibiscus breaking the stare of the highway. HAWAIIAN HOMES. There were other places like this on the island: Anahola, Kekaha. Places Hawaiians lived.

Between there and McBryde camp, there was Chickenland.

We let Robbie off on the side of the road. He scurried underneath a hedgerow. He didn't look back, though why would a chicken look back?

I still had the pierced ears. You couldn't just let those off on the side of the road.

Later my father joked that Robbie would probably be eaten that very same day, the eating habits of strangers always a good subject for jokes between my father and me.

Moekolohe

September 2002   Honolulu

HOMELESS WOMEN ARE THE SADDEST. SOMEHOW THE men don't seem as lost to me. It's like an extension of being a man, the vagabond life. Men seek that freedom. A homeless woman is naked, stripped of what gives her power—the domestic scene—and though she must be a kind of sorceress to survive on the street, a woman seems truly vulnerable there. Her beauty, her weapon, disappears little by little as she loses her teeth. Her cheeks draw toward the bone. Her death mask shines. She is fierce and perhaps even crueler than the men, whose cruelty seems by nature's design.

One last time downtown. It's been a few weeks since the last visit. Triangle Park is still empty. I ask a pretty woman hanging out near a building across the street whether she's seen someone named Karen. "Five-eight, red-brown hair—"

She spreads her hand in front of her face. "No."

"I'm sorry, I just want to—"

"Fuck you! Get the fuck away from me!"

I'm here on a tip: A few days ago Margaret told me she saw Mom on Fort Street in May. Margaret was waiting for her bus to dialysis. Mom was with a guy who Margaret thought might be a pimp. The sisters greeted each other. Then Karen disappeared into a doorway. It was the last time anyone saw her.

So I head down to the river. This time I ask Layla to come—she's on her lunch break from school—but she says she'd rather stay over by Triangle Park.

"She's not down there by the river, Tara. That's not where she hangs out."

I can't tell if my sister is being too innocent or I'm too dark. The river is where the prostitutes are. Am I trying to find her, or am I the worst kind of voyeur: the one who hopes for a bad ending?

In high school I used to drive down the Waikiki strip on Kūhiō with friends and laugh at the hookers. It seemed an innocent enough pastime. They were half glamorous, half freakish, an exciting combination. Back then Japanese businessmen came to Hawaii in great numbers to play *golfu,* so our giggles were tinged with awe.

"I heard they pay a thousand dollars a night for the high-class ones."

As if I knew.

Was this really all she had ever been good at? No, no. Karen helps people: Denise when she was relapsing and Margaret when she was sick, and at every party, there was Marsha, better now with the lithium.

By the river it's the same old scene. Girls walk back and forth across the bridge and along the banks, out of view of the satellite police station. Some are run-of-the-mill streetwalkers, a bit ripe in the heat. A few are terrifying. One in particular I am drawn to: sixtyish, skeletal, halfway across the bridge. She wears aerobics shorts, pumps, a bustier, and, over that, a white waist-length kimono. Her hair is long, dyed black, and has been pulled back into a tight ponytail. She is so pale she looks powdered. How shockingly old she looks in the getup of a young girl.

In Hawaii they used to call adultery *moekolohe,* sleeping rascally. Before the missionaries there was no such thing as adultery. Women and men partnered and unpartnered freely, choosing mates that suited them. In the 1840s, distressed by the burgeoning business downtown and at other island ports of call—Lahaina on Maui, for instance, where the whalers docked—a recently converted king proposed stiff punishments for moekolohe. A second offense brought drowning or banishment; a third offense, hanging.

But sleeping rascally was part of the story Westerners had told themselves about the South Seas, the Sandwich Islands included, and demand was hard to quell. Even on Cook's boats the lash had not been a convincing deterrent. January 25, 1779: "Will Bradley, for disobeying orders, with 2 dozen, and having connections with women knowing himself to be injured, with the Venereal disorder." After Cook was killed on that final visit—he died on Valentine's Day, oddly enough—and Captain Clerke was confined to his cabin, sick with tuberculosis (he would perish on the way to Alaska), discipline broke down further and recorded instances of the lash were fewer. The crew already knew the islands were infected. Upon their return in the winter of 1779, Hawaiians from islands the boats had never even approached the year before climbed aboard the ships complaining illness, pointing to clap-covered penises and then pointing to the crew.

When the boats left Kealakekua in the early spring of 1779, the village still burning, women stayed on deck in full view. The sailors stopped one last time on Kauai and Niihau, where a swain named Samwell wrote of the girls who slept aboard. He listed the words he'd learned from his "old sweethearts." It is a lover's list, gleaned from time spent intimately: hair, eyebrow, eyes, nose, teeth. She says, "Waheine," pointing to herself; to him, "Hekane." To the water, "Hevai." To the sun, "Hevah." "Herore," the pox, makes the list, as does "O wai tou e noa?" What's your name?

"Waw-whe"—*Ua wehe,* to go away—is the last entry, *wehe* meaning opening, loosening, unbuttoning, as in clothing; to cleanse of defilement, remove, forgive, satisfy. *Ua weheke akule i ka hohonu,* the akule fish has fled to the depths. *Wehe o uahi,* one who is quickly gone from sight, as smoke from a ship.

Over by the Section 8 houses I think I see my mother in a baseball hat and dark glasses getting into a Bronco. I watch her for a few minutes. She stands at the car door, her arm slung over its edge, talking and nodding. She looks my way before she ducks into the car, and though it is an accidental glance—I am too far away to be recognizable—for a moment I convince myself it's Mom. "Come and get me," she is saying. "Come and show me for who I am."

I don't. It's not her. I had wanted it to be, though. Sometimes even wrong—even really, really wrong—feels better than nothing.

Territoriality

⟡

1981   Lihue, Kauai

AT THE BEGINNING OF THE EIGHTIES, DAD AND DEBBIE and I moved to a subdivision called Ulumahi, a drab collection of concrete-block ranch houses xeroxed onto freshly paved streets. It was new; that's why we moved there. No doubt Debbie had gotten tired of the romance of living in the old plantation houses my father loved. In Puhi, where we had moved after Mokoi Street, the enamel sink bore the leaky trails of rust stains from sediment in the water. Birds nested in the eaves, cockroaches flew under the yellow garage light at night. The outdoor washing machine—never a dryer—shook violently on its small feet. Debbie would go out, readjust the towels and the jeans. I'd hang them on the line later. With all the rain, they wouldn't dry for days.

In Ulumahi, we were happy with our dishwasher, our microwave, our dryer. We were happy with Adaluz from housekeeping, who came every Thursday to clean.

Across the highway, where the fields started, at the end of a row of royal palms stood a white plantation house, complete with fluted columns and a porte cochere, ponds covered in scum and pathways that led into a weedy garden. Elena King and her husband, a realtor, lived there. Once Elena came over with a black eye, but when things were going well with her husband I'd play with their huskies, crack macadamia nuts on the pavement of their garage. Even when it wasn't raining I watched television after school instead of going to the Kauai Surf. "Why don't you go outside and play?" Debbie said.

"Don't feel like it." *What's Happening!!* was on.

Eventually the Kings divorced and left the house. A mainland haole girl named Anne moved in. Anne and I tramped around the garden looking for whatever, past the empty lily pond and the moss-covered statues and the macadamia nut orchard. Beyond the tall trees were cane fields, and those held few secrets.

I'd rather have been at Nina Madeiros's, anyway.

After a while I became distracted and bored. I'd pick a fight—something about how Anne never came to my house, how I always had to go to hers. I told her she could make it up to me if we could have a snack. So we went inside to eat ice cream, play *Sorry!,* watch TV. Her mom asked us in her icky mainland accent, "Whadja find?"

"Nothing," we said, which was true, even if I didn't want it to be.

"How about a hooker?"

Devika laughed and slapped me on the shoulder.

"No, I'm serious. I can get the costumes from my mom."

"Not."

"Uh-huh."

"When?"

"I can have her send them. From—"

I didn't quite know where my mother was. Texas? Last time I'd heard she'd moved to California with Margaret, to a town called Monterey. I had no idea where Monterey was. I'd only been to San Francisco and to L.A. Dad and Debbie took me to Disneyland. I had wanted to go on the Matterhorn, but when we got there it was closed for repair.

I remembered the costume. Red, with fringe. Back when I lived with Mom on Oahu we picked up her paycheck one day. Fort Shafter, Hickam, I don't remember which. In a brown room, louvered windows stretched across the wall. Light shone as if through paper over waxed concrete floors, aluminum folding chairs, brown laminate deuces. There was the stage, the bar, and further back a room, the stripper's dressing room, where the girls kept their costumes on a dolly. A red one—sequined, stringy—had been strewn across the back of a chair.

Devika stopped in the middle of the road. We were playing Charlie's Angels on our bikes. It was evening, mid-October. Unfinished houses ripped across the horizon. The road smelled like tar and rain.

"Like a real hooker costume?"

"Totally."

She took off her windbreaker and twirled it around her finger.

"Like this?"

I laughed, hand on a hip. "Hey there, mister, howsaboutagood-time?"

I almost peed my pants. It would be the best costume in Ulumahi. Everyone would crack up.

Cat. Fairy. Butterfly. Beauty Queen. Hooker.

When I lived in Tantalus, at Kinau Wilder's, I had been a cat. I still had the picture. No frame, just the photo stuck to a square of glass. I was holding the hand of a bearded Japanese man. He must have worked for Kinau, like Mom did. He wore a flashlight on his forehead. I wore a black leotard. Whiskers were painted on my cheeks.

"Hooker," I told Debbie when I got home.

She was at the sink facing Kona's pen. It was a weekday, so it was just us.

"Come and wash the lettuce."

She looked odd, as if she was trying to remember something. She dried her hands on a paper towel, rubbed her nose.

"That's not an appropriate costume for a little girl, Tara."

I knew it wasn't.

"It's just a joke."

"It's not funny."

"Yes, it is." I hated washing lettuce. I hated making iced tea. I hated scooping Kona's poop.

"No, it's not. It isn't funny at all."

*   *   *

Most of all I hated mainland haoles. Devika did, too, though she was one. On account of the fact that she picked up pidgin quick and all the *titas* thought she fought good, not like a haole, but like a real tita balling up her fists and using her nails and biting and spitting if she had to, no one thought of Devika as a mainland haole, or even a haole at all.

Why I continued to remain a haole confused me. I put it down to small differences: Devika, in spite of her ultrahaole hippie name (*Indian,* her mother, Carla, said, *it's Indian*), had *straight* brown hair and brown eyes. Her arms were hairy but Portuguese kind of hairy, thick and black. She shaved her legs in fifth grade. She talked pidgin as if she had been born here. She wore shorts to school. What did Hippie Carla care? In public Devika bullied me. This was the most important part about not being a haole. Making sure that the other haoles knew you weren't one of them.

The day she walked into fifth grade, Devika Benton was the most mainland haolified girl you ever saw. Number one, her hair was tangled, and I don't just mean tangled like Johnson & Johnson. Devika Benton's hair was a kind of nest for her long pale mouse face, wherein two beady brown eyes, nibbly mouse lips, and a delicate long mouse nose twitched. She had skinny arms and skinny legs and the worst thing about her, the thing that showed her for the haole she was, was that she *stunk.* A man's B.O.

She wore polyester aloha shirts. What was Hippie Carla thinking?

Someone called Devika a stink haole, some punk half her size, and right there she dropped her books, I mean dropped them, like in *My Bodyguard,* and fought the little shit right there. She scratched him and punched him and wrestled him and they were still on the ground scrambling when Mrs. Doi finally broke it up. *Eh! Rascal!* (Mrs. Doi has daikon fingers. Devika fake cries. Darren Fukuda trudges to the principal's. *Tree days' saspenshen.*) No one had to tell Mrs. Doi it was because Devika was a haole, and Devika never said anything about who had started the fight. What was important was that most of the people in the circle were rooting for her. She was winning, after all, even though just that morning she had been a stink B.O. mainland haole. What else was important was that I was in love.

"You have to think about *reputation*."

Debbie and I were driving up from the dump.

"A reputation is all a girl has."

Debbie's lips were already starting to crease from her pack-a-day B&Hs. They wrinkled on the word *reputation*.

"But she's cool. I like her. I like her."

I liked Devika's fingers. She had slim, long fingers. She painted her nails Wet-n-Wild maroon or metallic purple or glitter fuchsia. I liked to watch them bouncing across the numbers on the phone, prank calling. *Hi. Is Ben Dover there? No? How about Stu Pitt?* I even liked Devika's B.O. and the way her front teeth overlapped, and the buzzy things I imagined flying around her head, like Pigpen except she was a girl and eleven, and from Sacramento.

I liked her mom: fat, black-haired Hippie Carla. Carla worked at UPS. We'd ride around in the UPS van, doing errands, sitting three to a two-seater in the back. Neela, Devika's little sister, was loose-limbed, squishy; Devika was hard like a little carrot.

"She's not the right kind of girl," Debbie said, her jaw tight. "She's too grown up."

This was true. One night we had been sitting in somebody's—maybe Monica Burns's—Jacuzzi. (Monica Burns's mom loved the sun so much she had the skin on her face burned off with acid; I saw her at Kukui Grove shopping center with bandages and sunglasses on.) Devika and Neela said that when they had been in California their dad had been on coke and some men had locked them in a garage for a few days and did bad things to them. That's why they were sent to Hawaii to be with Carla. I wasn't sure whether to believe them or not. Something about the way they said it—both of them with their skinny arms looped around the aluminum railings, steam rising, chins lifted, like they were

bragging, but not. Plus, Devika walked around the track with Dawn
from Hale ʻŌpio, the bad girls' home in the old Wilcox mansion. Dawn
definitely had a reputation.

"Yeah. So?"

Debbie had her stern face on.

"Just stay out of trouble."

Trouble was that indefinable thing that girls with reputations got you
into. Trouble sounded fun.

"I know. I'll be careful. I'll be good."

Debbie shifted. "You'd better."

But Debbie was too strict, after all, and Dad was commuting, so I decided to run away. I'd camp out for a while; then try to find my mom. I
enlisted Devika's help.

It was a Saturday. Devika had slept over, and we were still in bed.

"Where're ya gonna go?" She had a funny accent. Part hippie, part
farmer. I wondered if it was because she was from Sacramento. "Excremento," my father called it. In Excremento there were farms and dusty
green trees the color of artichokes and lots of little long-haired ragtag
haole girls like Devika.

"I'm gonna camp out at the church," I said solemnly, burrowing my
hands under the covers. "Then I'm gonna find my real mom."

Since I could not picture where my real mom was, I thought of
the old Hawaiian stone church near Pualoke, where Devika lived.
There were a lot of big trees there. I liked the way the lawn spread out
flat and green. It reminded me of England. England seemed like a pleasant place.

Devika got out of bed and examined a piece of scab she had picked.
"All right. I ain't got a reason to run away but I'll go with you." She eyed
me. "But I can't bring any stuff."

Devika said "ain't." Only the Dukes of Hazzard said "ain't."

"That's all right," I said. "I have plenty."

We made plans to meet under the mango tree in a few hours. I packed a couple of garbage bags with food, clothes, blankets, sheets, pillows, Doritos, Chips Ahoy!, *saimin,* a couch cushion or two, butcher knives to protect ourselves. I gave them to Devika and told her to meet me there.

I never showed up. Dad, home for the weekend, found the note I'd left—something about not liking Debbie. Something about real moms.

"Did you write this?"

"No." I'd crumpled up a draft and left it in their bathroom wastebasket.

"Did you write this?"

"No."

I've always been a terrible liar.

Devika waited under the mango tree until dark. She didn't speak to me for a week. "I just did it for you," she sneered. "I didn't even want to go." She called me a pussy—her favorite word.

"You're an idiot and a pussy. I waited out there until eight. My mom was *pissed.*"

I looked at Devika's feet. Her toenails were purple, the polish cracked. Red dirt traced her toes.

"Are you grounded?" I asked. I had to spend two weeks weeding after school.

She sniggered. "No. What's your *problem* anyway?"

Eventually Devika forgave me and we hung out again until she decided to be Nina Madeiros's best friend. During a slumber party they had locked themselves in Nina's upstairs bathroom and shaved their legs. I wasn't allowed to shave my legs. I knocked on the door and asked to be let in anyway. They giggled. Later, during the midnight whipped-cream fights I felt distracted and left out but laughed anyway. It all had something to do with me being stuck up, Devika told me, but I figured it was because we were both haole. She traded up. Given the chance, I would have done the same thing.

*　　*　　*

I had shaved only once, with my mom on the north shore. We slept together then in a big bed with sandy sheets. It was after we left Neil Daniels. We lived with Renee Paty and Seabring. I didn't go to school anymore—maybe it was summer already. Mostly what Seabring and I did was play out in front of the house and wait for Renee to make us quesadillas or caramel apples. You could buy the wrappers at Foodland.

A little bathroom split off the dark bedroom. Mom lay in bed with a migraine. I stood in front of the bathroom mirror and shaved my arm, ran the razor across it, smooth. Seabring's arms were smooth. "It'll grow back black," Mom scolded when she saw me. She showed me her arm, her skin already webbed with fine wrinkles and speckled white with haole rot, what haoles get in Hawaii from too much sun.

"Do you want to look like this?"

I shook my head.

She passed a hand over her hair. "Well, you're going to."

I used to think it was just skin that made you a haole, a certain kind of skin: mottled pink, pale in parts, freckled in others, threaded with pink and blue and green, skin I inherited from my mother. She tanned herself until she grew slack. I tried. I got as tan as I could without blistering and hated myself if I peeled. You got haole rot then. Just that word: *rot*. Haoles ruined everything. You just had to look at Waikiki once to know that.

Haoles were fat and stunk and had bad breath. They ate brown bread and "health food" with weird, un-Hawaiian names like "granola" and "yogurt." They called their kids Aaron, Moon, Wolf, Tiger, Josh, Seabring, Forest, and Zach. They had curly hair. If you were Japanese, Chinese, Samoan, Hawaiian, Korean, Portuguese, Puerto Rican, Vietnamese, Filipino, Laotian, Tongan, Chamorro, Black, Indian, Native American, anything that could get dark in the sun, if you had brown eyes or smooth skin, you could be "local," the opposite of haole. Then you'd be spared some of the smaller agonies: *Fuckin' haole. Mainland haole. Hauna* (stink) *haole. Nīele* (nosy) *haole. Stuck-up haole. Stupid haole. Suckin' haole.*

If I could shave I would be hairless, as near to local as I could get, a partial answer to my daily prayer: *Make me Japanese, make me Japanese, please make me Japanese.*

Still, I went to school on Kill Haole Day and nothing happened. Maybe Kill Haole Day was for grunts, the military brats who had awkward haircuts, or for recent transplants, kids who spoke with dull, cowlike mainland accents, as if they had rocks in their mouths. *I'm from New Yoik. Howayah?* Pidgin was fast, staccato, syncopated: *You wen go Brennecke's yestaday, brah, was jammin, ah?* Even teachers fell into it. I tried out my pidgin with Edwina Loro. She shut me up quick.

"Eh, Edwina, I gotta go home."

"Why?"

"Cuz I gotta bade lidat."

"What you wen say?"

"I gotta *bade* lidat."

"Eh, *hanabata* head. Why you talk pidgin, you one haole, ah?"

"Hah?"

"You no can say *bade* cuz you one haole. Sound shetty. You say *bay-the,* stupid."

Devika never bathed. And Devika was a haole, too, but it didn't seem to matter as much to her. Maybe that's why she dumped me: I was too shame. As in, *Hanaokolele! I wen see you pick yo nose, hanabata head. Shame, ah, haole.* She didn't know what it meant, to be shame. She didn't know how it infected you and made you unable to see people straight.

The day Gabby Pahinui died in the fall of 1980, Devika and I went over to the park across from her house in Pualoke to play tackle football with some of the neighborhood kids: Mike, pink and tall and oblong; and Charity Cruz, whose father was a cop and whose mother drove a white Tercel (dream car). When we came back Hippie Carla was crying at the kitchen table, her boyfriend smoking pot next to her. Strands of long black hair stuck to the sides of her face. "Gabby died," she said. Her boyfriend nodded. They both stared, their eyes puffy slits. Gabby sang falsetto in the background, his voice wavery, caught up, the slack key sweet and jangly. *Kamaka ka 'ikena 'ia Hi'ilawe.* All eyes are on the waterfall of Hiilawe.

I didn't know why Carla was crying so hard. She wasn't even from here. She was from Excremento. She was trying to impress the local guy with the joint. They went into her bedroom after that, which was dark, and strung with scarves and peacock feathers. Probably to fuck. Devika and I went into her and Neela's bedroom, which smelled like rotten pumpkin from the jack-o'-lantern that sat on her windowsill.

Float

September 2002   *Honolulu*

YOU SEE PEOPLE CRUMPLED ON THE BENCH, PART BEAST, foul-smelling, very dirty, and you think—oh, they are so alone. But probably they're not. Some have kids and husbands, and wives and cousins and people who've got houses and maybe a little money, people who live places.

I want to find my mother—and I don't. If I did, what would I do? Come back and live here, rent a little house with a carport and a plumeria tree? Mom will set up a kitchen outside and we will bicker over salmon salad and grow old. I will never marry, never have my own family. I will work, and I will have a cat. I will invite my younger sisters over, and their children, and serve iced tea and we will look at photo albums. Only I will know what I have given up.

I thought I could do it but I can't. Being here and there and generally in too many places makes everything feel wavy, connections weak.

Yesterday Margaret told me a story about Patti—Patti from Monterey, whom Mom used to score with.

There is a Patti who exists outside my memory. This surprises me. Memory is how I remain close to people. Memory keeps them fixed, where they can't get away from me.

I remember my mother swimming. When my sisters and I were kids, Mom liked to swim at Sans Souci, far out, past the flag, so far we couldn't tell if we could or couldn't see her anymore. She'd stay out a long time. We sat in the sand and waited. We played in the break. We wanted to be out there with her in the drifting dark but we were scared, too, on account of sharks and riptides and the feeling of too much space. Finally she'd call, "Come in! Come in!" We'd meet her somewhere between the deep and the shallows, and she'd float. Sometimes on her back, sometimes facedown, limbs akimbo. She'd sink deep enough so that we'd dive down to shake her. She always came up laughing.

Today at Sans Souci tourists sit on towels; local families unpack coolers. We are here for *pau hana*—end of work. We watch the sun set over Waikiki. A few bums sit on the benches by the showers, drink from bottles wrapped in paper bags. Is she like that one? Barefoot and drunk? Or like the one sprawled in the grass, staring at the sky, his hand on his chest?

Two seem to be a couple. They're joking, laughing about a friend of theirs. The woman wears a sundress, frayed but clean. The man is in shorts and a T-shirt. They have their backpacks on. Should I ask them if they know her?

I don't say anything. One man holding a bottle watches me sullenly. I strip down to my bathing suit and walk to the sea.

The Forbidden Island

1981   Kauai and Niihau

W HEN I THOUGHT OF NIIHAU, I PICTURED IT AT NIGHT. People moved quietly against yellow bug-speckled light. Generators hummed (there was no electricity on Niihau, no phones). It was pure Hawaiian, and when I was eleven pure Hawaiians seemed a rather romantic construction. I ignored the Hawaiians I actually knew: Darlene, Percy, Uncle Abel, Uncle Bill, Patrick Cockett. They didn't register as "Hawaiians." Truth was, I knew very little about Hawaiians.

"We're going to Niihau!" Dad's hazel eyes shone. The diver, Doug Arnott—of the Arnott's Biscuit fortune of Australia—would take us. Doug Arnott: Indiana Jones gone tropo in a Speedo and a wraparound pareu, a long-sleeved T-shirt, shades, fair tousled hair, and Aussie-ruddy skin. He was handsome and no doubt my father found him dashing. To be led to Niihau by Doug Arnott of *Ahnott's Beeskeets* certainly qualified as an adventure. And Doug was a man. No wife, no child. Just Irene, a spectacularly figured five-foot-tall Korean gal. Or was it Rae, Tahitian, the diver. One of them was on the boat that day—Irene or Rae, or maybe Tai Over's girlfriend. Tai's father was Don Over, of Tihati, the Polynesian revue. Tai had foxy girlfriends, too.

So it was Doug, Irene/Rae, Tai, and my father on the boat that day, ready for anything.

Several million years ago, Niihau was an active volcano. Pele lived there then, black-haired, a younger goddess than she is now. Then she was chased down to the Big Island by her older sister Nāmakaokahaʻi, "Eyes of the Sacrificed," where she's likely to appear as a white dog, or a mist, or an old woman waiting for a hitch somewhere down Saddle Road.

After Pele left, wind and water wore Niihau down. What remains is a small, dry island roughly rectangular in shape, eighteen miles long and six miles wide at its spreading point, low plains tapering down from Mount Pānīʻau toward the sea.

When Mother Sinclair—Valdemar Knudsen's mother-in-law—bought the island in 1863 to use as a ranch, Niihau's residents numbered six hundred. Knudsen and Annie Sinclair got married there in 1867, and it's where Gampa Great and Maggie Lindsay would meet twenty-five years later. Knudsen even helped negotiate the sale of the last parcel of kuleana land on the island. An old couple had secured it during the Mahele and forbid the Sinclairs passage across their land. The Sinclairs appealed to Knudsen, who spoke Hawaiian. As his son tells it in *Kanuka of Kauai,* Knudsen took a bag of gold coins to the couple, spoke of the life they would have on Kauai, the plentiful *ʻōpae* in the Waimea River, the nearby stores, and they capitulated. The sale put the entire island firmly in the hands of the Sinclair-Robinson clan, where it remains to this day, the only privately owned island in Hawaii.

There are still two hundred Hawaiians on Niihau. It is, in fact, an island reserved for them. From birth until death, if they choose to stay on Niihau, residents—with the recurring surnames of Beniamina, Kanahele, Kaʻohelauliʻi, Keale, Kelley, Niau, Niheu, and Shintani—speak Hawaiian, use no telephones, live off what electricity their generators produce, and agree to follow a sober, moral lifestyle, as defined by Keith and Bruce Robinson, the island's owners, descendants of Mother Sinclair. The Hawaiians who live on the island are, as the Robinsons have put it, guests of the family.

Not much happens on Niihau these days, save the daily miracles of life and birth and death. Famous musicians have their lineage there; the island is celebrated for the quality and beauty of its shell lei, kiawe blossom honey, and woven mats. But it is a quiet and insular place. *Ni'ihau i ke kiku*—Niihau leans back firmly.

Except for this: December 7, 1941, a damaged Japanese fighter plane en route from Pearl Harbor to its carrier in the North Pacific made a crash landing on Niihau, thinking it was uninhabited. No Robinsons were on the island at the time, nor were its residents aware that Japan had attacked Pearl Harbor that day. Howard Kaleohano, the owner of the field where the pilot had landed, found the plane, took the stunned pilot's papers, and set guard over him while contact could be made with Kauai. After several days of waiting, the pilot, a twenty-two-year-old named Shigenori Nishikaichi, and a schoolteacher named Yoshio Harada, one of the only two Japanese residents on the island, took the entire population of Niihau hostage using one of the Robinsons' rifles and the downed plane's machine guns. The brouhaha ended a few days later, when a Niihau patriarch, Beni Kanahele, and his wife bravely countered the attackers, sustaining bullet wounds and finally killing the pilot with nothing but a rock and their bare hands. Harada committed suicide.

Kanahele and Kaleohano were awarded the Purple Heart. A song was penned—*The Jap was a sap to think it a snap when he set his airplane down*—and in January 1942, the actions of the two Niihau Japanese were included in a navy report to the U.S. government. There was a "likelihood that Japanese residents previously believed loyal to the United States may aid Japan," the report stated. A few months later, Roosevelt approved the internment of more than one hundred thousand Japanese-Americans.

No one ever located the weapons that were used during the battle of Niihau. The islanders had hidden them in the forest and they could never be found. The army eventually reclaimed the plane, but remnants of its wing remained under lantana bushes and kiawe trees at the edge of Howard Kaleohano's field. Eventually the Niihauans stripped the plane's carcass of its aluminum. The metal, they found, made excellent eyes for their fishing nets.

There was nothing special about the ride out—a few dolphins, and that was all. A glassy calm had settled on the ocean, so still and blue it seemed as stone. We passed the lighthouse at the bottom of Mount Haupu, caves perforating the rock. Bones were supposed to be secreted in those caves: Kamehameha's body had been hidden so well on the Big Island that no one could ever find it.

Past Poipu and the whitewashed resorts, then Brennecke's beach, where Mig-and-Ida passed their last days together in a salt-smeared cottage facing the sea. Spouting Horn next, waves pushing through a crack in the lava, a fountain of white water spewing fifty feet into the air. Hanapepe, sugar as far as the mountains, Makaweli Plantation. We were motoring up—past Waimea, past Kekaha, Mana, Polihale. I fixed myself on the prow of the boat and looked north and west. Niihau rose up, a squarish lump against the horizon.

Words like *snookum* had already passed between Tai and the girlfriend, or Doug and the girlfriend, I forget which. It must have been Irene: I remember a killer body, a Wicked Wahine body for sure. The Wicked Wahine contest had been Dad's idea for the Kauai Surf. A bathing-suit pageant, right on the beach. Only the foxiest girls could be Wicked Wahines, some with almond eyes, some with long 'ehu hair that turned light in the sun, some straight from Nebraska or wherever via California—blond, stacked types who popped Dexies and basted themselves in Hawaiian Tropic. Irene had won one year. I won the watermelon-eating contest that went along with it.

Snookum embarrassed me. I rolled my eyes at my father and he rolled his back. He patted my leg and looked ahead, at the ocean. My father would never use snookum to describe anyone.

A red bandanna twisted across his forehead, his aviators reflected the sun. He wore a black-and-white faded *palaka* shirt, the checked fabric plantation workers wore. His shorts were frayed. He sat on the boat's bench, his hands, sweaty-palmed, waiting on his legs. He sniffed the air around him, shook his head, and said, "Ah!"

I was my father's daughter. I had his blunt nose, his green eyes, apple cheeks, thick eyebrows, full lips. The space between my teeth—"Black Irish!"—was his. I looked like my mother, too—longer face, lighter hair, freckled skin. But I wasn't with my mother anymore, and there was little profit in thinking of her in such intimate ways.

We landed first at Lehua Rock. The men and Irene dove for a while, I read. Then it was my turn—just a snorkel, nothing fancy. Doug accompanied me. We treaded water side by side while I spit into my mask. He twirled his fingers and the boat revved and pulled away.

We were alone. Doug carried a bangstick in case of sharks, but I wasn't scared. Through curtains of light that ended nearly where we did we swam. So many fish. What was below was unfathomable. Even here at the surface I didn't feel like myself. I seemed not to end.

I have read about Hawaiians who swam in open ocean for miles, tossed from sunken canoes. Or the fishermen at Ka Lae, "South Point," on the Big Island, who tied hundred-foot-long ropes around their waists and allowed themselves to be pulled into the open ocean to fish, no land till Tahiti. If the ropes broke, they were lost.

Off Lehua Rock we filled two dive bags with *ulua,* rainbow runners, *'ahi.* Back in the boat I was roundly congratulated for my bravery.

I had pictured Niihau as more Hawaiian than the other islands, because it was reserved for them, and I associated Hawaiians with flowers, palm trees, jungles. The Hawaii I encountered on Niihau was plainly different from anything I had seen. It seemed, above all, very dry; the grass yellow and lowland beach scrub the only vegetation.

I was not impressed with the tide pools, though my father was.

"Lobsters! Just sitting in the tide pools." He had returned from a walk onto the reef. I had waited at the shore, pouring sand into our one pair of fins, bored.

And there are no telephones, and it's just like Hawaii used to be.

I lolled about, numbed by the dry grass and unending sky. On land there wasn't much to see: just a long stretch of beach, the bush up past the high-water mark, the suggestion of dunes further in. It was hot on Niihau, and I was sunburned.

Dad offered a walk.

Past him on the boat Doug stood astride something, his shirt off. Tai and Snookum had disappeared. Everything was very still.

"Okay," I said.

My father held my hand.

We hadn't gotten far when he pointed to something in the sand. "A skull," he said, and there it was, a baby's. It looked like how I pictured a skull looking, just smaller. I was shocked. Then they were everywhere: down by the water, up past the sandbanks. Forty people, or a hundred— I couldn't tell. They edged toward the ocean, skull here, leg bone there, bleached and scattered, the bones of little girls and old men. Some had tumbled to the shore; some were still banked along the dunes at the top of the beach where they had been laid. They were very white. Tiny holes opened where insects and the wind had eaten through.

"They bury their commoners by the sea," my father instructed.

"Why?"

He shrugged. "Not enough mana."

Already we were trespassing and now there were bones. I bent down to look at one.

"What happens to the nose?"

"It's cartilage." He toed the sand and rubbed his arms. "It disintegrates."

Hawaiians called the haole historian Jarves *po'o kanaka,* skull man, because he gathered skulls from the dunes around Oahu. Victims of battles, smallpox, typhus, TB—diseases the ships brought. Jarves sent them in bundles to his father in New England, plucked from sand dunes littered with skeletons by the thousands. Many more, said the historian Samuel Kamakau, than a man would care to count in a day.

All the way along that Niihau beach, picking up lobsters, stepping past bones, I had that sick-sweet feeling of wanting to open my eyes

wider so that I could take everything in, and at the same time wanting
to close them and run.

Tai appeared as if from the sky. He yelled as he ran: "The Hawaiians are
coming! The Hawaiians are coming!" Car wheels on a dirt road somewhere in the distance stirred up clouds of red dust. We grabbed the dive
bag filled with lobsters and green glass fishing floats. (*You can't find them
anywhere anymore* and *they used to be at every house in the islands* and *so much
has changed.*) My father took the fins and swam ahead of me. I followed
a few feet behind. I had never swum faster in my life. Each time I looked
up someone was getting on the boat: first Tai, then my father, then me.

The car stopped at the crest of the beach. A group of men stood in
an old army-issue Jeep. One in the backseat looked at us through binoculars, another held a rifle. We squinted through binoculars back. We
were in our white gleaming boat, bobbing on the calm blue sea, just
outside the reef. We had swum away as if for our lives, but they never
would have shot us.

I did not learn until twenty years later that while we were on the
beach tramping around, Doug had cleaned the fish we caught off
Lehua. Their blood had attracted two full-sized sharks. While we clambered aboard, the creatures had been resting below the boat's shadow.
Doug didn't know which was worse, the guns or the sharks.

At the most we would have been fined.

When I remind my father now that he had taken the fins from his
eleven-year-old daughter, he doesn't say anything. I think it's the best
part of the story.

"I was pretty brave," I tell him.

"You had no choice," he replies.

On the way back—we would dock at Hanalei, on the wind- and water-
carved north side—it was so rough that we huddled on the floor with
towels over our heads while waves crashed in.

"Lucky it's summah," Doug cried. Winter and the north coast would have been impassable. Water splashed. Our captain stood wide-legged at the helm. My father and I huddled next to each other, our backs raw against the sides of the boat. Tai and Snookum were on the other side, also bent low. None of us looked at the other, each in his or her towel tent, though when we'd take a particularly heavy fall we'd let out a *"Woo!"* and a gasp.

"Kirk, come and take the wheel, eh?"

My father got up, wobbling. I was proud of him for being asked.

Doug opened one of the benches behind Tai and Snookum and took out a crash helmet and put it on. This was an adventure, after all. Doug was wearing a motorcycle helmet. We were together at the belly of the boat; my father was at the helm, the first mate assisting his captain. We had fought some kind of battle and we were heading home from it. The summer sea was angry and roiled and we were elated. We had set foot on the Forbidden Isle. This was something I could tell my friends in school.

How many islands have you been to?

Seven. The magic number, the complete number, which meant all of them, Niihau included. No one counted Kahoolawe—the army still used it for target practice in those days—but I could claim the rest.

And Mom had only been to six.

I looked around. Everyone was peaceful, surfeited, glazed. It had been an adventure, nothing more. Circling sharks. Hawaiians. A gun. We had two dive bags full of fish, another of lobsters. We were happy.

The pictures we took came back blank. My father says it with particular reverence, in a low voice he reserves for things that he respects and believes in. We all believe in Hawaiians.

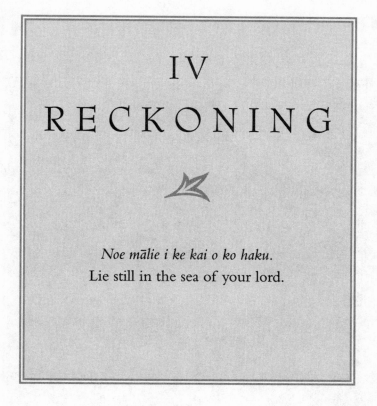

IV
RECKONING

Noe mālie i ke kai o ko haku.
Lie still in the sea of your lord.

Tara and Karen, 1988

Punchbowl

✄

September 2002   Honolulu

IN EARLY SEPTEMBER MY MOTHER CALLS. I HAVE BEEN home a little more than a month. She leaves the message on my father's answering machine. "It's your mother," she says, as if we spoke yesterday. No matter that this is not my house; or that my father has been divorced from my mother for thirty-one years, and this is his house, his girlfriend's house, not mine. No matter that no one has seen my mother in almost six months, or that she's been nearly missing from our lives for more than four years. "It's your mother," Karen says to me, and just like that it's the two of us, everything else falls away.

Ray must have told her I was looking for her. Her voice is huskier than I remember. She speaks slowly, as if she were addressing a child. "I don't have a phone but I have an address. Fourteen-sixty Puowaina Street, up on Punchbowl. It's a big pink house." She pauses. I scribble myself a note. "I don't know what's going on"—she sighs before she hangs up—"but I'll be home this afternoon."

The last time I spoke to my mother she was sleeping in the park. Maybe it *was* me. Maybe I needed to accept the way things were. This was my mother's life. Hadn't she said that? "This is my *life* now, Tara. My *life*." Our separation, which had for so long seemed the result of unfortunate circumstance, had come to define us. The search, after all, had been mostly academic.

I looked at the note. Puowaina. I'd never heard of it. Maybe I'd spelled it wrong. I rewound the machine. "Puowaina Street, up on Punchbowl," she said. *Poo*-oh-*why*na.

Pu'u-o-waina? Puowaena? Pua'aina?

Like a tourist: I'm sorry, can you spell that?

Punchbowl, Cemetery of the Pacific, an extinct crater turned into a national graveyard. You can't see the cemetery from the outside. From the road, from Puowaina Street, which curves up and around the hill like a grand staircase, Punchbowl looks like any old extinct crater, if you know what an extinct crater looks like: scabby brown and gray, gently ridged from millions of years of wind and rain, like an army blanket thrown over a bowl. Only on the inside do you see the thousands of tiny white squares, scattered like petals on a green pond. Twenty thousand vets from World War II and Korea and Vietnam are buried here, each grave marked by a single white stone. Wives and relatives, many Japanese, change the flowers every week: anthuriums, chrysanthemums, birds-of-paradise; stately, hardy flowers that look good on day six. Eighty percent of the men from Hawaii killed in World War II were Japanese, fighting the Jerries and the Dagos and the Japs.

Puowaina was the hill of sacrifices. *Kauwa,* outcasts, or kapu breakers or men captured in war were placed in underground ovens here and baked until the grease dripped from their bodies. That or drowned. Only if one could make it to a *pu'uhonua,* a place of refuge, could the *kahuna,* the priest there, absolve the kapu breaker of his crime.

On my way to Punchbowl I pass Punahou, its rock wall draped in night-blooming cereus. Past Kewalo, where Dad used to live. Then Punchbowl, drab in the afternoon heat, and Puowaina Street, and the big pink house she promised. Two junked cars rust in front, a broken stroller listing next to battered trash cans. I look toward the glassless win-

dows. A flowered bedsheet shades the screen. I can see my mother's silhouette. She's smoking. For a moment I stand there looking. I can hear
her laugh and her hand reaches to her mouth to take a drag.

I don't know what to call her. "Mom" sounds pathetic. "Karen," es-
tranged.

I don't know if she's high, sick, strung out. I don't know anything. I
really haven't spent more than a few hours with my mother in three
years.

I decide on Mom. As soon as she hears it her body responds. Past the
scrim of the curtain I can see her rise. She doesn't pull the sheet aside.
She knows it's me. And suddenly she's before me on the steps, in white
pants and a black stretch top and high heels. No one wears shoes at
home in Hawaii, let alone high heels. She dressed up for me. She knew
I'd come. She's skinnier, there are lines on her face, but she still looks
good.

"Hi, honey! How are you? Hi! God! It's been so long—" She
touches my hair. She hugs me. "You look so beautiful!"

I hug her back and we just stand there for a while below the stalled
cars.

"Where have you been?"

She shrugs, shakes her head. "I've just been here, getting off
methadone." She crosses her arms over her chest and scratches her back
with the fingers of each hand.

"I'm clean," she says. "I've been clean for two weeks."

She looks at me. I'm supposed to do something here, I know. It's part
of our old routine. She tells me how everything is looking up, and I say,
Wow! That's great! Then she says, *Yeah, I know. Really good, huh?* But I
haven't seen her for so long—a year, that last day at Jackass Ginger—so
I just look at her.

"I'm off the methadone."

"You said that already."

"Yeah, well."

We're quiet. I scrape the concrete steps with my slipper.

"Why didn't you call us? Why haven't you called Lauren?"

Lauren's alone in Texas with a family she doesn't really know. She's nineteen. I visited her in Houston before I came home. We drove her uncle Bob's SUV around and ate Mexican food. We waited in line to go to the IMAX but never got tickets. Instead we spent the afternoon in a gazebo in the park across from the theater and I tried to tell her that her mother loved her. Lauren nodded and said, "I know, I know." Then we talked about her new boyfriend, Ryan, a skateboarder.

Why haven't you called? This is what I really want to know, and I ask it simply, as if there's a simple answer.

My mother looks up at the sky, her hand across her eyes, as if she hadn't been out of the house for a while.

"Embarrassed? I didn't want you guys to see me like that." She rubs her arm, looks around. This is not a subject she'd like to pursue.

"Do you want to come in?" She motions to the window, to what I imagine is her and Ron's room. Smoke floats out; a television plays. "Come inside, honey. I want you to see my fish!"

"Your fish?" I shake my head. "No, no." Movement seems like a bad idea. I want us to stay right here, on the steps, where she can't get away from me.

Either you're with her or you're against her. I have just chosen sides.

"You're embarrassed of me, aren't you? That's why. That's all right. I know. I'm a fuckup. That's what you said: 'There's always something going on, Mom, when I come home.' I know. *Why can't I just be normal?* Well, I'm trying, Tara. Me and Ron are trying."

I adopt the attitude of calm. *Frigid,* a boyfriend once called me, though really I am just afraid.

I look past my mother. Some of the laminate has peeled off the front door so that it's just the pressboard showing. It looks raw, almost painful, as if its skin had been removed.

"God, you look like Gail. So rigid. Why are you so rigid?"

I look like Gail because we both do yoga and our hair is short.

"Come on, Tara. Come in. I want you to say hello to Ron."

I don't know why I give in, except that she's my mother. I haven't seen her in so long, and here she is.

I walk into the hallway. There is an open padlock on the door. Empty fish tanks stack to the left. Inside, the fading afternoon light has turned everything shadowy, the indistinct color of dust. A double bed squats on grimy linoleum; there's an old couch, a television, a coffee-maker, a fan, smoke. Various boxes are stashed under a cheap bureau. A blond man with a backpack coils on the couch, next to piles of folded clothes. Ron is on the bed, a wet towel over his forearm.

"I know. It's small," she says, as if the man weren't there, and Ron wasn't right now pressing a washcloth to a vein. "But here are our fish!" She points to a small aquarium atop the television.

I want to stare at the man, at Ron and his washcloth, but my mother is telling me to do something and I feel queerly impelled to follow her directions.

Aquariums, even nice ones, are depressing. This one is dirty and em-broidered with algae. Two minnowish things swim around listlessly, nib-bling at the glass.

She points to the far wall. "And that's the bed I've been lying on for the last twenty-four days."

"Oh, man," Ron says in sympathy. "Yeah."

This is the first time I've seen Ron in person. He looks even more like a hobo than I imagined. He's got brown longish hair and big brown puppy-dog eyes. He was probably handsome once, but now he's skinny and fuzzy around the edges and he's wearing pants that are far too big for him.

Mom places a hand on my arm. It's clammy. "This is my daughter," she says. "Ron, give her a hug."

Ron, abashed, shrugs at the man on the couch but gets up. He's holding his wet washcloth down with one hand and in that same hand holds a cigarette. He can't quite hug me, but he smiles a wide smile and leans in, kisses me on the cheek. He smells like smoke. "Hey, Tara! Good to meet you!" Both he and my mother have developed bum voices: the low and scratchy buzz of someone who asks you for a few bucks to get dinner.

I find it all extremely surreal. I kiss the side of his head, pull up, and nod to the man on the couch. He nods back, lifts his hand. I have a strong desire never to see any of this ever again.

My mother clears a place for me to sit on the bed. She seems bonier as she bends; she must be close to a hundred pounds. "Don't worry about it," I say.

"What?" she says. "Sit down, honey. Come on," and pats the mattress next to her.

"You're skinny," I say. "Why are you so skinny?"

"We haven't had food. We've been eating rice for the last three days. Can you imagine? Just rice? We're starving."

"Yeah," Ron chimes in. "Starving."

She gets up, fumbles through a pile on the top of the dresser, and passes me a letter.

"The guy downstairs wrote a note to the landlord saying we stole his saimin. Now she wants to kick us out."

I look at the letter, turn it around in my hands. It's laser-printed. Somehow this surprises me.

According to our agreement, you were only supposed to be here for a few weeks. . . . Missing saimin, missing morning papers. . . . Never used to have these problems . . . $250 by the 1st. . . . Esther Leung.

On the couch Ron shakes his head. "Oh, man. The letter."

Mom echoes him, sarcastic. "Yeah, Ron. The letter."

I'm confused. I feel like I am supposed to give them $250, but they're not telling me.

"Did you eat the saimin?"

Ron laughs. "Well, yeah!"

I turn to my mother. "I want to talk to you alone, outside."

"Oh, right," starts Ron. "I have to run out and get some food, too."

Suddenly the man on the couch speaks. "And I'd better be going myself."

We look at him as if we'd forgotten he was there. He's got a bowl haircut and wears stiff new jeans. He's stocky and his hair is straight and thick like thatching. He reminds me of a Tuffskins kid.

"Well, all right." My mother clasps her hands in front of her. It's all very polite. "Thanks for coming by."

Past the sundry junk piled in the hallway, past two more empty aquariums on the floor I hadn't noticed earlier. Outside, my mother waves good-bye to the man with the backpack. He is on a bike. He's definitely a drug dealer. She calls after him something about being careful with his leg. Is it code? I'm that discombobulated. The sun is bright. I can't look at everything at once. I concentrate on Ron loping down the hill toward downtown, then the broken baby stroller, then the hillbilly cars, then the long orange electric cord snaking up the front steps.

"Who lives here?"

"Two young Vietnamese guys." My mother is squinting again. "They're all right."

"Who's your landlord?"

She's used to it, this imperiousness.

"A Chinese lady Ron knew from his job at the photo place. It's an old run-down boardinghouse, but it's cheap."

I snort. Ron's *job*. At a *photo place*.

"Are they drug dealers?"

"God! No!"

She places one hand on her forehead, the other on my shoulder.

"Look, Tara. I've been really sick. I haven't been out of bed in three weeks. I'm sorry I didn't call. I'm sorry, I—"

"It's been almost a year."

"A year? I just talked to you in May!" She's right, of course, but it feels like longer.

"And before that? Not since September. You've been missing, Mom. You've been gone."

"Gone? God, I've been right here. I don't go anywhere."

She looks around. I look with her. The house is on the lower side of Punchbowl as it slopes into Nuuanu Valley. I can see almost to the Pali from here: Morgan's Corner, Jackass Ginger. I think about how small my mother's life has become. I touch her hand. The veins and the moles are rubbery.

"How are you feeling? How is your hepatitis?"

She looks at me, rubs her eyes with her thumb and forefinger. She shivers. "Listen, Tara, I'm not that sick. I'm not sick. I made all that up. My doctor said I split, my personality split. I was overidentifying with Margaret, with her lupus. I wanted to die, too."

"I don't believe you," I say, though I want to. "What about the pneumonia last fall? What about that?"

"Oh, that?" She waves her hand. "I was doing crack with that awful guy, Ted."

We sit. I rest my hands on the painted concrete steps. They feel smooth. I like smooth concrete. A lot of the old houses in Hawaii have it—cheap building material back in the plantation days. Now, like the corrugated-tin roofs of my childhood, yuppies want to have it in their lofts. I want to have it in my loft.

"Crack?"

She sighs. "Yeah."

A queer calm settles, a familiar fog inhabits me when I'm around my mother. All I do is fret about her when she's gone, but when she's here, in front of me, telling me that she lied about being ill and instead was doing crack, I can't actually feel anything but the miniscule fragments of rock under my hand, the smooth solid of the cement steps.

"Well, I'm glad you're not sick."

She's looking at me strangely, her eyes wide.

"God, do you know how long I've been worrying about telling you that? And you don't even react! Why don't you get angry at me, Tara? Why don't you get mad! Get mad at me! God!"

She's crying now. I hug her. I can feel the bones in her back. I almost feel something, but then it passes.

"My mother didn't like me," she sobs. "She broke my tooth when I was five. Do you know what it feels like for your mother to say she doesn't like you? I just got in touch with that this year. I felt it in here." She grabs her stomach.

I vaguely picture my mother getting in touch with it on her filthy bed, up in the pink house, comatose, with Ron going out to fetch her mission dinners or making beggar's rice in the urinal down the hall.

I thought you were supposed to get over all of that when you had your first child. I thought you were supposed to grow up.

"In here." She punches her stomach. "What that felt like. She hit me and broke my tooth. I was five. Can you imagine your mother doing that to you?"

She looks into my eyes. I'm inspecting her pupils to see if they are constricted. Junkies' pupils are supposed to constrict.

I can't tell because it's too bright on the steps.

"Did I ever abuse you? Were you ever abused?"

I don't have time to think yes or no so it comes out as an unformed blank. Really the answer is no, but I wanted to give it a moment.

"Five years old and she told me I had a black heart. Can you imagine saying that to a five-year-old? How cruel that is?"

The love story resumes. Suddenly my mother is there, next to me, and I am here, sitting on the steps, and I am her daughter again. Her eyes are so blue still, so round, surrounded by lines, deep and fine. She's cut her hair recently. It falls over her shoulders in copper waves. She used to be so pretty. I always think this when I look at my mother.

We've passed the climax, the part about the tooth and the black heart, so we just sit out here on the steps for a while. She wipes her face. She tries to ask me what I'm up to but I don't tell her much. "Nothing." I say. I don't feel like talking. "I'm home for a while, though."

She smiles. "Oh god, Tara! Really? Oh, that makes me so happy! Oh, I am so happy. Oh, honey." She hugs me again. "Oh, my daughter, my daughter." She's crying again. She hugs me. I let myself be held. I do a lot of crying alone, at night, but right now there's too much going on and I can't muster what I need to join her. I stroke her back instead. She still feels familiar.

Anyway, I like this part, where I come in to save her.

Ron's figure emerges from the lip of the road. "Brought you a sandwich," he calls.

"Oh, good." Mom is smiling now. "I'm so hungry!"

We follow him inside. "And look." He opens his palm. Five cigarette butts curl there, like little fetuses.

"I never knew what a snipe was until I met Ron."

She laughs when she says this, picks out the longest butt, pulls a lighter from her pocket, and lights it.

"Snipes." She exhales. "I smoke *snipes* now." She says it kind of fiercely, like she's proud. "This is my *life*."

Ron is delighted. "Heh, heh. Your mom found a con."

Ron the Con. Mom doesn't seem to notice this last sentence. "Ron has a good heart," she says to me, as if he weren't standing there next to us. Then she shrugs. "Who knows?"

She tugs at the curtain. "Need some air in here."

Ron and she smoke the snipe, passing it between them as if there were a burning oil drum in the middle of the room. Mom talks to me about something. I don't listen. I watch the ash of the snipe get longer between her callused fingertips. I reach for the ashtray. She puts her cigarette out.

"I love you guys," she says, meaning me and my sisters. "I know it's weird, because I've been here, on this bed, and I haven't called. But all I think about is you. Don't I, Ron?"

Ron nods. "Oh yeah. Definitely."

"I couldn't. I couldn't let you see me like that. I couldn't let that be your last memory of me. But all I think about is you guys."

I tell her she's been gone for years. This is my chorus. I sing it again and again.

"I haven't been anywhere!" This is her refrain. "I don't go anywhere! I've been on this rock my whole life. I don't go to Paris! I don't go anywhere! I stopped when I lost you back then, Tara. I got stuck. I got stuck!"

I want to talk about something else. What we'll do now that she's clean. How things will be different, what plans we'll make. How we'll go to the beach early in the morning, go camping and hiking, how we'll lose Ron and how she and I and Layla and Lauren will spend long evenings together, just talking. Mommy and babies.

I can't help myself. "But you're gone! You're gone!"

I keep saying this, as if by saying it I'll understand. As if it will be true, that she's been really missing all these years. Lost to something, drugs again, or a man, or whatever possesses my mother, takes her away from us: her daughters, the only ones who love her.

I'm the one who's been gone. Karen hasn't been anywhere. California once, when she got married to Ron, but I had to send them the money to fly home.

It was something I'd always envied about my mother. She had never left. She was as close as she could get to really belonging here, like a local. I even sort of liked her living here at the back of Punchbowl, by Papakōlea, Hawaiian Homes, where Katie Harden and I used to cruise to buy dime bags. Maybe Mom would get a union job, work in the fields like she did when she lived in Waimea, headscarf and all.

I walk with her to a store down the block and we buy bread and yogurt and Ensure and a pack of cigarettes, one of which I have before I leave. I buy her two phone cards and make her promise to call Layla and Lauren.

"I will!" she says, her blue eyes wide. "Let you guys know how I'm doing." She looks at me. "I got out of bed today, looked for a job in the paper. That's a big thing, you know."

I grab her hand and squeeze it.

It's true: she's been on this rock, and somewhere back there both of us got stuck.

Good Girls

September 2002   Honolulu

THE NIGHT-BLOOMING CEREUS IS HAPPENING, AS IT DOES each September. As soon as it gets dark the bloom opens, a great big insect of a flower arching up to the moon. They only come like this once a year, all at once, at night, and in such haste you can watch the petals opening. In the old days tourists used to gather to watch it happen. Hundreds of people at Punahou and Wilder, waiting for the petals to part. In the afternoon all the dead blossoms look like deflated balloons, trapped in crazy green barbed wire. "They planted it to keep the Hawaiians out," someone once told me, and this is what I always think of when I see the wall. It's probably not true, but night-blooming cereus is related to the cactus. Some ship captain from Acapulco gave it to a missionary wife and she planted it here. Anyway, it's something one does in Hawaii: diss the missionaries. "They came to do good and did well," and all that.

My mother isn't sick like I thought. She has a house, albeit pink and littered with old aquariums. Ron is not the canker of malevolence he once seemed. He is a junkie and a con, but he's a nice enough man and I think he might actually love my mother. And Mom? She's skinny and haggard and dubiously sober but she's managed to keep her white pants clean. She says that what she's been doing a lot of the time she's been out of touch is cleaning. "You know me and my cleaning." She laughs. "Even when I was detoxing I did laundry every day."

Layla and I take her to the movies. *The Good Girl,* with Jennifer Aniston. Mom sinks into her chair and bites her nails and laughs and talks back to the screen. *"What?"* she keeps saying. *"Come on."*

"Weird," she says afterward. "Those people were weird!"

Layla's boyfriend, Jack, is with us. It's the first time our mother has met him. She turns to him, puts her hand on his shoulder. "You know, life isn't like that all the time. Life isn't always so *dramatic.*" She shakes her head. "Like my life. My life is really boring."

Jack smiles. Layla looks for something in her purse. I grab my mother's hand. "So what do you feel like for lunch?"

At the Kaka'ako Kitchen Mom doesn't eat much. "Your stomach shrinks when you're starving," she says, dragging on a cigarette. Layla and Jack leave to go back to Kailua, where they share an apartment. I drive Mom back to Punchbowl to drop her off. "Bye, Mom," I say. "Bye, honey!" She waves and walks down the steps toward her house. When I get home to my father's I have to sit awhile in the car. I don't know exactly how I am supposed to feel. My mother is back. She keeps telling me she's back. I know why I don't trust it. What I don't understand is why I still care.

By the time I see Mom a week later, Layla and Jack have eloped. They do it at Honolulu Hale, just like Mom and Ron, but without the Hawaiian priest. I go over to Punchbowl to tell our mother, since she doesn't have a phone. "Am I supposed to be freaked out?" she keeps saying. "I'm not. Her father and I did the same thing."

I wish she hadn't said that.

This is how Layla tells her mother she's married: Mom and I and Ron are sitting at Esther Leung's. There's yet another guy with a blond bowl haircut, a homeless pal, on the bed next to my mother. He has blue eyes and greasy skin. "Don't mind him," she says, jerking her thumb. "He's staying the night. He's a guy we're helping." She pats him on the knee. He smiles. He's missing his front teeth.

Then he starts to fall asleep sitting up, his feet still on the floor.

Mom calls Layla from my cell phone. "Uh-huh, uh-huh. Well, congratulations!" The blond guy wakes up every so often then passes out just as suddenly, his eyes rolling into his head. Mom and Layla are trying to figure out how to see each other before Jack leaves for a tour in Okinawa in a week. "My dad has the car," I say.

"Tara doesn't have a car," Mom says to Layla.

"I can steal one," the guy suddenly offers from the bed, his eyes still closed.

"Oh yeah?"

"Yeah. I can jack it."

"Really." Mom is humoring him. She smiles at me, rolls her eyes.

"How are you going to do that?"

"Well, you gotta go in under the steering wheel." Now he's animated, gesturing. He seems to know what he's talking about.

"Uh-huh."

"And anyway, there's a wire in there—"

Ron's on the couch, his hands folded in his lap, smiling. I am watching the three of them like they are in a little diorama, the kind I made in fourth grade: "UNDER THE SEA," "WHITE CHRISTMAS," "MOM'S NEW FRIENDS."

"He's telling me to steal a car," she whispers to Layla. I can't hear my sister but she's obviously saying, "Who?"

"Just this guy that we're helping." And then to the carjacker: "Layla got married to a marine." She nods and points at the phone. "He's got tattoos."

The man rolls his eyes. "Marine. Great. He'll probably beat her up." He looks at the phone. "Oops."

Karen puts her hand over the mouthpiece and slaps him on the knee. She's laughing.

"God! Don't say that!" But she smiles and says to Layla, "Well, I'm really happy for you, honey. That's great."

On the ride back to my father's I call Lauren in Texas. She's starting to say y'all. "Something big happened last week," I say. "A surprise."

Lauren hasn't met Jack, but she has a boyfriend, too. Ryan. She's been dating him for almost two years now, since she got to Houston. He has a cabin in Colorado, she tells me. She's going to go there with him over Christmas.

"Wow."

"So what's the surprise?" Lauren yawns. It's late in Houston. "Did Mom get arrested?"

"No, no. It's about Layla. You'll have to ask her. But I'll give you a hint. Mom found out over the phone."

"What?"

"I went over to Mom's so she could call Layla. Some bum was spending the night. He fell asleep sitting up on the bed."

Lauren laughs. "What was Ron doing?"

"I don't know, just sitting there. It's all so crazy."

"Was she making it all dramatic? Was she making a scene?"

"Uh-huh."

Lauren sighed. "She's so fucked up."

"Yeah."

"God, I miss home."

I understand why Layla eloped, but the circumstances make me sad. I want my sister to have the dress, the veil, the bridesmaids, the tearful mother, the proud father. The flowers and the cake and the honeymoon. I want Lauren to be here and for us to be a family.

"The thing is," Mom said on the landing, saying good-bye, "open a door and one thing just leads right into another. Some famous philosopher said it. Ask your boyfriend. Aristotle or someone. One door and everything opens up in front of you."

The Flower Drop

✄

1981   Lihue, Kauai

AT THE BEAUTIFUL WEDDING OF FLIGHT ATTENDANT Cheri to Handsome Fred, my father got to go up in a chopper to drop flowers. This was part of his job at the Kauai Surf: to go up in Jack Harter's chopper with a big local guy and drop Vanda orchids on weddings and conventions, like the one where my father met Ray A. Kroc, the founder of McDonald's.

On the ground, on the grassy swale in front of Kalapaki Bay, where the Rices had their beach house a long time ago, before the tsunami wiped it clean and swept their gardener to sea, the wedding party gathered. Right past the lagoons, near the luau pit. (They filmed the dance scene of *South Pacific* there. Cousin Nan, half-Rice, half-Faye, played a chorus girl.)

Fred looked nervous. But they were happy. Cheri was pretty. Prettier, even, than my mother, though by this point Karen was starting to get vague. Cheri could be my mother. She had that glassy blue-eyed way about her, that particular kind of white skin that's seen too much sun.

Debbie and my father complimented me on how well behaved I was, how adult I acted, how intelligent. This was easy to do. I walked around and when I met adults I smiled and laughed at their jokes. I told them I was in sixth grade. Sometimes I recited Rap Replinger skits from the record I had: the drunk Hawaiian cook on the cooking show; the pidgin-speaking auntie who takes orders for room service. On the way home Debbie joked about how pale the groomsmen were. Poor Fred's family, from somewhere on the mainland.

What a gas. Groovy. Cheri is tan, her dress is tight, her shoulders high. The music is dreamy; Chinese lanterns dangle from the trees. Blush wine sweats, blue mascara bleeds. Everyone gets their feet wet. Cheri and Fred leave at the end of the night for Tahiti. We bid you a fond aloha.

Then the flower drop. Just at sunset, when the sky over Kalapaki Bay turns sapphire and yellow and the purple Vandas spin like little princesses in ball gowns. Everything is color-coordinated, like a good view should be, and the monkeypods spread their slender arms over us and the silhouettes of the palm trees rock—

Cheri and Fred divorced eventually, like everyone else. Dad was working for Dudley off-island and only came home on the weekends, so for a long time it was just Debbie and me. My mother disappeared deeper into the mainland. A few years later, during a flower drop at another hotel, someone's jacket flew out of the chopper, caught in the blade, and the whole thing went down. That was the end of the flower drop.

Psycheeatrick

September 2002 Honolulu

FOR HER BIRTHDAY IN MID-SEPTEMBER, GAMMA MAKES A dish called More. "That's what it's called," she says, laughing, "*More,* because when you eat it that's what you want." More is a kind of casserole involving macaroni noodles mixed with spaghetti sauce and canned olives, blanketed by cheddar cheese and baked. "Maybe the children will remember," she says, one hand in a green mitt. I think of a time when my mother and my aunts and my uncle Brew might have enjoyed eating More, when Gamma was the perfect Honolulu housewife, in the newspaper and everything.

The table is set. The pineapple is sliced. I've told Mom about the gathering but she doesn't come. She says she's sober, but something doesn't add up. She hasn't called Lauren; the day at the movies was the only time Layla and I have seen her, though I've gone over a few times. She still owes Esther Leung money and what about that job?

At breakfast the rest of the family wanders out to the plumeria tree facing the golf course. "Thirty years old, this house," Gamma says. "Like you, Tara."

I'm turning thirty-two in a few weeks. Gamma once gave me a Saint Christopher bracelet she'd had since she was a girl. Her father had given it to her when they lived in Berkeley. *For another September baby,* Gamma wrote in the card. I supply the rest: *On either side of a woman we don't understand.*

On the day of her birthday Gamma's philosophical. She holds up a grid she's drawn on a piece of paper, shows it to us. She's marked dots: one to a hundred, crossing one out for every year she's lived. "Look at this piece of paper," she says slowly. She's breathing a bit heavily. She has her dark glasses on. "There aren't many spots unmarked. I don't know what I did with the rest of this time."

We're all sitting around in the grass, at her feet. Layla's off to the side, blue eyes half closed. Gail's kids loll in the grass, their mother on her back looking up at the branches. Margaret sits tiny in a chair. She doesn't say anything because she's only fifty-three and in any case doesn't think she'll get to sixty. "That's where I'll stop," Margaret whispers and points. "No, Margaret!" Gail reaches up to stroke her arm.

Then my grandmother reads a speech about giving up things; the transitory nature of material objects. Layla and I look sideways at each other. Then Gamma says, "Let us remember those who aren't here: little Lauren in Texas, Brewster in his rig, little Melissa, Auntie Bubsy, Eleanor in New York, Mom and Dad and all those who've died—" and she lists everyone she can think of except for my mother. "And Karen," I say, loud, even before she's finished. Gamma doesn't hear. "And Karen," I say again, and then she says, "And Karen."

Up on Puowaina the fish have died. Someone propped a board against the aquarium and maybe that killed them—no light. In any case, they're dead, floating on the water like silver leaves.

"What are you doing tonight?" my mother asks. She's lying in bed, a sheet halfway up her thighs.

"Going to Deirdre's dad's forty-ninth death day celebration."

My father's girlfriend's father had died that summer. He was a Buddhist, third-generation Japanese-Hawaiian. His grandmother had been on the first boats to Hawaii from Japan; he himself had started in the plantation schools but got sick when he was young and started to draw.

In his adulthood he was a staff artist for the *Star-Bulletin*. He was a good man, a beautiful artist, and very kind. At his forty-ninth death day celebration his family could release him into the next world. They could go about their lives.

"Where?"

"Pālolo Temple."

"See, that's what I've been saying."

I didn't know what she'd been saying.

"What?"

"Other people lead normal lives. I tried." She sighs. "Remember? I tried. When Margaret was sick, I would go take care of her. Every day. I was working and I had kids and I would go and take care of my sister. That's all I've been doing my whole life. Taking care of everyone."

She's lying on her back, her face covered by her hands. "I am so worn out. I am so worn out. I don't even know how to take care of myself."

From where I sit on the couch across from her I can see three sores on the bottom of her chin. They are pink and raw. "What are those from?" I ask. "Picking pimples," she answers. Then she picks one, as if to show me how it's done.

"I got bitten by a centipede the other day on my toe. See?"

She wiggles her big toe. The nail is painted red and cut close.

"You can see the two bites. Look."

She offers me her right leg. It's pale and bony, and the foot at the end of it shifts in its bag of wrinkled skin. I hold her foot in my hand and inspect her big toe. There are indeed two punctures on the top, on a pink mound. She rests her foot on the bed again, reclines and pulls the blanket over her legs. She has lost so much weight since she started relapsing—almost forty pounds. Her limbs crook like a skeleton's.

"Anyone else would have gone into shock from those bites."

She's tough, she's telling me.

"I know, Mom. I know."

I go get her McDonald's. The woman behind the counter is Samoan but has cloudy blue eyes that look like marbles. I can't find the way home. I don't know this area—upper downtown, lower Nuuanu. We're close to Chinatown here. It's poor: L&L Drive-Inn, the Rehabilitation Hospital of the Pacific. Freeways shunt through. I can see Punchbowl but I can't get there. Pele Street bleeds into Captain Cook Street. When I first came back the little green signs helped orient me. Not in terms of directions—Honolulu I knew just by driving—but in the way that they gave me a story, a context in which to situate myself. Now they confuse me.

"I'll see you tomorrow morning," I say back at Punchbowl. I am going to take my mother to the hospital. *"Psycheeatrick,"* she had called it. I had come over on a whim the night before to find my mother on the bed, nearly catatonic. The television played and her face was blue-white from the light. She couldn't sit up. Ron was passed out next to her. "Mom," I said. "You're sick. You need help." She told me to go away. I said I didn't care what she said. I said I was taking her to treatment and that was that. "No." She turned away. Ron rolled over but didn't wake up. "I can't take Sand Island," she croaked. "They yell at you there. I'm too delicate for that right now. I need *psycheeatrick.*"

I thought if I could just get her in the car—

Today when I get back from McDonald's a wad of tissue paper spotted with blood is crumpled at the foot of the bed. I wonder if it's Ron's blood from the night before.

I give her the bag. She looks through it. I've gotten them double cheeseburgers, Cokes, french fries, and a chocolate shake.

"Tomorrow morning, then?" I get up to leave and accidentally brush her toe. She winces.

"Yeah, okay."

Ron pads in. He's been in the bathroom making rice. When he sees the McDonald's he smiles.

"Jeez! Thanks, Tara. That's real decent of you. Real nice."

The last thing I see on my way out the door is the garbage can. I can't help looking at it because last night there was a forty in the trash and a crumpled note. I had picked it up. "PLEASE DON'T LEAVE ME, KAREN! I STILL LOVE YOU!!!" It was written in an adolescent hand: block letters, all capitals. I stopped reading it when I saw that she had written him back. Had they even left the bed?

No, come to think of it, the last things I see walking out are the dead fish in the foyer aquarium.

The next morning when I arrive to take her to psychiatric, Mom tells me about the brown recluse spider that bit her a month ago.

"I saw the one that bit me," she says. "He was big. I saw the little sac of poison, everything. Ugh." She shakes her head. I nod. She does have a huge abscess on her leg—pink and brown and blue and swollen with a stream of pus leaking out the top—but it's strange how obsessed she is with the spider. I furrow my brow. I'm trying to be a good listener. I want to get her into the car.

"A brown recluse spider," she repeats. "Check it out."

"I will."

She looks around. "I can't believe I'm up. I took a shower even." Then she sits down on the bed again. She's still in her robe. "It's all so over-whelming."

Clothes are stacked on the couch. Vitamins and pill bottles crest the chest of drawers. There is the aquarium, the TV, the bed, the couch. None of it is my mother's. None of it is overwhelming. All it will take is a little packing—and I've brought boxes. I smile, hold one up. I'm try-ing to be cheerful. Karen's leaden on the bed. Her lips part slightly; she's staring at the television. She wipes her nose with the back of her hand.

"Mom?"

"Yeah, yeah. I know. Treatment."

Finally she starts to pack. I sit on the floor and go through her clothes. I remember them from happier times: a gold lace dress she wore to brunch at the Outrigger one Christmas, a blue skirt with yellow lilies for my high school graduation. The dresses are all too big for her; the jeans and T-shirts are stained. She asks me if I want anything; I say I don't.

In order to start over first you have to throw everything away.

I look at the TV. All Mom and Ron get is the Sci-Fi channel. *The Twilight Zone* is on: the episode where the doctors want to make a woman beautiful. She's scared. "No, no!" she cries. In the hospital she meets her twin. You have to tell yourself, "I am beautiful." Tell yourself, "I am beautiful." At the end it's revealed that she's the normal one; the doctors have pig snouts. The handsome man and the beautiful woman walk out of the hospital together at the end.

Mom sifts through papers in the hall.

"God, look at this junk. Cockroaches everywhere!"

And there are. Cockroaches climb along the side of the bed, along the floor, scurry into the box of tampons and notebooks and bottle caps and assorted junk she has stashed in the corner of the room. For a while she just sits in the hall, mumbling to herself: *This? This?* I wait on the bed, watch more TV.

Ron huffs in from Fort Street. This seems to be his day, as far as I can tell, deepening the goat path between Punchbowl and Fort Street, loaded or looking to get loaded. Mom tells me that last night Ron agreed to go into treatment, too. Today he's perhaps less motivated. To his credit, he sees my mother packing and picks up a box.

"Far-out! Boxes! Thanks, Tara, these are cool." He's holding one in his hands, turning it this way and that. "Hey, Karen, do you think that's weird, when I say *far-out?* People trip out when I talk like that."

"No." Mom looks at me and rolls her eyes. Then she softens. "Ron, did I tell you I saw the brown recluse spider that bit me? Out when I was doing wash? He had a big sac of poison on his back."

"No kidding," says Ron. He's still not sure what to do with the box. "Huh."

"Flap A first, Ron," I say, pointing. "Then B."

"These are cool! These are the best boxes, Tara. Thank you!"

Every so often Mom holds something up to ask whether she should keep it. I shake my head even before I see what it is. There are stains on all her clothes, Benzedrine on her robe. Brown smears, white smears. The whole room smells of puke.

"You get dirty when you're homeless," Mom says to no one in particular.

Ron holds a pair of jeans up to his waist. "How about these pants,

Karen? These are my favorites." He's laughing. They're ripped at the knee and far too big for him. They look like clown pants.

I suspect Ron actually likes this life.

Mom grabs them from him, starts rolling them into a lopsided ball. "Ron, you have to *fold* these." Her teeth show. Her mouth is dry. "What is this?" She holds up a shirt from a pile. "This is disgusting. Disgusting, Ron."

I try to ignore them. I put stuff into boxes, not really looking at anything, just concentrating on getting it out of here. This has been coming for five years. I am home. I am home and I am doing something. I am going to make her better. Finally my mother is going to get clean.

After two episodes of *The Twilight Zone* the room doesn't look much different than it did before.

"I'll just go and get the car," I say, trying to expedite things. "You guys say good-bye."

I like giving orders to my mother.

"Yeah, okay." She nods.

Outside, I stow boxes in the trunk of my father's car. He's lent it to me for the day, though I have to pick him up after work. After a while Ron follows me out.

"Am I giving you a ride to treatment, too?"

"Oh, no. I'm going tomorrow." Ron shakes his head. He's squinting. "Hey, thanks for the boxes."

"Sure."

He reaches a hand out. I hold it, thinking he wants to shake.

"Why don't you take this?" It's the key to his post office box, the one I thought was canceled. "I get my disability there. At least it's five hundred dollars."

It's a nice gesture, but that's all it is. Ron needs his money. Though I am intent on taking my mother to the hospital—she has government-subsidized health insurance, the state of Hawaii will pick up the bill—what I will do afterward I have yet to work out. She has not said that she wants to be clean. Ron is not the only one of us going through the motions.

"No, Ron, you keep it."

He scratches his arm, looks down at the cracked pavement, and I look with him. We are a bit shy with each other. His tennis shoes are remarkably white. I wonder if my mother washed them.

"How about the food stamp card?"

"No." I look over the valley behind him. "Mom should be doing that for herself anyway. You need some money?"

"Oh, no, no."

I take a twenty out of my wallet. "Here. Take it. Buy yourself some lunch."

He takes it, looks down at the bill between his fingers, then he folds it and puts it into his pocket. "Thanks." At the top of the stairs he waves to me, flapping his hand the way a kid does, from the wrist. "Bye, Tara. Bye."

"Let's go to Ross's," Mom suggests when she gets in the car. All her personal stuff is in the backseat, in a little bag. The rest piles in the trunk. I'm going to take it all to storage.

"I need some underwear."

"Okay." I am cheered by what seems to be her initiative. She must be planning to stay in treatment for a while.

We stop by Longs first. On Fort Street Mall old men sit outside on the benches waiting for their buses. Office workers walk in and out of stores carrying plastic bags. Fort Street doesn't look as bad now that I have my mother in my possession. In the store I buy her sensible things: toothpaste, shampoo, a brush. We walk around the aisles slowly. She holds my elbow. She laughs. We choose soap, razors, hair barrettes. ("What kind of hair barrettes do you like?" "I like the kind that you can pin both sides back." She spends the rest of the day pinning, unpinning her hair.) Shampoo, conditioner, moisturizer, two toothbrushes, dental floss, Birkenstock knockoffs, underwear, a pair of jeans.

At the register she puts her hand to her mouth and sucks her breath in. "Oh! I forgot reading glasses! Wait a minute!"

She runs over to the glasses, picks a pair out. I get in line again to buy them.

"I'll just wait outside." She smiles.

"Okay."

Why I ever let my mother leave I don't know. When I come out of the store she's gone. I look around. The sky is blue, downtown is busy, the bums are still here, and my mother is nowhere to be seen.

Fort Street fucking Mall. I sit on a bench and wait. What else can I do? I'm going to take her to the hospital. I'll sit here all day if I have to.

A few minutes later my mother appears at the corner, talking to Ron. He must have sprinted down the hill to meet her. He passes her something; she puts it in her purse. I can't see what it is. They nod at each other. They've already said their good-byes. Then she heads straight for me, smiling, as if she knew I were there the whole time.

"What was that?" I ask when she comes back.

"Oh, nothing." She's trying on her new eyeglasses. "Ron just had to give me a book."

She adjusts and readjusts the glasses, looking up Fort Street toward the mountains. "Thanks, honey," she's saying. "Thanks for all that stuff."

She squeezes my hand and takes the plastic bag from me.

"Want to get something to eat? I sure am hungry."

And just like that I believe her again.

Kaiser, the hospital where Karen has her insurance, is in Moanalua, almost to Pearl Harbor, across the freeway from the old Damon estate on Red Hill. Mr. Damon was a missionary, sent to Honolulu by the American Seamen's Friend Society, a temperance and retirement organization for old seadogs who had nothing to do but drink after they got off the boats. A Hawaiian princess willed Damon the entire valley back in the 1800s and he built his house on a hill. You can see the royal palms from the freeway overlooking suburban west Oahu like old maids from their windows.

My mother and I check in to the emergency room a little after noon.

Everything's fine. She nods when she's supposed to, fills out forms. She smiles and jokes with the nurse who takes her blood pressure.

"My daughter is worried about me," she says. "I've been depressed."

Her assigned room is empty save a gurney, a doctor's stool, and a security camera. "This one is for the psych patients," she says, looking around. She changes into a nightgown and empties her purse. "They'll probably want to look for sharps. I know. I did this all the time. *Assessment*." She wipes the sides of her mouth. They've gotten dry since Fort Street.

She sits on the gurney sideways, her legs dangling off the cot. She rubs the toe with the centipede bite fiercely, as if rubbing it will make it go away. I look at all the bites: the centipede bite on her toe, a mystery bite on her instep, and the brown recluse spider bite on her thigh, finally healing.

In the psych ward Mom pins and unpins her hair. She is so skinny she looks young again, gangly on the cot, her hair in double barrettes, pimples on her chin. Her legs swing.

"What's happening?" I ask.

She shrugs. "I'm just going to do whatever the doctor says."

The nurse who checked us in never looks for sharps, nor does she take anything away, like they do in the movies. Mom's clothes just sit in a paper bag in the corner of the room. She yawns.

"Might as well go outside, honey. This is going to take a while."

I wander out to the lanai. Two Hawaiian women wait there. They smoke cigarettes. One is laughing. She wears a shirt that says KŪ'Ē, resist. The other's shirt says HAWAIIAN. They're both sovereignty shirts. My mother's shirt says JINGLE in small letters in the middle of her chest.

I realize as I'm sitting here that Owen lived on the hill across from where we now sit. Owen Lee in his ugly little box of a condominium. Owen Lee and his waterbed, his visible veins, his bungee cords, and his pale, pale skin.

At about five I go back in to check on her. A social worker enters with a clipboard. Mom hadn't even rated a psychiatrist.

"We don't need to go to Mother Kaiser, do we?" The woman blinks, nods. She hands Mom two yellow pieces of paper. "These are your appointments for substance abuse intake, Karen. Two o'clock Thursday." She pauses, looks at my mother, then taps on the clipboard with the tip of her pen. "That's in two days."

My mother pretends to look at the pieces of paper, but really all she does is slip them into her purse. She won't look at them again. It's ridiculous what people think a drug addict needs. This pert woman before me has never seen my mother's purse. My mother's purse is a fucking mess. Empty pens—*Here's a lighter, you want this?*—a toothbrush, bits of dirty paper, pages from her planner, empty lipstick containers and envelopes, a plastic heart, her Alice in Wonderland glasses missing the earpieces, the watch missing the straps.

My mother and I walk out into the yellowing afternoon. We've been at Kaiser for five hours. She's jittery and pissed. I'm dejected and confused. To think I expected her to be admitted.

"See how she said that?" She snorts. "I told you. This is a waste of time. I shouldn't have come here. Fucking *Kaiser*. Fucking *social worker*. I could do her job with my fucking *eyes closed*."

I have no idea what to do now. The hospital isn't admitting her, and my father said 5:30 on the dot.

"I'm sorry," she says, though she sounds distinctly not sorry. "But I knew it."

She's shaking her head, pulling her hair away from her face. She gets out a comb from her purse and starts digging it into her scalp. She's obviously angry but somehow it all seems like a show.

I cast around. "How about Sand Island, Mom? I heard Joanna's at Sand Island—"

She looks at me. "Sand Island? Sand Island? I don't need Sand Island. That's not for people like me. That's for criminals and wastoids, not people like me. You want me to go to Sand Island?" She scowls. "No. No, I'm not going there. Just drop me off at my house."

It occurs to me I have nothing to offer my mother. I don't have a house, nor do I have money for a hotel. She can't go to Gail's, or Gamma's. Layla's living with Jack. I don't even have my own car. I had hoped that if I got her to the hospital they would see what seemed so plain to me: that my mother needed help, that she was not herself, that she needed a bed and food and a clean room away from Ron and downtown and Esther Leung's.

I had looked for my mother, I had found her, I had taken her to treatment. I had done what I was supposed to do. Now I wanted to leave.

We drive to Punchbowl in silence. She slams the car door on the way out, leaving the boxes.

"I hope you find a shelter or something." That's the last thing I say to her before I leave.

I call Layla. I call Gamma. I call Lauren in Texas to tell her about the bites. Lauren says, "Spider bites!" and then starts to cry. "My father's brother had spider bites. He had hepatitis C and an abscess on his foot and then he said he got a spider bite and that's when he died."

Layla says you can do heroin between your toes, between your fingers, on your feet. You wear shoes and people can't see the tracks.

"Spider bite, huh. More like abscesses from the needles."

"It's been this way since she was seventeen," Gamma says. "Andy wrote her a check for school. He said, 'I'll support you, Karen, I'll support you.' She was enrolled in the California School of Arts and Crafts. She took that money and went with your father and Michael Butler and that whole scene in the beginning of the seventies, late sixties. And Andy forgave her. Even when he got that check back and it said Karen Morgan on it, her signature. She took that money and spent it on drugs or whatever."

I think: Probably not. Probably just on living.

"And I've spent hundreds, thousands of dollars on Karen throughout her life. Don't you think I want to pay for a house for her, set her up somewhere and pay for her? But I'm angry. I am angry and I am taking care of Margaret now, and you and your sisters, you are responsible now."

"I am not," I say. "I am not responsible. The only person who is responsible for Karen Morgan is Karen Morgan."

I'm in a Honolulu library. I'm trying to whisper but everyone's looking at me. I'm saying it but I don't know if I totally believe it.

It's a year after 9/11. Earlier in the morning everyone gathered in the library plaza and sang Hawaiian songs and held hands. I stood outside the circle and watched. I don't know why I didn't hold hands, too. I wanted to.

"I'm not responsible," I repeated.

"No, but now, Tara, you're splitting my words. You're a stubborn, smart girl and you have your opinions but you're splitting my words. All right, you're not responsible, but you are responsible for yourself, for what you do and for doing what you can for your mother. I am not going to let her come in and kill Margaret, kill me. I'm just not going to let that happen."

She says good-bye. "I love you and I respect you." It's the only time I can remember her saying that.

I stop by Punchbowl on the day of Mom's intake appointment. Ron's there, squatting in his usual spot on the couch. I don't even ask him about his treatment. He's talking to me about getting clean. He doesn't quite get around to the clean part. "Hawaii's a *paradise* for junkies." He's animated. He knows this subject well. "You can sleep on the beach, the mission gives out free food." Then he notices my mother looking at him. "But we're going to change. We're going to get it together now, Tara."

She's heard it all before. She laughs: a bitter, hard little laugh.

"I'm just trying to be positive," says Ron, shrugging.

"This isn't *positive,* Ron."

"I know, I'm just saying."

"This isn't *positive.*" She scowls. This is my real mother, who tells it like it is.

I stand up, cross my hands in front of me.

"Do you have the money to get to the appointments?"

"Yeah. Ron scrounged a buck-fifty."

"Good luck, then." I pat her knee. I know I'm being formal but I don't feel like touching her. "Call me when you know what's going on."

"Yeah, okay."

She sinks back into her chair. Ron waves and smiles and I walk out into the sun.

I stay in Honolulu another three weeks. I don't hear from my mother again. Maybe she went to the appointments. A few days later she showed up at Gail's house chattering. *You know, you know, I'm like.* Gail said it wasn't heroin-high, but something else, something angrier. She asked Gail for a ride to a women's shelter. Gail said okay. "I've been clean for four days," she told Gail. "Ron split."

Once they got over the Pali Mom changed her mind.

"Just drop me off on Hotel."

Gail got angry; they fought. She told my mother not to come around again until she was clean. "You're a bitch," Mom yelled as she got out of the car. Two weeks later Gail's son saw my mother walking along Wilder, near Punahou, shoeless and dazed.

I go over to Punchbowl one last time, just in case. No one is there. No TV sounds waft out the screened window. No curtain flutters. There's a lock on the door. Esther Leung probably put it there.

I have a dream—or a kind of a dream. I'm trying to find my mother. No one will tell me where she is, so I go to a hotel. I am familiar with the landscape: the beige hallways, the hedges, the redundant balconied rooms. This one is full of drug addicts. Everyone's high and no one has anywhere to be. Mom lies in a dirty bed. She's wasted. She's a sack of bones; she can barely stand up. I pull back a sheet to tuck her in and I see her feet. They are horned like a lizard's.

I don't remember if I saved her or not. I only remember that I flew out of the building—I had resolved to fly and so I did. I floated out an open window and onto the wind, higher and higher, a variation on that dream I've always had about Hawaii where I'm flying around, looking at it from above. Green encircled by blue, waterfalls, that one perfect valley. I swoop toward the ocean. I can't believe I'm flying. And just when I stop to think about it is when I start falling.

Hurricane!

1982   Lihue, Kauai

SEVENTH GRADE AND THEY PACKED YOU UP AND SENT you to the dogs. Kauai High School was *rough*. Barely adolescent nerds of twelve played tetherball next to eighteen-plus toughs hotboxing in the parking lot. It caused more than a few problems. Or that's what everyone told me.

Lihue was town: one McDonald's, one Pizza Hut. Home of the Red (color of the dirt) Raiders. The best thing about Kauai High School? Night games at Vidinha Stadium. High school football was the shit. Hot *malasadas* and chili rice from the plate-lunch truck. Black-haired boys with dark eyes and high cheekbones and sagging surfer shorts and well-placed moles. *Nō ka ʻoi! Da Red Raiders stay da bes brah!* Devika stuffed her greasy LeSportsac with makeup pimped from Woolworth's: Wet-n-Wild eyeliner for the bottom lid, CoverGirl purple eyeshadow on top. Blue mascara. Bonne Bell pink lip gloss for smackable lips. Debbie only allowed *clear* lip gloss and *black* mascara, so when Carla picked us up for games I plundered Devika's.

No one really liked me, but I liked them, liked the sullen night-game boys who stood in the shadows of the concrete-block walls passing joints. Their absence, their studied disregard tugged at me. It felt familiar: a space I could fill. Devika and I strolled past and let them ignore us. I liked the dark floodlit Kauai night, soft and a little wicked.

Dad came home only on weekends so I pounced:

"Dad, if you were on a desert island, and there was only one other person there, would you eat that person?"

We sat cross-legged in the den in front of the TV. My father rolled a Zig Zag between his fingers, pulling it up to his mouth, licking across. *Hmm.* He was looking at the screen. Some war movie was on, an island somewhere in the Pacific. Sweat rolled down the soldiers' dirty faces. People yelled, guns rattled, joints piled in a stack to my father's left. A typical Saturday afternoon on Kauai.

Dad got the weed from Uncle Bill over on Maui who grew it in his backyard next to his dish. I loved Uncle Bill. At Uncle Bill's baby girl's baby luau, Lilia Something Something Demuth's Hawaiian name was so long it stretched on a banner all the way around the ceiling of Kawaiahao Church. I threw up from eating too much coconut pudding and pork *laulau*. It was Uncle Bill who made me a turquoise bracelet right around the time I left my mother, the one I lost Boogie-boarding at the Surf. Maybe it was still sitting on the bottom of Kalapaki Bay. Maybe the chain-smoking beachcombers with their metal detectors found it and gave it to another girl.

Bits of leaves floated in the sweat from my guava juice. I wiped them up, rolled them between my fingers.

"Dad!"

"Huh?"

"Would you eat the other person or not?"

I had asked the question because Dad and Debbie and I were possibly going to move to Fiji. Debbie was up for a job at one of the hotels there and we all might move, as a family, to Fiji. Just the word sounded exciting. *Feejee.*

He nodded once.

"*Eeeew.* How could you *eat* another person, Dad?"

"They're dead, aren't they?" He twirled the end of his cigarette.

That's what they were called on the Zig Zag packet, cigarettes: premium cigarettes.

"That's gross, Dad! What parts?"

"Well, the legs. I'd eat the ribs, too. Then I'd finish off with the fingers."

He ran his head back and forth like a typewriter, clicking his teeth.

"But you can't eat a human, Dad!"

"Why?"

"'Cause you can't!"

"Survival of the fittest, Tee."

In Fiji, a long time ago, the natives ate people. I read it in the guidebook Dad gave me. It was called "long pig." I wasn't scared, though. It happened a long time ago; no one was eating each other now. It was the thought of my father eating people that scared me.

"But, Dad, would you eat your best friend?"

Who was Dad's best friend anyway? Jim Carter? I didn't even know what he looked like. Bill? Dad seemed to prefer women. *I'm glad I never had a boy,* he once told me. *Then I would have to play baseball.*

"I would eat my friend." He plopped a Triscuit into his mouth. "Sure."

I cracked a knuckle.

"But, Dad, would you eat me?"

He stopped. A few crumbs clung to his mustache. He wiped them away and winked.

"Aye, I'd eat ya. I'd eat yer little toes."

In Fiji, I decided, I would change my name. No one knew me there. All the schoolchildren wore uniforms. All day long you floated in the blue lagoons among the pretty fishes and drank coconut milk from coconut shells. There weren't any sharks in Fiji. What was Hawaii exotic to Fiji exotic? What could you do on a desert island? Anything.

I bought a spiral notebook just like Elayne did in *Sweet Dreams* romances and wrote about all the ways I was going to change. I would be called *Terra,* not *Tah-rah.* I would wear only Gloria Vanderbilt jeans. I would use Sun-In in my hair. I would become tan. I would lose weight.

I would change my handwriting. I would get a retainer and click it in and out of my mouth like Jocelyn Kawamoto did. Debbie and Dad and I would move far into the Pacific, where I wouldn't know or care if no one was trying to find me.

Watch the line of cheerleaders raise their shaved legs in unison, black hair swaying behind them. Kalei. Kalei who was so ethereally popular she could even be nice to me. Watch the cheerleaders and the football players. The *mokes* and titas, too. Big girls, big boys in baggy tees and surf shorts, tattooed with Hawaiian things: warriors with helmets and spears and names in Gothic letters. Big fat femmie Hawaiian boys were called *māhū*—they liked *oofing* other boys. Maybe they looked at the slim boys I liked and wanted the same thing. Maybe the titas looked at Jocelyn and Kalei and wanted that, too. What was it I wanted? My mouth on something. Like in second-period jam session, the ubiquitous haole counselor's idea (always a Mr. Bryant doing good). Get kids together in a steamy empty classroom, shut the windows, shut the fluorescent lights, hot. Mariah Quezon (Sun-In blonde) dancing with Chad Kubota to "Faithfully." *They say that the road ain't no place to start a family.* My Bonne Bell mouth, my Babe-scented neck, covered in someone else's Aquafresh breath.

First period. Homeroom. Mrs. DeSouza took roll. *Hea. Hea. Present. Hea.*

Second period. Mat-matics wit Mistah Kobayashi. Mistah Kobayashi crack jokes. *Okay Gang-y. First, one joke. Knock-knock. Who's dea? Portagee burgla brah! Okay, gang-y. Two times two. Foah. Tree times tree. Sex! Foah times foah. Sexteen!*

Third period. Half-year Hawaiiana, half-year Sosho Studies. In Sosho Studies I memorize the state bird of Maine. Right now in Hawaiiana. Mr. Hamburger, that's his name, Mr. Hamburger, is reading from a textbook. That's what he does. *In 1778 Captain James Cook and his boats the* Discovery *and* Resolution *landed at Waimea Bay on the west side of the island of Kauai. The Hawaiians, celebrating the harvest season of Makahiki, received him*

*as their god Lono. On a return trip the following year he was killed at Kealakekua
in a scuffle with the natives.* Mr. Hamburger was from the mainland. He was
black-haired, genial. Sometimes he mispronounced the names.

"There's a storm coming," Mr. Hamburger said. We turned our eyes
to the classroom windows. Mr. Hamburger had been stuck in one of
the crappy trailers with louvered windows along one side. A half-bare
plumeria tree stretched its bony branches toward nothing. I couldn't
quite see the sky, but I expected it to be sort of blue-white, as it often
was on a day in late November. It had rained the night before; the grass
steamed. I could almost hear the buzzing.

A storm. Maybe it would be like the one that knocked out the old
Lumaha'i Bridge. But that was a tidal wave. I wished I had seen a tidal wave.

Fourth period, language arts. We'd been memorizing poems. I
couldn't seem to get mine down. Something was happening to me. I was
losing my touch. All I wanted was to sit in Kalei's lap and have her
groom me for Red Raiders games. I wanted Troy or Kimo or Chad or
J.J. to do something to me, something close enough to smell their Old
Spice. At Wilcox I was the teacher's pet. At Kauai High School I forgot
everything. While Devika and Dawn sewed up the track, closing in on
the night-game boys, I was at home reading guidebooks for Feejee.
Dawn had been molested; Devika had been molested. They wrapped
their joints in tinfoil, snuck them behind the temporary buildings. I
wanted to walk with them, tulip jeans tight, a little leather bag swinging
off my shoulder, my Candie's clacking, but I always lagged behind.

I didn't cry alone at night anymore, I was too old for that now. But
there was something missing. A hole inside that I kept to myself, making my need for things seem larger than my ability to express it. Debbie
loved me. My father loved me. But I wanted something else.

We got dismissed at noon. Buses would pick us up from the front circle and drive us home. But I dallied in the halls, and by the time I
reached the circle Mr. Gomes's bus number 202 was gone.

A hurricane! Funnel clouds and houses aloft. Trees and whole buildings
and shards of glass flying. Like *The Wizard of Oz,* which played on TV

every year. Dad and I watched it together. I got excited when the screen turned to color; he told stories about the actors. *They ruined her,* nodding at Judy Garland. *She had a beautiful voice.* And at Scarecrow: *Wonderful actor, wonderful man.*

"All the munchkins were getting drunk and doing drugs on the set. It was a real party. A real fucking party!"

He laughed until he cried.

Good witches, bad witches. Poppies, poppies.

The thrill of being abandoned at the onset of a hurricane and having to seek shelter among the brown temporary classrooms of Kauai High's intermediate wing lasted only as long as it took Debbie's Karmann Ghia to inch its way around the drop-off circle. I would not be forced to face the storm alone, a few furry jungle creatures my only companions. Too bad. The Ghia's black seats were, as usual, hot, nearly tarry. I started sweating. Kalei never sweat, even in her Red Raiders sweater.

"I thought I'd lost you," Debbie joked, reaching over to give the passenger door a tug. "Just went to Foodland. You should have seen it— batteries and macaroni and cheese flying off the shelves! Crazy! Everybody needs to just calm down."

She felt next to the gearshift for cigarettes and lit one, flicking her ashes out the window. She looked excited, and it made her pretty. Thirty-two, sixteen, I thought. That was the age we'd be when I was half as old as her. Right now we were twelve and twenty-eight. Twelve and twenty-eight seemed far apart. Thirty-two, sixteen seemed closer.

She flicked her thumb toward the backseat.

"Take a look at the loot."

We had water and a pack of batteries, tape, macaroni and cheese, crackers, saimin, canned soup, ice. Not much different from what we usually bought, except for the tape and batteries.

"They told us to tape the windows—that can be your job."

It was a chore, but I didn't mind. I was out at noon and a hurricane was coming. Maybe I'd get carried away.

★   ★   ★

Kona was already going crazy when we got home, barking that weird, wailing bark that makes you think everything is about to go awry. We didn't have much of a view from the poured-cement patch out back we called a lanai, but we could see the neighbor's house, his dog penned in back.

The dogs crooned, the cattle egrets that stalked the fields flew as if the cane itself had shaken them out. It started raining like it did in winter: sideways, in gray sheets. The royal palms over Grove Farm twisted.

Debbie and I watched TV while the signal held. Civil defense said there was a hurricane heading straight for Kauai. The eye was supposed to hit us at two or three.

"I can't believe they didn't tell us about this until noon! The eye is at three for chrissakes."

I was taping crosses on each of the picture windows. I started from the top, pressing the tape down firmly like Debbie had instructed, no bubbles. I made sure the lines were straight.

Debbie sat in her chair with an iced tea and watched me.

"What's the eye?" I asked.

"That's when everything gets calm." She looked into her glass, picked something out of it.

I kept taping. I wanted everything to get crazy first. I wanted to see a house blow away.

All it did was get really dark. I lay by the sliding glass doors of the lanai and watched the sky thicken. The TV went out, then the lights. I still didn't see the funnel cloud.

We brought Kona inside and he scratched at the guest-room door. The neighbor's dog finally got taken in. Mabel Wilcox's palms curved like the bottoms of canoes. Bits of things flew through the air but too quickly for me to identify them. Debbie smoked at the dining-room table. We turned on the transistor radio. Dad called before the phones went down. "You two okay?" He was on Oahu, at work. The storm wasn't hitting there so bad. "Yeah." I was a little disappointed.

We had sandwiches at two and when the eye hit I knew I was going through a storm because here was the calm center of it. Afterward the roof of the house belonging to our unfriendly neighbor who screamed at his dog blew off. I watched it detach and smash into the house next door. I had a hard time seeing what that meant, though, because there was no one to watch reacting. I yelled to Debbie, "The neighbor's roof just blew off!"

"Really?" She lay beside me on the floor but she didn't tear her hair or cry.

More bits. The coconut trees looked as if they would snap in two. "This is fun."

Debbie and I held hands. Hers were cool and dry. Mine were a little wet. I felt that she was my mom, taking care of me. My real mother was somewhere else, far away, and I didn't think of her once during the hurricane except to wonder whether she'd find out that I had been in one. After a few hours in the dark Debbie said it was time for bed. I don't remember how late it was but I was tired. I had just gone through a hurricane, even though nothing really happened except Debbie and I sat together at the dining-room table and she smoked cigarettes and I ate sandwiches and we felt close.

Kona stayed in the guest room all night. I even went in to say goodnight to him. He looked okay, though he paced and whimpered. Closing the door, I could hear his big paws clicking.

It was called Hurricane 'Iwa, we found out later, after the 'iwa bird—the white frigate bird that heralds a storm. Civil defense hadn't seen the hurricane coming; that's why we were in school at noon when the eye was set to hit at three. Everyone said someone should have known, should have warned us. But what were we going to do? Fly away?

The Torrid Zone

$\measuredangle$

October 2002   Waimea, Kauai

T HE DAY I ARRIVE ON KAUAI ANOTHER HURRICANE
threatens but it sweeps to the south. Swells are up; cars park out in
front of Pakala's just before Waimea, where the Robinsons used to pa-
trol the beach in front of their house on horseback. They carried guns,
it was rumored, and picked on surfers, hippies in particular. One of my
cousins got set up with one of the Robinson boys once, she told me.
G.G. had him over after church. He was quiet and sober and religious. It
wasn't a match.

It's been exactly ten years since the last hurricane, 'Iniki, which hit on
September 11, 1992, and twenty since Iwa. I was in Portland during
Iniki, living with the Tupperware guy. We didn't have a TV so I missed
most of the storm, but I knew it hit Kauai the worst, especially Waimea.
Most of the cottages were gutted. G.G. was there. Gampa had died in the
eighties so they had moved her out of the manager's house by then and
into a little cottage facing the sea. She rode out Iniki alone. She was ninety-
four. Most of her belongings were washed out onto the lawn.

It's been weird Kona weather on all the islands: hot winds from the
south instead of the normal trades. The Big Island is green as a meadow;

Waimea's wet when Hanalei is clear. Some say it's El Niño. Others say it's God-willed: hurricanes keep tourists away.

I am staying with Mina, Gamma's first cousin, at the Cottages. I've come to get my head clear. Not much doing on the west side since the plantation left. There are the seed companies, a shrimp farm, a couple of restaurants, and the Cottages. The tourists heading for the Waimea Canyon or the state park up in Kokee usually breeze by.

The biggest thing around is the missile range, PMRF—the Pacific Missile Range Facility—down at Barking Sands. The first simulated interception of a launcher-phase dummy nuclear missile originated, in part, here, at Barking Sands, named so for the peculiar *woof* the dunes make when someone walks across them. Hollow skeletons of coral, coupled with the extreme dry heat of Kauai's west side—Mana gets less than sixteen inches of rain a year—are responsible for the phenomenon. Senator Inouye, of World War II's 442nd (mostly Japanese from Hawaii, the most decorated battalion in U.S. history), got $683 million for Hawaii defense in 2002, $175 million of which went straight to Kauai. Barking Sands is going to help save the United States from terrorists and North Korea: we're building a huge shield over us; that's what Star Wars is, a shield, though it's got a different name now. After 9/11 Donald Rumsfeld renamed it BMD, Ballistic Missile Defense. Future wars are going to be fought in space, or this is the idea, rockets against rockets. Brilliant Pebbles—that was Reagan's term for them—will blanket us like a thousand points of light, each specially trained to bring down a nuclear Goliath. It's a weird anachronism. Everyone knows America's the only big guy around.

Besides the PMRF it's quiet on the west side, and lovely. Gampa Great's palm trees still creak and rock in the wind; the dry foothills of Kokee rise up ocher and gold behind them. I run on the beach with Mina's dog and watch the sun set behind Niihau, all the clouds alit. The beach is still dirty from the river, and the water is brownish red, but it is pretty here and it feels familiar. The horse corral is down toward the pier; driftwood and kukui shells litter the beach. All of this soothes me.

At night I make Mina tuna on the stove and we have gin and tonics and she tells me stories about the family. She's had troubles, too. "Your mother reminds me of my mother," she says. "My mother was a beautiful woman. She had a drinking problem—that's what we called it then—but she was charming and people loved her. Just like your mother. I loved your mother."

I don't know why she says it in the past tense, but I appreciate it anyway.

After dinner we get in the hot tub under the moon.

Mina's seventy, still a good-looking blonde, with a pointed tan face and intelligent brown eyes. She grew up here on Kauai's west side. Her father was manager at Kekaha, even ran for territorial Senate, though he lost. He built the Kekaha pool. He and Mina's mother, Lani, threw parties, were beloved. Mina was the ragtag curly-haired plantation gal whose mother drank a little too much, but Mina says she doesn't regret a thing.

I remember this one time: Waiting for the convoy ship to take the girls to California during the war. Mina hid in the closet with her sister. All the adults were drunk. There was a brawl. Then all of them got on the convoy along with Gamma and Bubsy and Mina saw some of the people she'd grown up with on the plantation in the hold. Until then the war had been fun: gas masks and dugouts and plotting guerrilla warfare with Korean Kokee Yi, who lived up in the mountains and hated the Japanese so much he lined his cabin walls with Molotov cocktails in Coke bottles.

When they got to California, Lani set herself and the girls up in the Saint Francis Hotel. They lived for a week on what was in Mina's penny jar. Then Lani got them a house in the Haight and the first thing she did was buy Mina a cocker spaniel and herself a parrot. The parrot knew how to laugh the way Lani laughed, throaty. One night mother and daughter went to Fisherman's Wharf to pick up some crab. Lani said, "Wait in the car, Mina." Mina got down into the well of the backseat and stayed there, fearful of the tramps and the wharf rats. After a while the pleasant strains of "Sweet Leilani, Heavenly Flower" wafted from the bar. Lani tottered out several hours later, cracked crab under her arm. Mina, twelve or so, drove them home.

Mina felt from then on she should never tell anyone anything.

Her head is back, the water bubbles up around us. I can't see Mina's eyes—it's too dark out here, even with the moon—but I know what they look like. They're my eyes. I got them from her family: deeply set, a little too close together. A smear of blue underneath, like a thumbprint.

Seventeen-Mile Drive

1984 Pebble Beach, California

MY THIRTEENTH SUMMER I GOT STRETCH MARKS. I don't know who I got them from—the lines, the breasts. My mother's were small and baggy. *From feeding you, Tara.* Two summers visiting my mother in Monterey and I was a woman: stretch marks, boobs, two younger sisters to watch out for.

The summer before, my mother had greeted me at the San Francisco airport pregnant. "Surprise!" And there she was, standing at the bottom of the escalator holding Layla's hand. She had her nice shoes on, and a big belly and an overpacked smile. I pretended I was surprised, but Margaret had already let the cat out of the bag. "Your mom is pregnant again," she said. "Fertile Myrtle." Dad sighed.

My stomach was tight for a month—Mom didn't have money for another kid—but everything worked out. She befriended a rich lady named Beth who lived across the street from Margaret. Beth was a Southern grocery-store heiress who had cerebral palsy, so Mom helped her, did things around her house, drove her places in her specially made Volvo. Really Beth helped us. She installed us in a garage apartment in the Italian section of Monterey. She bought us a washer and a dryer and a sewing machine. She paid for a nanny for Lauren.

I liked it by the Italians. We had kittens and Layla befriended a girl named Antonella who lived next door. Beth bought us sheets and towels and comforters. I drew things for the walls. We picked the carnations that grew along the side of a neighbor's driveway until Mom told us to stop. On the mainland you can't just pick people's flowers, she explained. I didn't understand. Flowers grew back, didn't they?

When she came home from the hospital with Lauren, stitches in her stomach, I snuck a few. I went down the street and cut white roses from a neighbor's yard and put them in a glass bowl. When Mom got home she wasn't angry. All she said was, "How did you know to put roses in a bowl like that?"

But the second summer felt different. It was 1984. Karen had been in Monterey for two years and all the habits she had tried to elude by leaving Texas had started to take hold again. She was living in a motel room on a strip with too many convenience stores and fast-food restaurants. Then there was the boyfriend, an army guy from Fort Ord. When I arrived in June I tried to resume the life we'd had a year ago. I saw the friends I had made the previous summer, a minister's daughter named Becky, a little preppy girl named Lee; we went swimming at Beth's club. But it was embarrassing to live in a motel. When Becky's father dropped me off he'd say, "Are you sure you're all right?" I said I was fine.

The woman I wanted to become lived in Pebble Beach, anyway, not Monterey. Pebble Beach was the community on Seventeen-Mile Drive, across the peninsula from Monterey. Beth got us a house there after a few weeks in the motel. Fifteen hundred dollars for one and a half months. The landlord would be "doing Europe" with her daughter. A letter posted in the kitchen set out the rules: Mom was to start the car in the garage every month, collect the mail, mow the lawn. We were *welcome*. Our family was to *enjoy the house*.

It was nothing special: a rectangular ranch house, dark brown, trimmed in red. Two bedrooms, a fireplace. A little playhouse, a miniature of the real one, occupied a corner of the backyard. But it was inside Seventeen-Mile Drive and that's what counted. Seventeen-Mile Drive was private. To drive there in 1984 cost a tourist eight dollars or so, but you didn't have to pay the fee if you had the Pebble Beach sticker, and despite the rules we were using the landlady's car.

There were only two entrances to Seventeen-Mile Drive: one at Fort Ord, one at Carmel-by-the-Sea. Security shacks sat at each one. At the Carmel-by-the-Sea entrance, the one that proclaimed PEBBLE BEACH for the tourists who came to buy Italian ice and cappuccino and shoes, the guard shack was more elegant. A patch of forest grew there; if you looked down the long tunnel of trees you could imagine the ocean and the mansions further in, and it enticed you to spend the money and take the ride. For a few minutes there was just forest, thick and dark green, and then the houses began. They were made of great stone blocks and they were romantic and brooding and leaned on their haunches at the edge of the ocean as if they were considering throwing themselves in.

I was thirteen, she was thirty-four. Close enough, I guess is what she thought.

We were making dinner for two brothers: Randy, the grunt my mother was dating, twenty-eight, unmarried, bony, mustached; and his younger brother, Matt, eighteen, a senior, a sandy blond with ruddy skin. It was a double date. Mom had set it up, even arranged it so that my sisters would stay the night with Beth. Mom wanted me to feel grown up. If the kids were around, I'd feel like one of them.

I was thirteen. My concerns were more straightforward.

"What will we make for dinner?"

We were in the kitchen. Sunlight slanted through the open porch door.

She wasn't listening. She was looking for something to eat. There wasn't much: tuna, a few eggs, mustard. A stand of celery wilted in the crisper.

"Mom?"

She picked at the back of her teeth, dislodged something, and chewed on it.

"Oh, fuck, this is stupid, Tara. I don't want to do this. Randy's a creep. Anyway, who's got money?"

It was true. We didn't have any money. I had a few bucks left from the money my father sent me—at the motel room she had stolen it, so now I hid it in a shoe—but we were out of the last welfare check and wouldn't get any more till next week. Still, I wanted that dinner. It was just a grunt and his teenaged brother, but I wanted it.

She pulled a whipped cream canister left over from one of the girls' birthdays from the door and closed her mouth around the spout.

"He's a grunt." Her mouth was full. "And we're broke."

She raised her eyebrows, passed the canister to me. I squirted.

"What about that grill?" I didn't want to give up. We had food stamps and a house. They could bring beer. "There's that grill. We could have steak."

She cackled. "Men like steak, yeah? And potatoes? Steak and potatoes?" She slammed the refrigerator door shut. "Fuck."

Sometimes there'd be no food in the fridge except for eggs, mustard, ketchup, wilted celery, a can of Vienna sausages, and a box of Cream of Wheat. She'd fry Cream of Wheat for dinner and let Layla and Lauren and me eat the whole thing. I didn't know where she ate, but I knew it cost her something to do it.

"But, Mom!"

"What?"

"We have to have dinner!"

Dinner seemed respectable, and fun. I had gotten my period. I took care of my sisters. I shaved my legs.

"All right," she said abruptly. "I'll go to the store." She swiped her purse off the kitchen counter. I followed, though I hadn't been invited. In the garage the landlord's mauve Mazda coughed and sputtered. Though Mom had promised me she wouldn't use it anymore—the odometer kept climbing, she'd gotten in a little fender bender, and one of the taillights had blown out—this time I didn't mind.

From where I sat in the passenger's seat, a mint chocolate chip ice cream melting in one hand and Lauren in the other, I had one thing free: my eyes, and they fixed on the rearview mirror and the cop trapped inside of it. I was going to tell the future: my mother would get busted big-time or she would get a date.

We had gone shopping. The steaks were duly purchased, we had potatoes and tomatoes for salad, and Mom had even taken some of the landlord's pennies from the penny jar and used them to buy my sisters and me ice cream in Carmel. The *shoppe* had called the flavor "crème de menthe"; my mother showed off by ordering me a double scoop. The lady behind the counter waited patiently while we counted out the pennies. I was embarrassed; a double scoop was too much. We were still in town when I dumped the top of it out the window.

We had broken the law three times over: one count of no infant car seat; one count car theft; one count of littering the streets of Carmel-by-the-Sea with green ice cream. In the rearview mirror the officer leaned his butt against his motorcycle, cradling his radio. His hair was red and he had a mustache.

My mother *loved* men with mustaches.

"Anything between my teeth?" she asked. The cop hung up his radio and adjusted his pants, running his thumbs along the inside of his waistband. He was trim and short, muscular, and captioned. CAUTION: OBJECTS ARE CLOSER THAN THEY APPEAR. Even before he got to our car he was smiling.

"Here, take Lauren," I said to her, and she did.

He came to my window. I fancied it was because I looked responsible. Where did we live? Where was our insurance and registration? When did we plan to get a car seat for the infant? Didn't I know that littering was illegal?

I tried to point out that ice cream was biodegradable.

"Still littering." He crouched outside the window and rested his hands on the sill. Dimples cusped the corners of his lips like parentheses.

Smile. Tilt head. Appear motherly.

He walked around to her side of the car. She fluffed her hair.

"Officer, my wallet got stolen. We're borrowing the car from a friend. And hadn't we been saying, honey, hadn't we just been saying how we needed to get a car seat for Lauren?"

Despite the lies we got let go with a warning. No ticket, but no date, either. We had the steaks; I made her promise she wouldn't drive the landlady's car anymore.

At the guard shack the security guard squinted. Leaving they just waved at you, but coming back you were inspected. Was he wondering how we lived in Pebble Beach? The car, did he know we were stealing it? Could he tell that all of us had different fathers and that Mom was dating a grunt and that she stayed out sometimes all night with her pal Liza, who was, as Becky said, a *major cokehead*?

He waved us in. We had the sticker, after all. It was affixed to the windshield of the landlady's car—the one that must have seemed like a kind of serendipity to my mother when we first moved to Pebble Beach, just sitting there, cozy in the garage, keys in the ignition, ready to roll and, except for the odometer, mute.

The sun got in my eyes and I sneezed. "Bless you," she said. We were on the deck. The air was dry, cool, sunny, ticklish. Perfect California weather. I was to cut her hair. I had been begging for weeks to give her a bob, and our date was my opportunity. A respectable bob. Cut to the chin, glossy, horsey. It was 1984 in Pebble Beach and I wanted my mother to look the part: bob, plaid dirndl skirt, Polo shirt, sweater wrapped around her shoulders.

We were barefoot, barelegged, tanned from a California summer. The haole rot along her legs dusted her skin. One of my hands rested on her shoulder; the other brushed her hair. She was hot, like I remembered her being when we would go to Kahala Beach and I'd ask her to swim. She always would but first she'd say, "Wait until I get hot, honey. Wait until I get warm."

"So what are you gonna do to me?"

I pulled the brush up from the bottom like they did at salons, watched it fall again to her neck. Some was dark honey-colored, some the dull copper of an old penny from where she'd dyed it. I wanted to cut off all the old-penny hair. I bunched it under, approximating a bob. I leaned over her head to look at her face. She wore sunglasses. Her cheeks tilted toward the sun.

"A bob, like the one I showed you."

She laughed. "A bob! A bob. Well, okay." She didn't seem to care either way. Her hands spread on her thighs. She wiggled her toes, pointed and flexed them. I had a sudden urge to hold her hand.

I didn't. She tucked her fingers between her thighs.

"All right," she said. "Ready."

I wrapped the towel around her shoulders. It was peach and not quite big enough to stretch all the way. I made it fit by fastening it at her collar with a clothespin.

"You can't move or the towel will come off."

"Okay, honey."

She moved and towel came off. She cupped her hand over her eyes and shook her knee. She scratched the bottom of her feet, stretched her neck.

She wasn't taking the haircut seriously. I pulled a clump of hair and her head jerked up.

"Stop moving so much."

She turned around to face me and lifted her sunglasses.

"Watch it."

I got the idea from *The Preppy Handbook,* which I had discovered in the daughter's bedroom, wedged between her high school yearbooks. I had never seen *The Preppy Handbook* before. I studied it: tartan, rugby shirts, pearls. I had never heard of a rugby shirt. Girls who wore rugby shirts had androgynous names like Sloane and Evans. They went to boarding schools and in college played something called squash. The rules for preppies were compellingly precise. Acceptable art included portraits of ancestors, not children's drawings; Martha's Vineyard was classier than the Cape; and under no circumstances were you to install track lighting.

I read the book cover to cover, only slightly aware of its being a parody, finding comfort in the chummy black-and-white drawings, the clean jaws, the lips curling into smirks. I would engineer our entrance into this tartan-covered, diaphragm-and-pearls-wearing world. All we needed were the right clothes and a bob—and even I could do a bob. I cut sanitary-napkin and International Coffee ads from *Redbook* and *Good Housekeeping* to show my mother what hairstyles I liked. She said, "Make a poster for me. Cut out the head and the clothes and then show it to me." I cut heads across the collarbone and pasted them on white typing paper that I found in the daughter's bedroom.

Mom could pull it off. She had the face. She had the name. *Karen Brewster Morgan.* Hadn't she told me that someone related to us had been on the *Mayflower*? I showed her the different styles: parted on the side for gardening, parted in the middle for shopping, double barrettes for cooking or housework. A grosgrain ribbon at the back for church or PTA; a plaid headband for golf. A rumpled Brooks Brothers pink Oxford cuffed at the elbows for the movies; flats and pearls for entertaining; sandals for poking around the yard.

It could happen. It happened in magazines all the time. It was called a makeover and it took only two pages. We were already living in Pebble Beach. We had a car and a house and a fireplace. Hadn't the lady who handed us the keys called us a family? My oxford was a Hunt Club— though I did have a pair of salmon-colored Ralph Lauren socks that I stole from the daughter's bedroom. And my sisters: ragamuffins. Layla had a mullet. We never did get a car seat for Lauren.

Add to this my mother's mirrored gypsy skirts, her home dye jobs, her taste for balding military men with mustaches, her unblended blush and makeup on only one eye, her food stamps. (They had to be colored differently than real dollars, food stamps did. They had to be bright pink and blue and green and had to come in a pack, so that everyone in line could see when you took them out of the envelope they came in.) Karen Morgan's nail polish bore toothmarks where she gnawed at her fingers, her cuticles red and ragged; she left my sisters and me in public places for hours while she "went to the store." She evaporated some nights and didn't come back till morning, even when rich boarding-school girl-friends named Lee who wore real Polo shirts were over.

But that summer we were living in Pebble Beach, and Mom's latest con was paying for my equestrian lessons at the Pebble Beach Club. Layla knew how to order fettuccine Alfredo when Beth took us out for brunch. I knew what cappuccino was. We could certainly cut our hair.

"I'm starting to get a migraine. This is giving me a migraine."

"No, Mom. It looks good. It looks good."

It didn't really look good. It twisted at weird places. It didn't curl under; it looked singed. I sprayed, cut again. She moved her head under my hands.

"I can't cut it straight if you keep moving. It's going to look like shit."

Mom wouldn't care if I swore.

She snorted. She crossed and uncrossed her legs. She bent down without telling me to pick up her glass of water. I pulled her hair back again. I was snipping at the back now, trying to even it out. She reached her hand to her nape. Then she looked down at the hair on the porch, of which there was suddenly too much.

"God!"

She jerked in her chair and the glass of water that had been at her feet spilled and rolled, throwing light.

"It's so short! What are you doing?"

"I'm not done yet. Just hold still."

I tried to put my hand on her head and she jerked away.

"I didn't even want a haircut, dammit. You know?" She took off her sunglasses and shaded her eyes with her hands.

"Yes, you did. You said you wanted one yesterday, in the morning, when I showed you that picture. You said you liked that. You did. You said you liked that."

She looked back over the lawn, toward the playhouse. She ran her hands through her hair, wiped the cuttings off her shirt.

"You know? You come here and think you can tell me what I should wear and how I should have my hair and what kind of a job I should have. You know? I am your *mother*. You understand what that means? That means that you need to *listen* to me, you know? And you need to *mind*. Goddammit."

She was wheezing. "Are you listening to me?"

I nodded and folded my arms across my chest. The scissors were cold.

"Brat." She got up out of the chair and stamped across the porch. "And don't *ever* tell me what to do."

She was wrong, I was right. She needed a haircut and I would be the one to give it to her. I had a right to be embarrassed.

I looked at the playhouse, the hedges at the border of the yard, the pale blue sky above them. A small plane flew low in the distance. If I had money, I could have gone to a movie that afternoon. I liked movies, matinees especially. I liked how, when you walked out from a matinee, you expected it to be night and it wasn't. It would still be bright out, but something would have changed. Walking down the sidewalk afterward it would still be light—cars would pass, all the stores would be open— but it wouldn't feel like afternoon anymore.

Was it strange, this double date? No. "Your mom is so cool," Becky said, and she was. Mom wasn't a Christian, at least. She talked to Becky and me about sex and boys and danced with us to Madonna.

Anyway, Matt and I had *separate* chaises.

We were on the porch: Randy and my mother, Matt and I. We faced the backyard, like spectators at a drive-in. We were getting to know each other. Mom and Randy had a head start. They tilted their knees in; they shared a cigarette. Kools, the kind my father smoked. I found it strange that Mom smoked Kools, like it was strange that on her California license she still used my father's name. KAREN SMITH, next to her picture.

Mom scratched one leg slowly with the other foot. She scratched Randy's, too. He wore denim cutoffs and his legs glowed from a matting of strawberry-blond hair. Below the chaises light shone past the plastic slats—long strips of pale yellow, like a basket.

They talked about silly things, like the way they had danced together when they first met, and what my mother had worn, and how Randy had told his buddy Jerry what a fox Mom was. She laughed in response—a throaty laugh, louder than the quiet night called for. When Matt and Randy got up to tend the barbecue, Mom smiled, nodding at Matt. "So what do you think? Cute, huh? He likes you." She winked. "He's a hunk."

Before that night I'd seen Matt only once, when Randy had come over one day to say hello. I stood at the front door and peered through the screen. Matt was in the car. I saw only half of his head and some chest. He wore sunglasses—black Vuarnets, though I was too far away to tell if they were real. He had full lips and spotty skin. I looked at him for a second, then I turned and walked back into the house.

"He's cute," I offered.

"Just cute?"

She tickled my leg with her foot. "I think he likes you." Mom always thought everyone liked me.

"He doesn't."

She tossed her head. "Well, I know. I know men."

Matt was a tall boy with nice hands lined with blue veins, like rivers on a map. Maybe he would kiss me. Maybe he would put his hands around my waist, like the boys used to do in jam session. Me, I could hardly see at all, just brown lines slung together, a pair of gold hoops at my ears, looking more like my mother than myself.

"That's a weird little house," Matt said after it was quiet for too long. Mom and Randy had squeezed themselves into the same chaise and were necking. Smacking noises punctuated the otherwise still night. I tried not to pay attention. I tried to focus on Matt, who was at this moment clacking his first two fingers together to make that stupid cracking sound.

He tipped his beer toward the playhouses. "Who's it for?"

I shrugged like I didn't know, though I did. It was for playing, obviously. For Layla and Lauren, and occasionally me.

"How old is the girl who lives here? Isn't she in college already?"

I nodded.

"Maybe they should tear it down."

"No," I shot a hand out over the spaces between the chaises to slap him. It had been an angry gesture, but once I touched him I sort of liked it.

"Shut up!"

At Dad and Debbie's I wasn't allowed to say shut up.

It was starting to get dark. Moths circled under the outdoor light. There were rings on the red wood of the porch where I had set my beer bottle, staining the wood an even darker red, black-red. All the circles ran into each other like the hoops on the ground at a ring toss. I was careful to try to place my beer in exactly the same ring I had placed it in before.

"That means you're a virgin, you know." He pointed at my beer bottle. I'd torn the whole label off in one piece.

I hit him again. This time my hand lingered.

I had tried earlier to start conversations with Matt, ask him about his school, the basketball team he played on, what it was like to be a senior. Once I caught him winking at his brother. Sometimes he looked at me and told me a few things, but they were scraps. Mostly he talked about the cars of the men he'd caddied: BMW Si and Si twos, Mercedes, Jags. I knew their logos, but that was all. Other than Beth's Volvo I had never ridden in a fancy car.

"Aw, man, the Si. That's a car. My ex-girlfriend's mom had one of those and she let me drive it. I took it to one-ten one night on the Drive. It was sweet. You know."

I nodded like I knew.

Matt chuckled to himself. "It might be small"—he cupped his hands behind his head, scratching the back of his neck slowly—"but you can do a lot in an Si."

Someone in the other chaise growled.

Matt wasn't a boarding-school boy. He was a caddy, albeit at the Pebble Beach Club. So his sister babysat for Huey Lewis. Big deal. He was as dull as the golf turf he spent all day on. If I had been older, fifteen—

He had nice hands, though, like I thought he would.

I gathered the beer bottles, three to a hand. They clinked as I walked. Cleaning up was something I was good at. I did it without being asked—Mom, too. She cleared away the plates from the floor, barefoot in her spaghetti-strap dress, glowing as she moved. When she bent, one strap loosened and slid over her shoulder. Randy watched her from the chaise.

She swung her ass. The hip slide, the jelly slide, the grease slide, slide me over, slide on some eggs, soft, supple, dimply. I followed her. Randy stared after us. I didn't swing my butt like she did, and I was dressed like a normal thirteen-year-old girl, white Bermuda shorts cuffed, pink Hunt Club, feathered hair parted on the side. Topsider knockoffs, braided leather belt. No straps to slip.

"Careful now, girls!" Randy said it good-naturedly, but it felt ominous—it was so quiet in the backyard. I didn't turn around but Mom did, and I saw her face before she walked into the kitchen. She was smiling, her one yellow tooth duller in the light.

She held the door open and stared through me.

"*Raaandy,*" she called. "Why don't you come in here and help me with the dishes?"

Before she got an answer she laughed. I shook my head from inside the kitchen, mouthing no. I didn't want to go alone outside with Matt. She was still laughing when she turned and walked toward me, the door slapping her back as it closed.

"Watch. He won't come in here and help. Men are lazy pigs."

She smiled when she said this, but it was just her mouth smiling.

I didn't think men were pigs. They were just unfamiliar—Mom's family was mostly women, and I didn't think of my father as a man; he was Dad. Men seemed to me like plumbing. Necessary. Perhaps not very interesting.

In the kitchen I rinsed the plates and loaded them into the dish-washer. Mom stood next to me, inspecting a mole on her shoulder. Her chin doubled.

"Did you see the way he was drinking?"

"Who?"

"*Ran*-dy." She rolled her eyes.

"No."

"*Al-co-ho-lic*," she stage-whispered, her tongue thrust between her teeth.

"You are?"

She bumped my hip and laughed.

I liked to stack the dishes in the dishwasher so that all the plates lined up against each other, an even two inches apart, their surfaces rinsed clean of blood and potato skin, gristle, chewed-up fat. I liked to put the big plates in first, arranging them so they matched. Smaller plates to the right, bowls to the left, pots in back. Glasses stacked above; silver in the rack. There was a small happiness in looking at this kind of order, like look-ing at a style of handwriting I'd copied in order to perfect it.

Mom disappeared into the bedroom, past the fireplace, in which we made fires until the living room was black with soot because we didn't know that you had to open the flue. We'd get in trouble for that later, along with the pennies and the car, but now, standing over the sink, I wanted to follow her, have her take care of me, put me to bed. Read me something, rub my back. Let the men find their way home.

I stood against the counter in the kitchen, listening. Randy and Matt laughed hoarsely about something outside. They were waiting for us out there under the yellow light, where I had swept away my mother's curls just that afternoon, and the dead moths collected like ash.

I felt a penis for the first time that night. What else was I going to do? After I finished the dishes, Randy went inside and Matt and I started kissing on the porch. I put my hand on top of his jeans; he put it un-derneath them. He wore boxers. I felt his pubic hairs first, which were both rough and soft, and sparser than my own. Then he pushed himself against me. At first I moved my hand away but Matt kept moving it back so I started to do something I thought might be similar to a caress. We frenched. I moved my hand back and forth. That was all. He told me about blue balls, then he said he'd better get home. It was 11:15. His curfew was at midnight and he lived in Monterey, a half hour's drive away.

But it was weird. The whole time I was out there, making out with this person, this *man,* my hand around his dick, while my mother was probably screwing his brother inside, all I could think about was that playhouse in front of us. I kept sneaking looks at it: its little windows reflecting the porch light, its miniature roof, its girdle of hedges. That house was the real one, and the big one behind me—with the fireplace and the mother, the dishes, the dark rooms—that was just a summer's mirage, not real at all.

It was August already; nothing had gone the way I planned. I was counting the days until I had to leave. I'd go back to Hawaii, to my father and stepmother, to bedtimes and rules and ninth grade. I didn't know where my mother would go.

Matt gave me a kiss before he got in his car. He was a foot taller, but when I stood on the front steps my mouth reached his. We kissed with our tongues. It was a tender kiss. I watched and waved while he backed his car out. There were a few hedges he had to navigate, and Randy's truck, a Ford, big and black, but he made it out okay.

Westward the Star of Empire
Takes Its Way

⚸

November 2002   Waimea, Kauai

T HE DESIRE FOR SOMETHING SWEET STARTS IN MOTHER'S
milk. Perhaps that's where I got my sweet tooth. I love sugar.
Lemon drops, rock candy, Blo-Pops, Lik-m-Aid, Sweet Tarts, Smarties,
Sugar Babies, Pop Rocks, the closer to pure sugar the better. Chocolate
doesn't interest me—too many ingredients. When I was a kid I could
put an entire jumbo pack of Wrigley's in my mouth. At Wilcox School
I was known as the girl who went around during recess, my hand out-
stretched, begging for snacks: *"I like, I like."* And I was crazy for cut
cane. I loved cut cane so much I once tried to grab a stalk right out of a
field. I didn't know then that the immature plant is covered with tiny
hairs up and down its spine, as irritating as fiberglass to bare skin. This
was why cane workers wore such thick clothing—long-sleeved *kasuri*
shirts, pants, hats, handkerchiefs—all under a noonday sun.

It felt confusing to be so intimate with something—know its many
smells and faces: spindly and wind-tossed when young; turgid, wildly
green when mature; smelling like caramel after burning—yet to not
know any of this when it came to actually touching it. The desire for
something sweet makes you stupid.

243

There are nearly seventy separate jobs in a mechanized harvest of sugarcane. From nearly two tons of stalk and leaf, 225 pounds of raw sugar is made. From there, 95 pounds to every 100 is refined.

A pound of white sugar requires five hundred gallons of water, as well as plentiful sun, a difficult balance to strike without serious irrigation. In the 1920s Hawaii's sugar plantations consumed more than 150 times the water per day used by the entire city of Boston. Fortunately, Hawaii is a well-watered place. Waialeale, the mountain at the center of the island of Kauai, is drenched with more than four hundred inches of rain a year. Much of this water drains into the ocean, but some soaks into the water table, which floats above Kauai's lava core like a lens, providing a year-long supply. H. P. Faye Sr. drilled the first artesian well on the island, out at Kaunalewa, in Mana. He consulted a Hawaiian water diviner for the job. When the artesians dried up after ten years or so— the water table had sunk by a third by 1909—Faye dug ditches to bring water down to the fields from Kokee.

Water was my great-great-grandfather's passion. It was what made Kekaha profitable; some of the highest sugar yields recorded in the world grew in his fields, despite the fact that Mana gets only sixteen inches of rain a year. It was also the cause of one of his life's great tragedies: when he first came to Hawaii in 1880, he brought his younger brother, a sixteen-year-old named Christopher. They worked first at Olokele, on the west side of Maui, for a planter named H. P. Baldwin. One day while Hans was engaged in business on Oahu, Christopher was sent to pick up a recent boatload of Norwegian laborers, who had been convinced to come to the islands by Faye and Knudsen relatives back home. A freak storm met the horse train on the way back. Christopher tried to help the terrified newcomers across a rising freshet. His horse slipped and tumbled over a waterfall. He drowned, along with his little poi dog companion. Both were found downstream after the storm, the dog's jaw clamped to his master's pommel slicker. Faye was said to have never set foot on Maui again.

And sugar is expensive. (The pre-annexation reciprocity treaty that gave the United States Pearl Harbor allowed Hawaiian sugar to enter the

States duty-free. Artificially high prices allowed a profit of two cents on the pound to go straight to the planter. Even today Americans pay over three times the world market price for sugar.) Until thirty years ago almost all of Hawaii's arable land was invested in its continuance, thousands of trees cut down and then planted in the mountains as watersheds to slake its thirst. Trillions of gallons of water were diverted from streams and sucked from wells to water it, and hundreds of thousands of people were born, raised, and trained to work in its fields. It is the cheapest source of carbohydrate in the world, and yet somehow it made my family rich.

The Robinsons still have a plantation down the road from Waimea at Makaweli. I stay on Kauai long enough to see their sugar tasseling. Faye never let his cane tassel, said it wasted the sugar, but how beautiful it is when it flowers: purple and silken and feathery against a most astonishing green. Down the driftwood beach I run every day, walk Mina's dog, do things slow. I'm wasting time, waiting for something to happen. My mother never calls.

At night the waves roll in and the roosters crow and then I wake up and it starts all over again.

I make a visit to the last functioning sugar mill on the island, Gay & Robinson. Still the west side produces the most tons of sugar per acre in the world—a record 17.42 tons in 1987. Wilfred Ibara is our guide. He used to work at Kekaha. I have seen him walking on the beach out in front of the Cottages with his dog. He's a handsome, thoughtful-looking man. Nineteen years, nine months he's been in sugar. His father worked at Waimea; his grandfather at Kekaha. These days sugar is grown in Brazil, Africa, China, India, places where wages are what they were on Kauai a hundred years ago. At G & R everything is mechanized, efficient. Ripeners are used; drip irrigation has replaced flooding in the fields. Harvesting is done by machine, too—except for the seed cane. One field is reserved for ratooning, and seed cutters still use the Martindale "Crocodile" cane knife made in England, with the little hook at the edge for grabbing the stalk. In the fields Wilfred delicately slices open a length of cane and offers me a wedge to suck on. "The cane fields used to be our playground," he says. "And this used to be our snack." Then he hands me the knife, "perfect for opening coconuts." I cut a stalk and suck on it.

Later in the mill we stick Dixie cups into a centrifuge and eat our fill. Raw sugar tastes grassy, vegetal. We stand on a catwalk and watch a cataract of sugar juice pour. I am reminded of Willy Wonka: bad girls fall in, get crushed by the grinding wheels.

When we leave we pass a cemetery near the edge of the ocean. The graves are marked in Japanese; some of the stones are broken. Everything is coated with red dust, as if it had been rouged. There are broken mayonnaise jars, a few scraggly impatiens that have taken root. I wonder when the last visitors were here. Across the dirt road is a boneyard, as Wilfred calls it, where old equipment goes to die.

If there could be a plant for forgetfulness, for the desire to wipe everything away and start all over every so often, it would be sugarcane. So green and uniform, so plangent in the wind. Green gold, to those who reaped its profits. Mind-numbing, backbreaking, monotonous, hell on earth to those who worked in the fields.

When Mom lived in Waimea in 1996, Lauren's best friends were Makanoe, Sanoe, and Eyleen. Lauren knew everything. Rode her bike all over the place. Played with the strays, built bonfires, swam in the Cottages' pool. She clambered barefoot over the suspension bridge in Waimea Valley (the only way out when Iniki hit), got shave ice from Jo-Jo's. Lauren never felt like she was out of place, like she wasn't supposed to be there. She never thought since she was haole she didn't belong. She felt connected. She could beat some ass. All her friends knew that.

One afternoon I'm awoken from a nap by the loudest, longest boom I've ever heard. It's bone-rattling and deep, like an earthquake. It's the Ballistic Missile Defense, Star Wars, I read the next day, out at Barking Sands.

Barking Sands: Aunt Isabel and Maggie Lindsay used to go there on picnics. They'd ride out in one of the open cane cars along a ten-mile track from Kekaha all the way to Polihale. They'd bring cold chicken and bottled sodas from the Waimea Soda Works and slide down the dunes. They'd tell stories: the one about Hali, the overseer who robbed the Kekaha paysack and made his getaway in a cane car, Hawaii's only train robbery; the story of Na Wahine O Li'ulā, the Lady of the Mirage, who appeared each day at dusk to wait under a palm grove for her lover, Limaloa. Before she moved to Hollywood rich on sugar, widowed Annie Knudsen would come down from Waiawa with her grandkids, toting Welch's grape juice and seven varieties of mangoes.

Barking Sands don't bark anymore. It's not dry enough out there, or the missile range has screwed up the vibrations. It's harder to get to the beach. You've got to go through a bunch of checkpoints, and now that there's no sugar in Kekaha, there's not much reason to visit, except to surf. It's a long ride from Lihue, where the airport is; the road to Polihale is pocked and ill marked and the rental-car companies warn tourists away. Besides, Mana is just boring: dry and flat and hot, nothing like green, clefted Hanalei or sunny, placid Poipu, where the condos and the Spouting Horn are.

Anyway, it was so long ago, those stories about Isabel and Annie Knudsen, 1905 at least. Everyone is long dead; sugar, except for G & R, is gone. Tourism's the thing, though even that's dicey. The real money is in Senate appropriations.

Hawaiians tell a different story about Barking Sands: nine dogs are buried in the dunes, they say. Their owner left them tied to posts to go fishing. He was caught in a storm, and when he returned, all that was left were three little mounds. He could hear their barking, though, from under the sand. He dug and he dug, but he never could find them again. He died of a broken heart soon after.

The Rip

⚞

1982–84   Kona, Hawaii, and Hanalei, Kauai

THE DAY DAD AND DEBBIE AND I MOVED TO THE BIG
Island—January 18, 1982—Kilauea started erupting and never
stopped. Fiji hadn't worked out; Debbie got a job at the Kona Surf instead, this time as conventions manager. So that's where we moved—
to Kona, on the island of Hawaii—a few months after the hurricane.
Power had barely been restored on Kauai before we left. We packed up
midyear and lived at the Kona Surf for a few months before we got a
house of our own.

I was twelve, then thirteen. Bikinis and *Cosmo* supplanted Boogie-
boarding and *Seventeen*. I drank Diet Coke now, with lime, and did my
homework by the pool, floating occasionally under the fake waterfall
when I got hot, the long tan legs of Bain de Soleil–buttered eighties ladies
surrounding me like a border. The Kona Surf was a more grown-up hotel
than the Surf on Kauai. The pool, real saltwater, had a sophistication to it,
its outer lip jutting up to the lava at the edge of the sea. During storms
waves broke over the pool and all the chaises had to be cleared away.

And the sea itself: different than on Kauai, vaster, more solid. On
a day when Kilauea was really going, the vog would erase the horizon,
the ocean bleeding into the sky. The horizon was there, you knew,

but it eluded you. It felt as if the island were suspended in a cloudy bubble. Sunsets were spectacular in Kona: the color of a perfectly made Mai Tai.

The Kona Surf was even shaped like a volcano. Smooth white stucco encircled a roofless atrium, each floor narrowing as the building approached the sky. From the outside it looked rather like a behemoth, a white lump set in black rock, but look inside and—*lo!*—a swinging jungle nested among the stucco folds. Balconies lined the interior. An adult bar—the Poi Pounder—sank among palm fronds and ferns; colored disco lights twinkled. I could walk around the entire perimeter of the hotel in a few minutes, and some afternoons when I didn't have anything else to do—I was the new girl again at Kealakehe Intermediate— I did just that. I trailed my hand along the balcony railing, chewing gum, looking down at tourists lugging their bags to various elevators. I stopped, leaned over, elbows on the rim. I dangled my hands. I threw small things—bits of paper, a penny—and watched them drop down unnoticed. It was easy to be unnoticed in a hotel, until you finally were.

I don't know when he saw me first. Was it walking alone to my parents' room? Was it out by the back pool near the shuffleboard courts, an orchid soggy at the bottom of my glass? Signing my name, now to virgin chichis, at the Nalo Bar? (I was there for the free popcorn.)

No, it was in the elevator. I remember him. We stood on opposite sides, as one does, but I could feel his attention like a column between us. It took him a day, but he did it.

"Hello." He was a lank-haired creep—somewhere in his thirties, skinny, white.

"Hello."

"I've seen you around the hotel."

I nodded. I was polite.

"I was wondering if you could babysit for my children. I'm staying right over there." He pointed somewhere behind him to a brown door. It was afternoon and his side of the balcony was in shadow.

"Oh." I felt surprised and not surprised. He was no father. "I have to ask my parents."

"Okay. You can just come by. Right over there." He pointed again. His other hand rested on his waist.

I pretended to look at the room. Instead I memorized his face: long, narrow, pale, waxy. Brown hair. Metal-rimmed glasses. I did not ask my parents, nor did I tell them about the man. I stayed in my room and did not walk around the atrium for a while. After a week he was gone.

Sometimes you get lucky and nothing happens to you. People did terrible things to girls, I knew that.

At Kealakehe Intermediate I made friends: Crystal, Dionne, Sina, and Paige. Paige's dad owned Dorian's, the restaurant overlooking Magic Sands, one of the Big Island's rare beaches. The newness of the island meant most of the coral hadn't yet eroded. Magic Sands disappeared in winter and showed up again in summer, when we were out of school.

Paige Dorian's dad had only one arm. I heard he had a martini shaker screwed in where his missing hand should have been.

I was growing up. In home ec I made a log cabin quilt for Lauren and a stuffed Siamese cat from a kit for Layla. In shop I made a lamp shaped like a shell that matched the wallpaper in the bathroom of the house Debbie and Dad and I lived in on Plumeria Road. We never plugged it in. For my last project in home ec I tried to make a chocolate bombe from Debbie's *Bon Appétit* magazine, just like she had for a party, but it deflated and I cried. I told her she wasn't my mother. She shrugged, kept slicing tomatoes.

Debbie endured my brattiness. She woke me up for school in the morning and cooked dinner for me at night. She comforted me when I cried over deflated cakes, and still I wanted something else. How hard it must have been for Debbie to stay quiet, go to work day after day— another beige office, more Xerox machines—make me do my home-work, send me to gymnastics lessons, buy me shampoo. I cried and cried about things she had no control over and a woman she barely knew. Debbie took it, lips set, and kept slicing tomatoes.

I snooped. In the cabinet in their bedroom, notes on a legal pad from my father splotched by what I imagined were his tears. *Please don't leave me.*

Something was clearly unraveling between Debbie and my father. When Dad came home on weekends, my stepmother disappeared. They didn't joke like they used to. Maybe it was the heat, but things around Plumeria Road felt dead. One night Debbie was out so late I called Grandma Betty. When she finally came home she apologized. I wouldn't stop crying. She told me to get over it.

Plumeria was a stupid name for a road. On Plumeria Road we had a mouse. Only one, but Debbie and I laid traps for it everywhere. "We have a mouse," I told my father on the phone. "Oh, a mouse!" he said. One night Debbie saw it run into my room. She roused me, shut the door. We slept in her bed. "We'll think about what to do in the morning," she said, resting her fingers on her chin. "Maybe poison." In the morning my door was still sealed, but there was a chink at the bottom and a little pile of shavings where the mouse had chewed her way out. I hadn't wanted her to die anyway.

Mom called. She was sick of California. She missed the beach! She was going to go back to college. She wanted to see her baby, by which I guess she meant me.

"How is Lauren?" I said.

"Lauren's fine. She misses her sister."

"How is Layla?"

"Layla is good. Brew sent her some makeup. You should see her. She puts makeup on Lauren. They're so cute."

"Do you have a job?"

"Yeah." *I take care of an old woman, work at a little shop, answer phones, help Beth, sell rugs, waitress.* "Beth's helping me out right now. And you know what?"

"What?"

"We're coming home!"

*   *   *

When Mom and Beth arrived, Lauren had left behind on the plane her quilt, and Layla, her Siamese cat. Or maybe that was just the story Mom told me. Maybe they had been lost a long time before, for reasons not so apparent.

Beth and Mom stayed at the Surf. I worried about Debbie and her running into each other, but they didn't. Hotels can hide a lot.

They were going to be on the Big Island for only for a few days. Then we were all supposed to fly to Kauai, where we'd stay at the Hanalei house for a week. I slept with Mom in the room. She wanted to see where I hung out, where I went to school. She wanted to meet my friends. Mostly what we did was drive around and hang out by the pool. Once we went out to the Hyatt on the coast to swim with the dolphins, but when we got there the dolphins were sick.

Mom drove us back to the hotel. The road was black; the lava black, too. It was difficult to see where the highway ended and rock began. I was quiet. I had not seen my mother since Pebble Beach. She tried to ask me about who I was, but I was almost fourteen, and my mother, with her endless scheming and frenetic visits and fake jobs, bugged me. So I looked out the window. A few yellow lights blinked in the distance. I thought about what I had learned in Hawaiiana: When Kamehameha was conquering the Big Island, the island where he had been born, he trapped his enemies in a lava field like this one. There was an eruption going on, so he simply encircled the warriors and waited for lava to cover them. Hundreds of men, dead at once. It seemed a brilliant maneuver.

A dog trotted in front of the car. I saw a flash of flank and yellow eyes. Then it was under the wheels.

The car hiccuped.

"Mom, a dog! We ran over a dog!"

She slowed down. We looked behind us—as if we could see anything. There were no cars, no streetlights. There seemed to be no dog, either. Layla woke up, confused.

"What happened?"

"Nothing," Mom said, and accelerated. Lauren slept on.

"Mom, we ran over a dog!"

"No, we didn't."

"Yes, we did! I saw it!"

She set her mouth. "No. We. Didn't."

Layla whimpered. "A dog, Mom? A dog?"

"Tara, we didn't run over a dog. You're imagining things."

"We did! We did! We ran over a dog!"

Something bad would happen to us now, surely it would.

"Oh god!"

"Enough! Enough!"

"I want to go home."

She quieted, then sped up. The rental car jerked.

"You want to go home? To Debbie? To your *mom?* Fine. I'll take you home."

She swerved and made a U-turn onto the dark road. Layla slid in the backseat. Lauren started wailing.

At Plumeria Road she slowed down and unlocked the doors, staring ahead.

"There. Happy?"

I got out; she pealed away.

We left for Kauai a few days after that, stopping on Oahu, where Beth took us to the Royal Hawaiian and bought us all fancy robes. Mom and I made up. Then we flew to Kauai, to the Hanalei house. Auntie Margaret, who was back in Hawaii taking care of the Japanese green-tea baron's fake grass-shack mansion on Kaiko'o Place, came, too.

In my grandmother's day the opium drops would come in off Hanalei Bay, the crescent of white sand at the far north shore of Kauai where the sea in the summer is exquisitely glossy, and the green mountains rise up behind in elaborate folds. There is copious food, taro and bananas and lilikoi vines and opae in the streams, and at night, swimming in the bay, fluorescent plankton coats your body, making the whole experience of Hanalei ridiculously pleasant, laughably paradisiacal. A local proverb put it this way: "See Hanalei and die."

Opium seemed hardly necessary, but there were addicts on the island from the plantation days, and so steamships coming from Hong Kong would veer close enough to the shore to drop off tarpaulin-wrapped parcels of dope, which would bob on the waves until a passel of fishing boats, emissaries of the tongs back in Honolulu, motored by to pick them up. Only one of the boats would get the real loot, the others acting as decoys to confuse the coast guard. They'd stop a boat or two, but all they'd find were dummy goods. By then the boat with the drugs would have gotten away.

When the opium came in, everyone in the run would split it, but the fishing boat that got the drugs would take the lion's share. From there it went to the plantation stores. At Ching Young in Hanalei, the store where the Fayes kept the keys to the Hanalei house, Cousin Mina remembers an old Chinese man sitting on the front lanai. She and her brother would go in for *see moi,* dried plum, and there the old man would be, sitting and rocking and smoking his opium. He made himself useful, though. A string had been tied to his chair. It ran over the road out into the rice paddies across the street. The strings attached to pulleys, the pulleys to bells, and the bells scared away the ricebirds.

In the sixties the Morgan kids—Mom and Margaret and Gail and Brew—went to Hanalei, too. The *koa* sailing canoe would be shipped over from the west side and the whole family would spend the summer there, shopping at Ching Young, inner-tubing down the streams, picking fruit, camping and hiking down the Napali coast. Instead of backpacks they carried tied-up blankets. Mom liked the scene, so after my father left she moved us to Hanalei for a few months. Elizabeth Taylor's brother lived there in his commune, Taylor Camp. For a while we stayed with Bunker Spreckels, Clark Gable's grandson, another sugar kid. He rented a room to us. One day he died sitting up in a chair.

So that's where we lived, Hanalei, in corrugated-tin shacks alongside the sea; in valleys where only a rusted mailbox announced a turnoff, and the tree-tunnel dirt roads smelled like rotting fruit.

At Lumahai Beach on Kauai's north shore—you will know it as the cove immortalized by shampooing nurses in *South Pacific*—a river, fifty feet

across, rolls into the ocean. The Lumahai Stream is neither too broad
nor too deep, and during the calm summer months its mouth is a pleasant place for children to play, its brackish water the color of moss, its
bottom a fine silty sand.

Come winter, everything changes. Waves hit the beach from every
direction, from off Kolokolo Point to the west and Pu'upoa Point to the
east, whipped up by currents and cold northerly winds. The waves ram
into each other, the result a gray and white mess that surfers call soup.
It's too soupy, they'll say, on days when the waves lose their shapely curl
and instead dissolve into unridable mush.

The water must land, and what lands must find its way back to sea.
At Lumahai, a current forms. This current is called an undertow, rip
current, or riptide, and it moves swiftly and inevitably past the break out
to open ocean.

A Lumahai day in winter without a little rain is an impossibility. Get out
early enough, though, and you might catch some sun.

There were maybe ten of us on the beach that day. There was a
bodysurfer of the young thin blond variety who rode mostly inside the
break—the waves were too soupy for boards. There was a tourist with a
military cast—short hair, aviator sunglasses, thick waist—whose white
legs extruded from sagging navy blue swim trunks like turnips. Daikon
legs, we used to call them at Wilcox, the bane of tubby Japanese girls
everywhere. He waded in the river while his wife, a slight Asian woman,
and his son, a two- or three-year-old boy wearing diapers, sat in the
sand. Another knot of sunbathers, then us: Karen and Tara, Linda and
Mahina, and Lauren, pale, bean-shaped. Layla had gone shopping with
Beth.

My littlest sister was a wild thing in a ratty bathing suit blown out
at the butt. An impulsive and emotional little girl, she had blue wells for
eyes—as if, as soon as she was born, she'd seen everything there was
to see.

Mom had met Linda thirteen years before in Hanalei, when I was
one. Linda was from Detroit and moved to Hawaii in the late sixties. A

little older than my mother, she, too, bore a generational name: *Linda,* beautiful. In Hawaii she met a man and they had a baby together. Linda named her *Mahina,* moon. Mahina's dad left and my mother and I moved in.

Mahina was my first friend. We'd known each other since we were babies. We bathed together. We touched each other's privates.

So focus on us: Mahina's wispy root brown hair strung with gold. Her nose, splashed with freckles. A little-girl face even though she was fourteen. Long, muscular arms and broad shoulders like her Hawaiian father. Skinny and tough as a Detroit girl.

Mahina was a teenaged star. She had been on television. A mainland film crew had come to Kauai to shoot a Mountain Dew commercial: kids jump off a waterfall and land in a green pool below. Mahina was the girl who did a flip into the water, her long hair flying back behind her. Everyone remembers that commercial from eighth grade. Everyone remembers Mahina.

It didn't make her stuck-up, though. She laughed a lot and took me crab-catching at the Wilcox house over by the pier. But she had nice bathing suits now, and zebra-striped sheets. At Lumahai, Mahina wore a black wedge French cut. A triangle top cupped her breasts. She had a Hawaiian bracelet already. Her stomach was tan and flat; she did aerobics every day up in Kapa'a. She was beautiful and tall and looked like a woman.

Adolescence had fallen on me like a wet towel. I was pudgy and short and my hair, curly in the heat, never seemed to do what Mahina's did naturally: fall long and straight onto her lovely back. I kept sneaking looks at her until she told me to cut it out.

Look at Mahina, tumbling alongside a waterfall, revolving once, her body a circle, before skin slaps the pool.

The winter did strange things with the bottom at Lumahai. Only a few feet from the shore, a trench formed where the break pounded into the sand. Oddly, this meant that a little further out it was shallow enough to stand. A few yards past that the bottom dropped out, and suddenly you were in deep ocean.

"Can you touch?"

Mahina and I had just come up from swimming out. The trench was in front of us now, toward the beach.

I knew she could, but you ask things like that when you're in the ocean.

"Yeah. I'm taller than you though," and as if to prove it, she stood up and ran her hands over her head, squeezing out the water from her hair. Then she pulled her freckly nose between her thumb and forefinger, in the way that surfers do, to clear it.

Even the way Mahina cleared her snot seemed cool.

I paddled to stay afloat. An easy roller swept toward us, just beginning to crest. I swam to catch it but it slipped by. There's nothing more embarrassing than missing a wave. It's like calling to a stranger. I watched Mahina ride it in.

Past her on the beach my mother sat with her arms wrapped around her knees. She was talking to Linda, gesturing. Her mouth moved, her hands waved, she nodded. She looked excited. She was probably talking about a boyfriend. I didn't know who my mother was dating—the grunt disappeared soon after I left Pebble Beach. She dug at the sand, scooping at it to cover her calves. She looked young and pretty and I liked the view the ocean afforded me. Obscured by the rolling waves, I could watch her all I wanted.

How had she gotten from here, where I was as an awkward girl at thirteen, to there, laughing on the sand with Linda—no job, no man, three kids, juggling love and guilt and proud carelessness? I knew it had something to do with my sisters and me, but there seemed to be something else, something missing that I didn't understand. Linda, though she was only a few years older than Mom and just as much of an ex-hippie, seemed different, more of a grown-up. Linda cut hair in town, lived with a man named Danny, who carved wooden bowls and occasionally took tourists down the coast in a pontoon boat. How had my mother missed that? Was she what I, with my failed home-ec projects, would become, running over dogs willy-nilly, the hanger-on of rich people I'd conned, alone, still wanting to party with the girls?

She was thirty-four. I was thirteen, at the cusp of girlhood—the time that my mother was trying to grow up from, the days I had left behind too soon.

Lauren's legs straddled a pail. Linda put her hand to her eyes and waved at Mahina. The military man waded in the river, his wife watching from the sand, their son running back and forth between them, his diaper sagging. Suddenly I felt far away and scared, even though I was only a few yards out at sea. I realized I wasn't supposed to be facing the shore—it's the first thing you learn as a child in Hawaii: Don't turn your back to the ocean. So I dove under again, and when I came up, Mahina had returned, and though I had only been under an instant, the clouds had shifted into afternoon and I sensed rain.

There is something very queer about the way the water pulls you in a rip: currents move in two directions. The one closer to the surface, the one you think you are swimming in, gently holds you. The current beneath is far stronger. You move and yet you are not moving yourself. Your arms begin to circle. You lower your head to clear your eyes and your nose, brush your hair away from your face. Just a few minutes ago you were much closer to shore; now you seem to be at sea. You decide that this would be a good time to start making your way back to the beach, but it seems far away and you are seized in your chest and in your stomach by fear, which would ordinarily make you sweat except you are too cold. Someone cups a hand to a brow—can she see your arms waving?—and you realize you have raised them too high, swallowed too much water, and are now out of breath.

You should not swim against the rip, but instead let it carry you as far from land as it needs to, sometimes several hundred yards past the break. Eventually the current will sweep you in again. But this is against instinct. The ocean is huge and rough, and there are creatures much bigger than you swimming below. What you feel like doing when caught in a rip is swim, with all your might, back to shore. You will swim and

swim in a riptide and never go anywhere. You will swim and swim until you feel your arms detach and float away. You will swim and take in
water and start to cough, and again you will raise your hands and try to
signal the people on the beach, who will see you and wave back, but you
are still on one side of a great mass of water, with large animals swimming under you, and for now you will just have to wait.

Perhaps we knew early on there was something wrong. The man who
had been wading in the river was now slowly drifting to sea. But what
could we do? Tourists came and went and did what they pleased. They
got stuck on mountaintops and in blowholes; they fell down cliffs and
waterfalls; were stung by all manner of creatures; burned preposterously;
and complained about the facts of life on an island in the mid-Pacific:
flying cockroaches, cane spiders, daddy longlegs, geckos, and the heat.
Always the heat. They fell on lava rock and got lost in caves and floated
off to sea. Better to pay as little attention to them as possible.

The little boy waddled from the river to his mother and back again,
carrying water in his pail. Sometimes he went in as far as his ankles. His
mother called him back. Otherwise she stood and watched her husband—now past the rocks—her hand shading her eyes.

Why didn't she call to him? To us? Not once had she run up and
said, "My husband is out there. Do you see him? He is not a good swim-
mer. Please help me." I had assumed it was because she couldn't speak
English; I had assumed that it was because she was a foreigner. I do not
know if any of this is true. She watched her husband and, as far as I
could tell, did not speak a word to anyone, only stared at the sea with
her hand cupped over her brow, occasionally fetching her son from the
margin of the stream.

Did she find us as callous as I did? No matter. It was too late for such
soft sentiment, as it was clear now, looking at the ocean and the rising
waves and the man's hands getting smaller, his head bobbing, that her
husband would drown.

Linda frowned. "I told him," she said, lifting her sunglasses from her
eyes. "I said, 'Get out of the river. It's dangerous.'"

She was pointing at the ocean. I looked past her finger; all I could see was water. The woman walked to the stream. She shook her head and patted her thighs for her son to come.

"She doesn't understand," Linda said. Mom nodded and looked sad.

Mahina inspected the beach. She wiped her sunglasses on her shirt. "If I had my board I could go get him."

"Nobody with a board," Linda shook her head. She looked at her watch. "I'm calling Danny."

"Poor lady." Mom sighed. She had suddenly become nervous. She chewed at the corner of her thumb and with the other hand motioned for Lauren to come. Once she had Lauren in hand she looked at the ocean and frowned and then announced to no one in particular: "Oh, god. That guy's gonna drown."

It was all so horrible. I had played in that stream many times. I used to surf with Dad right out past the rocks.

Lauren stood dumbly staring at the water, hand in her mouth, in the way children will look around and sense something is wrong, but not know what.

You get to the point you just want them to die already.

Mom took Lauren and walked over to the lady, bent down, and stroked her back. The woman's hand moved from her brow to her eyes.

From then on I watched the water almost exclusively, except when I was looking at my mother or at Mahina, who was now down at the shore, clearly wishing she had a surfboard. I was glad I couldn't go out. I wanted to leave. I wanted Beth to pick us up in her air-conditioned rental car. I wanted to go back to the Hanalei house and wait there until I could fly away.

No one came to fetch us. I stood and watched the man's head bobbing and his hands waving, watched to see what a dying man would do with his hands.

On an island we face in. The horizon is only the first boundary. Each round binds you tighter: the shore, the roads, the houses, the mountains

at the center. An island is like that: everything you need right there next
to you. If what you think you want is not there, then you don't need it.
So what do people do on this island on this day? They sit on their towels and watch a man drown, encapsulated, as if by a bubble. They play
listlessly (as my little sister does) in the sand and the sand feels soft and
insubstantial in their fingers and there is suddenly too much sand, when
you think of it. They try to say things but all they come up with are the
commonplaces of a teenager: *Those sunglasses are cool.*

It seemed a very bad sign, the drowning. And though it had nothing
to do with my mother, the day I first saw a man die has since gotten all
twisted up with her.

It was afternoon by the time Danny came with his boat; the sun had
begun its descent toward the mountains behind us. Mahina put a long-
sleeved T-shirt around her shoulders. White, with a red stripe down
each arm. BIG BEAR SURFBOARDS, it read. HANALEI, KAUAI—a fictional surfboard company from the movie *Big Wednesday.* I bought one just like it
before I left Hanalei.

"These guys come from the mainland and they don't know the water."

This was what Linda said, hands on her hips, her skinny arms tensed.
There was our knot of people—Linda, Mom, Mahina, Lauren, and me,
all women—and then there was the knot collected around the wife and
the child, still trying to run to the river with the pail. We had abandoned
them now. Other strangers tried to console them.

Danny scooped the man out of the water and brought him to the
sand. It appeared as if they would do CPR. Linda walked toward them.
"I'm going to go see what's going on," she said. Mahina followed. My
mother and I stayed behind. "God," Mom moaned. "Look at the wife.
Poor thing."

Lauren ran to the edge of the little group. She sucked a finger and
stared.

"Lauren!"

I called her and she didn't hear. I was angry at my sister for looking
and angry at my mother for not minding. It wasn't something that a

child should see up close. I would not look at it and I was almost four-teen. So I went to fetch my sister and when I did I saw two things: the tourist was dun blue; and an arm splayed outside the circle of people surrounding him. I grabbed Lauren and led her back. It was the only time I have seen a dead person, and my sister, with her old man's face, would not look away.

V

HOME

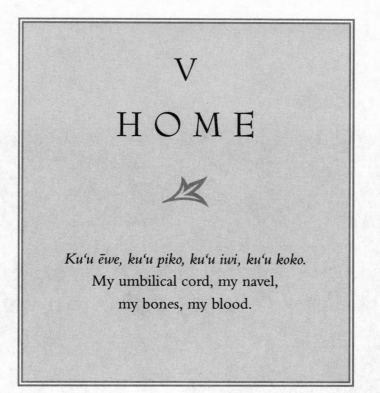

Ku'u ēwe, ku'u piko, ku'u iwi, ku'u koko.
My umbilical cord, my navel,
my bones, my blood.

Sisters, 1998

Little White Panties

Thanksgiving 2002   Honolulu

THANKSGIVING INCLUDES ME, LAYLA, AUNT GAIL AND her children, Margaret, and Gamma. No one has heard from Karen since September and anyway who knows if she'd be invited.

Gamma makes WASPy fifties dishes: creamed onions with horseradish; spinach sprinkled with fried onions; candied yams and coconut. Layla, who is moving to Virginia with Jack when he returns from Okinawa, says she wants to write down all of Gamma's recipes because she loves them so much, especially the candied yams.

Margaret helps by peeling onions. At some point she becomes agitated—stress over the onions—and her fistula explodes all over the kitchen.

A fistulary blowout, I find out later, is common among dialysis patients. The vein-artery that carries the blood for twice-a-week dialysis is distended, the whole thing like an old plastic bag filled with water. Eventually a spell of high blood pressure will break it, and the blood from the vein-artery will go everywhere.

Everywhere is where Margaret's blood went, two liters of it, when her fistula exploded around eleven o'clock on Thanksgiving morning. Gail called me. I was at my father's, making a dessert. "Margaret's fistula broke," she cried, and I started crying, too. Thanksgiving seemed a horrible day to die.

I called my grandmother. She was panting.

"Margaret. They took her to the hospital."

"Is she all right?"

"She lost a lot of blood. There's blood everywhere."

"Oh, Gamma!"

"I have all these vegetables here. I was cooking all morning. I can't leave—I—can you come down and get them? Take them to Gail's?" She paused, caught her breath. "I want you to go on. This is what you must do. Carry on. Gail's children have to see this. You have to carry on."

I wondered why Gail's children needed to see this especially.

I asked her if she needed help cleaning up. There were places that did this kind of thing, I told her. Cleaned up blood after accidents and such.

"Oh, Tara. You know me better than that."

This was to mean she was private.

When I arrived at Gamma's it was noon. The lychee tree was full and green; the asphalt of the carport, hot. Puddles reflected light a few steps past the garage door. Gamma emerged from the kitchen. She wore a short white nightie; her legs were bare. Her hair swept to the side. She looked strangely sultry. There was blood on the nightie: a solitary smear right down the center.

"Who's there?"

"Tara."

"Oh god, Tara."

I stepped into the shade where my aunt had assembled her outdoor kitchen and where we once had lunched a long time ago, when everything was hypothetical.

Gamma had already cleaned the kitchen floor. Reddened towels lay in a heap next to the washing machine. Blood on the punee; blood on Margaret's pillowcase; blood pooled on the black cement of the lanai. Gamma was pale and damp and in shock. Blood flecked her arms.

"She was in her little white panties and she was running around crazy and, oh, it was horrible, blood going everywhere and I thought immediately, *Call the ambulance,* and I pressed a towel on her forearm but then we used all the towels and Margaret was starting to go. 'I'm scared, Mom,' she said. She was getting faint—and just then the ambulance came and they said, 'What you did saved your daughter's life, Mrs. Morgan,' and I watched her leave in the ambulance. I had to stay here and clean up this mess and the vegetables, oh, the vegetables were in the oven—"

Later my grandmother would say that for weeks she was finding blood in the strangest places: along the lintel above the door that led to Margaret's room, in the crevice of a light switch.

At some point I hugged my grandmother and she cried briefly in dry, shaking heaves. She kept her hands in the air because they still had blood on them and she didn't want to stain me.

"That's little Margaret's blood," she said, pointing to the puddles at the foot of the washer-dryer. "That's my daughter's blood."

Blood is very dark in great quantities, almost black.

"Gamma, you need help cleaning this up."

"No, no. I need to do this myself."

"But, Gamma—"

"Do you see. This is *life.*"

I tracked blood into the kitchen. I looked down and there my footprints were, on my grandmother's floor, their shape stamped in blood.

Later I could think, *No, this is not life,* but in there with the blood splashed on the wall where Gail's children had their height measured in notches—Karen's children were never measured, we grew up too fast anyway—I did not think this. I helped Gamma carry the creamed onions, the spinach, and the candied yams to the car.

I had been called to be a witness. She needed someone to see it and there I was.

Gamma gave me a card Margaret had written her and sent by post only a few days before, even though they lived in the same house. It said, *Thank you. I learned from you. You learned from me.* She was taking leave. I cried and hugged my grandmother again. She said for us to carry on.

"Tell them what you saw." She handed me a canister of fried onions and a baking tin with the balance of the Thanksgiving vegetables. I told her I would. She went back into Margaret's room. As I was leaving she was struggling with the mattress.

I told everyone at Gail's they didn't have to eat anything. Margaret's blood had splashed on the fried onion canister. Now it was on my hands. "You don't have to eat a single thing," I said to them.

We ended up eating every last bit of the Thanksgiving vegetables, which were quite good, even the fried onions.

One Day at a Time

1985   Honolulu

POT-SMOKING DADS KEEP THEIR STASH IN HEFTY GAR-
bage bags in the closets of the extra rooms in their houses. The
year before my stepmother and father got a divorce she gave him a small
plastic canister for Christmas. It was wrapped up with all the other presents under the tree, along with the makeup caddy for me, the blouse for
Debbie, and the surf wax for Dad. The box was rectangular and had a
clear plastic top and metal clasps—a step above Tupperware. Debbie
smiled and laughed when my father opened it, but it seemed a little
mean. She said, "I got it for your stash," and stash sounded dirty. My father said, "Ah!" and thanked her. "That was very thoughtful of you,"
but his eyes were in his lap. The room, though open and airy, facing the
plumeria grove, felt stuffy.

"The metal detectors, though. The clasps."

I had a pot-smoking dad and we spoke of it only once. We were at a
pizza restaurant in Kona. Cars skimmed Alii Drive. I guess it was my
drug talk. Dad said, "A while back I developed a habit that I regret."
Across the table I nodded and tried to look serious, though my face
warmed. It's embarrassing for someone to admit something you already
know. We never talked about it again.

★   ★   ★

High school had begun. I was at a boarding school now, Hawaii Prep, on the Big Island, the one Debbie had gone to before she met my dad. I met Lauren Nevin from Chicago my first weekend of school, at Hapuna Beach. She had a Ralph Lauren black maillot bathing suit and several pairs of Guess jeans in varying shades of denim, from dark blue to stonewash, like the color of the sky as it changes during the day. She blew out her hair. I didn't know anything about blowing out my hair. I did not know about Guess jeans. I knew about malasadas and different kinds of sand and when to pick up a lilikoi from the ground and when not to—when it would be sweet and when it would be bug-eaten. I knew about chopsticks and sashimi and *aku* bait and Hello Kitty and pickled mango and sticker books and what a wave looks like when it's glassy and what it looks like when it's soup. I knew about haoles and Japanese and Chinese and Portuguese and Filipinos and Hawaiians and when all of that was important and when it wasn't. I knew about fathers and mothers and stepmothers and stepfathers and stepgrandmothers and ex-stepgrandfathers and half siblings and how no one is ever innocent. I knew how pot smelled: in a joint, rolled with tobacco, in a bong, in the dark, on the beach. I wanted to know how to be brave. I wanted to know my mother like I thought I once must have, at some time in the past, before memory and thinking happened, when there weren't words for anything. I wanted to go back there and I didn't want to go back there. I wanted that time to be real.

The first year at Hawaii Prep, I was a day student, commuting forty-five minutes each way across the face of a mountain thirteen thousand feet high—so high there was snow at the top in the winter and a telescope to which the Nevins took Lauren and me to view the rings of Saturn. It was the year Bobby the Vietnam vet bought me my prom dress. I made earrings out of fishing lures and wore Keds with double-fluorescent ankle socks and wrote teary self-revelations in my ninth-grade English journal, which someone lifted out of my locker and promptly passed around the boy's dorm, even correcting a few factual errors about a boy I liked.

I had fallen in love. John Doyle was from Papua New Guinea—*Pay En Jay*. We made out in the tall grass behind the chapel, went running through the dung-dotted pastures above the school. (Hawaii Prep had been built on a cattle ranch.) I could stare into John Doyle's green-yellow eyes all day. All I wanted to do was touch him. He had floppy blond hair and freckled hairy legs and chapped lips from all my kissing.

He broke up with me. He told me by the commons—Hawaii Prep had been started by an old Choatie. I cried. He said to pretend he was going away on a trip; maybe that would make me feel better. I knew all about what going on a trip meant.

The autumn I turned fifteen I counted my calories on a green steno notepad. Grapefruit with Sweet 'N Low, 30; Crystal Light, 10; extra gum, 2 sticks, 16; vegetable sandwiches with mustard for lunch, rice and corn for dinner. I allowed myself two Fig Newtons for dessert and did sit-ups and push-ups and waist twists in the narrow space between Lauren and my twin beds. I tried on Lauren's size-two Guess jeans while she was in class, but no matter how much I lost I could not fit into them. I weighed myself after cross-country practice. The day that I was 102 I was so elated that I had to sit down on the infirmary cot. The nurse watched me come in. She called Debbie, who told me not to be stupid about food. Sometime later, I ate two hamburgers at a cookout after a football game and tried to make myself throw up, which I accomplished, but Sonia Bauer from Guam, whose boyfriend looked like Bon Jovi, was a bulemic and her teeth had turned brown and she still had a butt, so throwing up didn't seem like the best idea.

Then the divorce: My father and Debbie told me about their impending split on Super Bowl Sunday, which was funny, because Super Bowl Sunday had always been a day when everyone got along. I cried. My father, probably trying to make it easier on me, said, "Now, you knew this was coming." I cried more. "Now, Tara," Debbie said.

It had been hard on her, the commuting. Or maybe she wanted her own life. She was only thirty-one. We'd always made fun of nuclear families anyway. *Why do you think they're called nuclear?*

"We want you to know that we both love you and that nothing will change," they said. "Nothing will be different at all."

I went to Oahu for spring break to see my mother, who was living with Bobby a few blocks from Gamma's in Kahala. Bobby ran a bike shop and had bought my mother a bike with a Cookie Monster baby seat in the back for Lauren. I rode it around Kahala by Peace, Love, and Joy's house—those were their names: Peace, Love, and Joy to the World— three towheaded brothers I had a crush on. We had tacos one night. I washed the dishes and then I watched MTV and put my sisters to bed: Layla, seven; Lauren, two.

Maybe Mom and Bobby had a fight. For whatever reason, she came into my bed and stretched out next to me and I curled into her like I used to when I was younger and she would sing to me. She said something about how I was almost fifteen now and there was something that she had wanted to tell me but she had wanted to wait until I was old enough. And now I was old enough.

I had an older sister, she told me. Her name was Elsie.

The room was still dark and we were still close but everything had shifted around us. I was now only one of her daughters.

Mom told me the whole story: San Francisco and Mrs. Rasmussen and the flasher in Golden Gate Park. Making pie and how she hadn't wanted to give up the baby but Gamma made her, even though she was eighteen and could have made up her own mind.

"I could have kept her, you know. I would have kept her."

She touched my hair. "And then you. I didn't know what to do. And then you."

My mother didn't stay with me that night. I had wanted her to, but she didn't. I couldn't fall asleep. I had had too much Coke. Not the coke that Bobby did, that gave him flashbacks some nights and made him pace in front of the bathroom mirror, but regular Coke, which did this weird thing to me, a kind of chaos behind the eyelids. I couldn't erase it, except when Dad took me to the dentist, Dr. Scott on Kauai. *You want a little gas, hon?* Fake leather cool against my thighs—sun slanting in and everything glowing.

The next morning I couldn't wait to tell everyone about my new sister, but Mom said it had to be a secret, so I called my friend Miranda, who sucked in her breath. But then we ended up talking about Jean-Marc, my new French-Vietnamese boyfriend whose dad worked for the telescope, and the prom and the color of my dress.

Elsie, the eldest. Four paper dolls joined in a row. Not one of us shares a father. Only Lauren and Layla grew up in the same house.

Sophomore year I memorized the serenity prayer. Mom sent a photocopy of it to me in a letter from Women's Way. *God grant me serenity to accept the things I cannot change; courage to change the things I can; and wisdom to know the difference.* She said I could call it a higher power, if it made me feel comfortable, but really she knew it was God. When we talked on the phone finally after silent time, she told me that God was watching out for the both of us and for the kids, and that if she just trusted in God everything would work out okay for everyone. She asked me about Jean-Marc. I had moved on to a doctor's son named David. She sent me glitter decals that counseled "Let Go and Let God" and "Easy Does It."

At Hawaii Prep, I worked on getting skinny and forgetting John Doyle, who had, by that point, sampled the school's prettiest blondes. God would work that out, too, I hoped.

I called my mother from a pay phone in the lounge of the dorm where Valerie was rumored to give Eric head and where we watched the Bears win in 1985 and where I sang sentimentally along with Whitney to "The Greatest Love of All." It felt good to have a number where I could call my mother. Miranda showed me how to stick safety pins into the receiver, touching it to the metal of the pay phone to get a free call. Every time I called my mother that year I got shocked.

She started saying how she wanted me to go to school at Punahou, where she went. It would be like finishing up where she left off. Beginning, middle, and end. I thought so much about it I started acting like I already left. So a freckly dean at Hawaii Prep called me into his office. I never got called to the office. "Don't burn your bridges," he said. I nodded. I didn't burn my bridges. But I didn't cross back over them, either.

★   ★   ★

The first time I saw my mother after she had gone into Women's Way, she was working on step nine: making amends. I was on Oahu visiting my father, who had moved to a two-room add-on up Wilhemina Rise and had just started dating Deirdre. I slept on his foldout couch and I visited Mom in the afternoon.

"I stole that money," she said.

We were sitting in lawn chairs on the Women's Way terrace. The plastic roof over us had tinged everything green. Mom looked queasy. A woman I didn't know observed the proceedings, dragging on a cigarette now and again. I had no idea what my mother was talking about.

"The shoe? Are you talking about the money in the shoe? In the motel? I knew about that. I knew about that already."

Mom stared and shook her head.

"No, Mom. I knew about that."

She was still shaking her head. The stranger next to her started shaking her head, too. Mom ashed on the concrete, dusting it away with a bare foot. For some reason the gesture surprised me.

"The girl. Your little friend, in Pebble Beach."

"Becky?"

"No, not Becky." She smiled. "How is Becky, anyway? She was cute."

Becky was fine: in tenth grade, like me. She'd finally moved on from Duran Duran.

"She's okay." I stopped. "Was it Lee?"

"Yeah. The preppy girl. Lee." She wiped around her mouth. "The twenty dollars. I said it was Lauren. That was a lie."

Lee had lost twenty bucks at the Pebble Beach house one night she stayed over. Mom felt around the couch, looked under a few chairs, then blamed Lauren, whom I spanked.

"I'm sorry." My mother's face crumpled and she started crying. The stranger put an arm around her shoulder. Mom cried into her own hand, then she moved into the lady's shirtsleeve. "I'm sorry," she said again, and hugged me once, but when you're making amends it's a personal thing, something to be shared only with strangers, which was okay because I had forgotten about the whole thing anyway.

We went inside to eat. Mom showed me the room where the women had group. She showed me the kids' bunk beds and the social workers' desks and the kitchen. A schedule hung on the refrigerator determining who cooked when and who cleaned up. She pointed to a woman who had a resentment against her—that's what they called anger at Women's Way, resentment.

"She has a resentment against me because I told her not to slap her kid." Mom's voice echoed into the living room, and I had a resentment against her for talking so loud.

We ate. I had my meeting with Evelyn, Mom's counselor, a pretty Japanese woman with short black hair and a soft voice. She asked me how I felt about "Mom," like Mom was Evelyn's mother, too. I told her my father smoked pot. Evelyn asked me if I could tell him it hurt me. I said no, I didn't think I could. Evelyn said it's like when there's a big pink elephant sitting in the room with you and everyone sees it but no one talks about it. "That's what it's like," she said. "Can you talk about it with him?" I shook my head. I felt like telling Evelyn to mind her own business. My elephant was different. Rhinestones dropped from my elephant's ears. She wore a gold satin saddle and she sat erect on her hindquarters on the orange jungle-print ottoman we used to have at Dad and Debbie's in Ulumahi. My elephant was happy. She ate Doritos and watched TV.

I didn't like it at Women's Way, though I could tell it was good for my mother. There were rules and chore wheels and higher powers. Slogans to repeat. People to help and have resentments against and kids to mind and a cot to sleep on.

When I left that afternoon, the women of Women's Way locked themselves in again. I looked at them through the fence, my mother scratching one leg with her toes, blowing me kisses, the other women waving. I walked by the Waioli Tea Room. The carved wooden sign read WAIOLI TEA ROOM, like it was still open, but the windows and doors were all closed.

West of Then

Christmas 2002   Honolulu

I DRIVE AROUND DOWNTOWN LOOKING FOR MY MOTHER the day after Thanksgiving to tell her that Margaret is in the hospital. The last time anyone's heard from her was that afternoon in late September when Gail dropped her off on Hotel Street, a few days after we went to psychiatric and I left her at Esther Leung's. Though I am not sure this is where she'll be, downtown, Triangle Park seems as good a place as any to start. This is, after all, the closest thing she has to a home now. It holds her in the way a home does. She orbits around it like one does a home. She's safe here, and it's close to CHAMP and within walking distance of Fort Street Mall and the mission.

Of course it's sunny. November, a dreary month on the mainland, is lovely in Hawaii—hurricanes notwithstanding. Wetter weather brings out the green. Even gray Punchbowl has an emerald sheen. There is a part of me that doesn't want to believe I can just come here, look around, be patient and search and there she will be, but I must. My mother is here, and wants to be here, for more complicated reasons than I can imagine.

Anyway, here she is right now, walking toward me up Bishop from the ocean.

She's wearing what looks like a suit: mauve pleated skirt, tweed

276

jacket, black pumps. Ron is in jeans and a button-down shirt. If you're
from here you know what they are: the telltale mission castoffs, the bony
shoulders, the hunted expression. Proud and also crestfallen, a discom-
fiting mix. It makes you want to avoid them.

This one is my mother, so I can't. I pull up; she peers in.

"Tara! Hi! Wow! What are you doing here?"

It is as if I saw her yesterday, though it's been two months.

"Hi." My hands are still on the steering wheel. "Get in."

She furrows her brow, glances at Ron.

"What?"

"I have something to tell you."

"Okay." She motions to Ron and he opens the back door.

"Not Ron. Just you."

She looks confused and not entirely comfortable with the idea. How
long has it been since she's been in a car? Alone without Ron? Still, she
walks around the passenger side and slips in.

"We went to the beach," she says, adjusting her jacket. "We saw a
movie at Waikiki. I haven't done that in a year."

"Yeah. Listen, Mom. Margaret's sick. She's in the hospital."

My voice is stern. I nod to signal my earnestness. It is all in the service of news, but really I am pissed. How dare she be seeing a movie.
She should have been there at Gamma's. She completed that triangle,
not me.

She looks like a child, an adult imposter in her tweed and her pumps,
in her mask of wrinkles. I have shifted: from beloved lost daughter to
adversary. I am surprised by how easy the change feels.

It's too sudden. I haven't prepared her. Her face falls. "What?"

"Margaret's really sick. She's in the hospital. You should go and
see her."

"Why? What happened?"

"Her fistula broke."

"Oh god! Oh god!" Mom starts bleating. She shakes her legs up and
down. It's too much, I can tell, but I want her to understand. I want her
to see how serious things are now. I want to make her feel bad.

"You know, Margaret really misses you."

"What?"

"It's hard, having you live out here."

She knows what I'm getting at. Karen knows it's all her fault. That everything, in the end, is Karen's fault.

"I'm not going to let you blame me for this, Tara! I'm not going to take the blame!"

"I'm not blaming you. I just want you to—"

"You made me throw away all my clothes! Now I don't have any! I'm not good enough for you!" She cries; she shakes her head. "I'm not okay. I'm never okay! There's always something wrong with me. Well, I'm not taking it anymore, Tara. I'm not taking it!"

I decide she's gone crazy since September.

I take a left on King and by the time we are halfway up Alakea I am yelling. I slow, then stop the car. She gets out, slams the door, and marches away from me, pulling her jacket close. I drive around the block and by the time I pull up next to Triangle Park, she has disappeared.

A half hour later, in the grass, Ron, who never disappears, is talking about getting off the disability titty.

"We're getting things going. Making a change. Your mom's made a schedule. Right, Karen?"

She's back and nodding. Sores open like little pink pools on her face.

"What are those?" I say, touching her.

"Pimples." She doesn't elaborate.

"Oh."

We sit around Triangle Park, talking. She says she's going to go over to Queen's to see Margaret right after I leave. She takes out her day planner and looks through it.

"*Three P.M. Visit Margaret.* Ron, why don't you write this down in yours, too." She starts reaching over to Ron's backpack but slips before she gets it. She dusts off her jacket, laughs a little. "*Whoa.*"

It's the moment I've been waiting for.

"Mom, I think you need to go to treatment. You're not well. You're skinny, and you've got sores—"

She scowls. "Not well! I'm not well! I'm *fine,* Tara. Ron and me are fine." She's sitting up now, pulling her hair back away from her face. "We're *great,* in fact. Aren't we, Ron?"

Ron nods, but he looks at the grass.

"I don't need Sand Island, Tara. I've been to treatment. I know all about treatment. You know what they do at Sand Island? Huh?" She's shaking a twig at me. Her eyes are wide and her teeth are bared and the sores on her face look redder against her exposed gums.

"They *yell* at you at Sand Island, Tara. Did you know that? They tell you you're *shit.* You want that for me? Huh? I don't need Sand Island. I've *got* a program. My program is *here.* With *Ron.* See? See this?" She holds up her organizer and shakes it. "I go to *meetings.* I have a relationship with *God.* You know? Sand Island's not for me. You think they can teach me something at Sand Island? I know that guy, that director. I know what they do. They force you to go on welfare and then they take your money. It's a scam. Sand Island is a fucking *scam.*"

Ron sits on his haunches, nodding. I hate the way he sits like that, as if he's about to sprint away. For now Mom's planted; her legs cross in front of her. She still fingers the grass, but if Ron were to leave she'd split right after him.

"Mom, I just want you to get well."

"Well. Huh." She snorts. "You threw away all my *clothes.*"

What that has to do with anything I don't know.

She shakes the twig again: "You've got *problems.* You're *cold.* I'm your *mother.*"

And why don't I come and visit her more often, she wants to know.

"This is where I *live.* Why don't you visit me? These are my *friends,* Tara." She waves back behind her, still looking at me. Over by the fire station Brenda sits at the edge of a concrete planter laughing with a few backpacked men. She slaps one of them on the arm and smiles.

"You know I'm married now, Tara. I have a *life.* Ron is my husband."

"Ron's a junkie," I say, even though he's still sitting right next to us. Ron shakes his head, sighs.

She cuts her eyes. "There are people and there are behaviors, Tara. Being a junkie is a behavior. I am not a *junkie*. Ron is not a *junkie*."

She keeps saying it: *junkie, junkie.*

"We are people with ad-*dick*-shuns. There is a difference. *Okay?* Just wait until you have kids, Tara. *Okay?!*"

"Okay."

She stares. "God! Why are you so cruel? Just like your father. I'm trying, okay? Can't you see I'm trying?"

It's the *okay?* that gets me. That and the sad-looking wrinkles around her mouth, and her big floppy ears, and her large teeth, the yellow one in front, fake. She's looking at me. But not really at me, rather, at something past me, past my head. Then suddenly there is something on her chest: a pimple or a freckle or a mole. She peers down at it, doubles her chin, sticks out her tongue. She's moving her mouth around now, engrossed.

She's not really listening anymore. She's gone, picking at herself. I wonder if she'll be back.

That horrible stretch between Thanksgiving and Christmas, the season of AA meetings and family flare-ups and *Mele Kalikimaka* and Santa Clauses in canoes, marches on. The first Christmas ever celebrated in Hawaii was on someone's ship: Vancouver's, I believe, off Kauai. They lit fireworks, which the Hawaiians did not like, and played violins, which they also did not like. Cook himself missed celebrating the holiday here only by a few weeks; instead, Christmas 1777 was spent on a spit of an island further south, in what used to be called the Line Islands and is now part of the Republic of Kiribati. He named the atoll Christmas Island, for the day the ships departed, which it is still called to this day.

Christmas has ever been a strange and disorienting holiday in the mid-Pacific. There's the pidgin English version of "The Twelve Days of Christmas," which features pounds of poi, *beeg fat peegs,* coconuts, and one mynah bird in one papaya tree. "Mele Kalikimaka" doesn't actually mean anything in Hawaiian. It's just a Hawaiianization of merry and Christmas, each consonant sound a syllable, like others: *kālā* for dollar, *buke* for book, *palapala* for paper, *huipa* for whip—things that didn't exist here until Westerners came.

Palm trees sway, things are green and bright. The sun shines by day and so do the stars at night. Mainlanders who've moved to Hawaii will get nostalgic around this time and say things like "I miss the seasons," even if they are from California. But most are happy, and Christmas passes like any day: seventy-eight degrees and sunny, tradewinds out of the north.

I've never loved Christmas. Something to do with all the houses. After the divorce it was always Dad's for Christmas Eve and early morning, Gamma's Christmas Day. Fly to the Big Island, to Debbie's, for Christmas night. I liked being with family—and of course I liked the gifts and the food—but I spent a lot of the holiday in transit.

Gamma made it festive, lots of wrapping paper everywhere, but she gave Mom gift certificates for haircuts and my sisters shampoo and that depressed me. Auntie Margaret wrote poems, that was nice, and Aunt Isabel, when she was alive, sent Advent calendars and Peter Rabbit books. But really Christmas seemed an overlong opportunity to get lost in the family bramble. Since I moved to New York I mostly spend the day quietly.

One Christmas, sometime in college, I was given an old chest. It had been my great-grandmother's back when she lived in New York: pine, nothing fancy, though it had a certain sentimental value. It had gone through two hurricanes, as G.G. had. Grayed by sun and sea, it had sat on my grandmother's lanai for a few years before she dragged it into the Kahala house one Christmas to give to me. She'd refinish it, she said. But no one ever did, and it languished for years, holding up the television. Every so often Mom would bring it up, telling me that she was going to get that chest and refinish it finally, and that it would be my hope chest, a memento of my great-grandmother.

When G.G. died in 2000, things had already started falling apart. So one day when Gamma was on Kauai my mother took the chest. She called it my rightful inheritance and she left it in my father's garage for me to claim when I got home.

"Your great-grandmother left you her hope chest," Dad said over the phone. His voice was soft when he said it, and I was surprised. I didn't expect G.G. to leave me anything, and I didn't put this hope chest together with the one Gamma had almost given me all those years before.

A few nights later my grandmother called New York, late. Time difference again. She wanted the chest returned. She hadn't been ready to give it to me—she was waiting until I got my own house—and Mom had stolen it from her.

"Your mother is a thief," she said. "Did you know your mother is a thief?"

I didn't argue. It was very dark in my room and I was sitting up in my bed. Gamma's voice was low, and she seemed rather lost, talking about the chest and Mom, forgetting that she had given it away already.

The last Christmas my great-grandmother was alive, Christmas of 1999—Gail's house again—G.G. kept asking for glasses of champagne. Mom made a terrine and brought Terry and wore too much pancake makeup. She had just gotten kicked out of Mrs. Delacruz's and was staying with friends for a while.

The doctor had fitted G.G. with a hearing aid that drooped below her chin, so that she looked like a sports announcer. She wasn't deaf; she wasn't senile. She was just less interested in what took place around her. "I can't work anymore," she told Gamma. "I don't have anything to do. I'm not useful."

One day in defiance she took the garden shears to the bougainvillea hedge at Gamma's house. The thorns dug into her papery skin. "I'm fine," she kept saying. But she wasn't. Later that year she died, lucid till the end. "I know, I going *make*," she said at one point. Make means "to die" in Hawaiian. It is what you'd say about a dog that has gone off or a cockroach you are about to squash.

My great-grandmother had been born August 1, 1898—ten days

before the official annexation of Hawaii to the U.S. When she first arrived on Kauai in 1917 as a guest of the Faye family (she had become
friends with Mig-and-Ida after she met Gampa back East), the only car
on the island had picked her up. She spent the rest of her life there. She
was 101 years old when she died in February 2000. Gamma put her in
the back room, next to Mig-and-Ida's books about heroic dogs and or-
phans named Nab. She and Margaret dressed her in flowers and candles.
G.G. stayed there for two days. Aunt Gail cut off a curl and sent it to me
in a card with no signature. It was soft and tiny, like G.G. herself, and I
appreciated her sending it.

Mom went over afterward and screamed, "I'm sick! I have hepatitis!
I'm dying!" She told me she said it loud enough so that all those fuckers at Gamma's tennis club could hear.

The same day, Elsie started looking for her mother.

Mom was looking, too, haphazardly. She had contacted someone
from the state and he sent her a copy of Elsie's original birth certificate.
After Mom relapsed I inherited the folder, with the letter from Kenneth
Ling, the adoption specialist, and Elsie's birth certificate folded into a
square. Contact could be made only if both parties were looking, so
Mom let it be known that she wanted to find her daughter, and information trickled in. At last, she got ahold of a wedding license. She went
down to the state library one day in early 2000 and called me crying.
She had found her. "Magee-Hamilton Wedding Held Yesterday," she
read over the phone. *The bride wore a gown of ivory peau de soie styled on
classic lines. Her veil was of heirloom Brussels lace and she carried a spray of white
cymbidium orchids. The reception was at the Pacific Club. Eddie Kinilau and his
troupe serenaded.*

"The Pacific Club, Tara! Can you believe that? God! I bet Gamma
knew. I bet she knew!"

Gamma did know. My sister's name was Claire. She'd been adopted
by a good family, a kamaaina family, Gamma said. It was Gamma who
called Claire first. "This is your grandmother," she told her. And to me,
later, I guess by way of explanation: "Karen said, 'Promise me that you'll

tell her I did it against my will. Promise me you'll tell her that.' And I did. I said, 'Your name was Elsie. After Karen's grandmother, whom she loved very much.'"

When Mom found out that Gamma had called her daughter she cried. She was at Terry's. I was home for a few weeks and went over to his house and tried to calm her down.

"She took her twice from me. Twice!"

She put her head in her hands and sobbed.

Even if you find what's lost it doesn't make you whole.

August of that year I went to San Francisco to meet my sister. We hiked in the Tennessee Valley; took pictures with her husband and her son, who brought me daisies. I started crying. Claire told me her story: she grew up in a mansion in northern California. The schools she attended were schools for rich girls: Marin Catholic, Santa Catalina. She went to a few schools, she said. She drifted around a little.

Her mother had adopted three babies altogether, Heather, Richard, and Claire, all under age three. Claire was a last-minute gift. "Heather and I always had boyfriends." Claire smiled shyly. I can see why. Claire is lovely. It is a blessing and an irritation at the same time that Claire could be so pretty, as if she got all the genes I wanted: the straight hair, the toothpick bones, the wide smile. When I described her to Layla on the phone, I said she was small. Five-three, 109 pounds. I heard a little sigh on the other side of the phone: "Why are we the fatties?"

Claire drove me to the airport and we cried and hugged each other. She looked just like Mom when Mom was the age she lost her.

For a little while I had a sense of lightness. Claire was the eldest now; she could be responsible. This is what I told Mom when we spoke. "You've got the chance to resolve this now," I said. "This has been a se-cret for thirty-two years." Our conversation was full of big statements like this, as if finding Claire would remake my mother's life and my own. But families are choice and care and patience and pain and time as much as blood. I should know that.

Mom was the last one to meet her daughter. Spring of 2001, Claire
came to Hawaii. Mom and she spent a week together: taking pictures,
going to the beach. Layla and Lauren said it was weird. Mom was on
methadone by then, so her moods were erratic. One day the foursome
went swimming at Lanikai. Mom held Claire while she floated, out-
stretched, in her mother's arms. *My baby,* Mom crooned. Lauren and
Layla watched from the shore.

Before she fell apart she had written down on a Post-It when we
were all born; now I have the note:

2. Tara 11:55 A.M.
4. Layla 10:51 A.M.
3. Lauren 10:09 A.M.
1. Elsie 9:50 A.M.

She got the order wrong, but we're all in there.

The Board of Water Supply has hung its Christmas lights. It's always a
big show: mountains and passing showers and rainbows. I don't know
many places in the United States whose Board of Water Supply is so
elaborately adorned, but then this is Hawaii. Water is in our name.

Fred Lunt has seen Mom in Triangle Park. And friends of Layla's
have spotted her on Fort Street Mall. They walk close to the buildings
to avoid her, but later, with Layla, they're sympathetic: "Your mom's not
home*less,* she's home-*free.*" It's a nice thought.

At some point I'll have to go through her storage. All of Layla and
Lauren's baby pictures are there: Lauren on Layla's lap at Gamma's; Mom
on a rock at Jackass Ginger; me holding a rose at Lauren's baptism in
Monterey. It was how you knew you were at Karen's. The walls would
have changed, but the pictures were the same.

One day after school in mid-December Layla sees her in the park.
Mom has on fake nails; a few are broken. She stinks. With her is Celeste,
another one of Layla's friends from high school. Celeste has lice—'ukus,

we called them at Wilcox. Layla told me she could see the eggs. Celeste reports on Joanna: she is back in San Francisco, Celeste says, working for a pimp named Showboat.

A guy comes over. "Um, hi, Karen, can I talk to you?"

"If you go over there," Layla says, "I'm outta here."

Mom is agitated. "I have to get money from him."

"I'm outta here."

"He owes me money," Mom says, and walks away.

Later, on the phone: "Layla, I am so sorry."

It's always worse when it's not me.

On the sixth day of Christmas, Mom calls from the River of Life. "I need that cell phone you talked about," she says. "Come and pick me up."

I had offered to give her one. "Where will you be?"

"The park." She laughs. "Where do you think I'll be?"

When I arrive it's early evening. Work has ended and downtown is quiet. I can almost picture the old town here—the ships creaking and the greasy low light of the whale-oil lamps. It is too warm for Christmas.

Ron and my mother sprawl in the grass. They seem to be fighting, though their motions are slow and uncoordinated, as if underwater. I wait for them in my father's car. I don't know exactly what I'm doing here, though I suppose the answer is simple: I still come when called.

The sky over downtown darkens. Eventually I call to her and a few minutes later she gets up. She throws her planner at Ron; she limps to the car. She has a duffel with her. It's so heavy and she's so skinny she bends under its weight.

When she gets in I see that her right foot is bandaged and swollen— a sunburst of yellowing pus and blood seeping through dirty gauze. She notices me looking.

"I got bitten by another spider." She tugs at the door. She's slurring her words. Then she grabs her jaw. "It's my *toof*. My toof broke and it's rubbing the inside of my *mouf*."

It takes her a few tries but finally the door closes. She puts both feet on the dash. There's a sore on the other one, too.

"What's that?" I point to her left foot.

"What?"

"That."

"Thassa blister from where the shoe hiss my foot. Nevermine. Ron broke our schedule today. He broke our *schedule*."

"Okay."

"I'm leaving him."

"Okay."

She paws at the gauze, lifting her foot off the dash weakly, then putting it down again, as if she can't decide what to do with this thing attached to her leg. She's trashed. I have no idea where to go so we just drive around: toward Waikiki, up Ward, past the hospital.

"Margaret!" she cries when we pass Queen's. "Margaret is dying! My sister is dying!"

She never did visit Margaret after Thanksgiving.

"No, Mom, she's not dying. She's just sick."

"Gamma wants us to die! I see through her. She fucked me. She fucking *fucked* me. She fucking ruined my life!"

"No, no, Mom."

"I ruined your life."

"No, no, you didn't." I'm shaking my head. "I'm happy."

I try to touch her shoulder. She sobs. "Oh!"

We've made it to Honolulu Harbor. Part of it is a foreign trade zone now—tax benefits for Chinese businessmen and the like. I've never been down here. Hibiscus hedges encircle corrugated-steel buildings; roads are split by monkeypod trees. I feel like we should go somewhere from here, but where? Mom doesn't know anyone anywhere else. We're on an island. And she's wasted. I don't know where to take her. Sand Island? They're closed. She's too loopy anyway. I can't take her to my father's. Her family doesn't want her. Lauren's on the mainland. Now that Jack's in Okinawa Layla's staying with friends. It strikes me that no one will have us.

We pass under the shapely limbs of a monkeypod and she gets an idea.

"Pull over here."

She straddles the curb, pulls down her pants and starts pissing, ass to the moon. Cars pass. She teeters and straightens up.

"What are you doing?"

"Nevermine."

In the car she's focused. "I need some coffee. Let's get some coffee. I need to sit somewhere."

"Okay."

There's a Jack in the Box on Ward so that's where we go. It's got coffee; its sign makes it easily locatable; it isn't far from here. "Jack in the Crack," Ron calls it. Jack in the Crack is where we'll go.

In the parking lot the orange light cast by the sign turns our skin yellow.

"Fuck! You're taking me here? Here? Fuck!"

And she had been doing so well after she peed.

"What? Mom, what? What's wrong?"

"You're embarrassed of me!"

"No. No. Let's go to Starbucks."

"I don't want to go to Starbucks."

"Let's just go."

Her head hangs. "No. This is fine." She sighs, fingers to her eyes. "If this is where you want to go, this is fine."

Her hands curl in her lap. A few of the fake nails hang on. I really don't care where we go. I just want her to stop crying.

Actually what I really want is for her to go away.

At the drive-through I buy her a fajita and a cup of coffee.

She taps my shoulder. "Ask for extra milk and sugar."

I stare at her. What do you say to your hysterical high mother? Something intimate? Something to jog her memory? I'm your daughter. You're my mother. It's Christmas. It's not supposed to be like this.

"You always like so much sugar in your coffee."

What I've said is vaguely cruel, though I can't put my finger on exactly why. It's not in the words. It's in the delivery. I'm too calm. Rage has eaten me up and replaced me with a replica of myself.

"There's something wrong with you," she says between bites of fajita. We're driving again, aimless, down Ward. "You don't have empathy. You don't know how to feel. Why don't you have children? Then you'd know."

I would like to have a child. I don't have anyone to have it with. I have relationships; they peter out at a year or two. An old feeling comes over me, the desire to move on. I am doing it now. How long have I been here? Five months already. The philosopher is too good on the phone.

But I took care of my sisters, didn't I?

Lauren: I'm glad she isn't here to see any of this.

Karen slurps her coffee, her eyes squinting over the rim of the cup. She's moved on. She turns to me. She's found her target.

"Why don't you get mad at me, huh? Why don't you react?"

It's anger she wants and I won't give it to her.

"Because you take up all the drama, Karen Morgan."

I've been wanting to use her name all night.

She stares. The streetlights sweep across her face as we pass under them. Now that she is skinnier her eyes seem bigger and more luminous, as if her whole face were just teeth and eyes.

"What? I take up all the drama? What?" She's crying again, heaving wails. The coffee between her knees sloshes. "What is that supposed to mean?"

We're driving around the back alleys of Kapiolani, where the taxi companies and parking lots for the exotic clubs are—Saigon Passion, Rock-za, Club By Me. Buy me drink, buy me champagne? The shower show, the ping-pong show, the scrambled egg show. I went to Rock-za once, a few years ago, with a guy I met when I first moved to New York. A woman with long black hair danced in a G-string on a stage around which women and men drank and chatted and laughed. I wanted to put money in her underwear. My date encouraged me. I tried to meet her eyes but she only smiled and looked up at the lights over my head.

My mother points to the streaked stucco wall, the tin-roofed carport, the gas station beyond, all the colors of rot.

"Here. Here's where I got raped. Somewhere **around here. Back** there. Here! No, here! Take a right."

Everything's going too fast. "Raped? You got raped? What?"

"Yeah, I got raped. Over by Kapiolani with Naomi."

I don't know who Naomi is, so I picture Serena's flaccid blond hair and her missing teeth. I can't help thinking it: Does it make a blow job easier?

"We were walking down Kapiolani. These guys picked us up and raped me."

"Here!" Mom whispers. "Those fuckers. And Naomi, that bitch, left me. She ran away from me." She's casting around; she finds me. "Do you know what it's like for someone to want to kill you? For someone to look in your face and want to kill you?"

My hands sweat on the steering wheel. I try to meet her gaze. I'm confused. I want to say yes, but I can't tell if that's because I'm seeing my mother's face and she looks like she wants to kill—if not me, then some-one—or if I want to kill her.

"No."

"No. That's right. No, you don't." She sniffs, laughs. It turns into a hack. "Now slow down, slow down." She clears her throat. "This. Here."

We pull up behind a battered red Datsun, darker in the alley so that it looks almost black.

"I remember. An old car. They had me in the front seat. They were grabbing me." She grabs me. "No—" She's changed her mind. "Let's go. This isn't it."

She waves her hand. I drive nowhere for ten minutes, my mother muttering, *I'm going to kill them! I'm going to slit their fucking throats!*

"Those sorry motherfuckers. I'm going to get my transvestite friend, Brenda. She's like a feminist, but a guy. She told me, 'I'll come with you Karen, I'll kill those fucking bastards.'"

Then she puts her arm in front of me, like she used to when we didn't wear seat belts in Pebble Beach and she was braking. "Wait! Where are we?"

We're off Kapiolani, heading west. We're less than six blocks from the ocean. Three blocks away is Ala Moana, once the biggest outdoor shop-ping center in the world, built in 1959, before time stopped. A few blocks beyond that is Ala Moana beach park, where Mom and Terry used to go in the afternoon before Anna Banana's and she would swim and he would jog. We're about a mile from downtown, where she now lives in Triangle Park with Ron, and a mile from Punahou, where she spent nearly every day of her adolescent life, kindergarten through eleventh grade, and about as far from St. Andrew's, where she got married.

Queen's Hospital, where she was born, where Margaret was born. Where her sister was now dying in a hospital bed in the very room she had been born in. ("Can you believe it?" Gail had said. "Can you fuck-ing believe it?") Four or five miles from Kahala, less than three from Waikiki. We're in Honolulu, my mother's home for fifty-two years.

"Which way is the ocean?" She says it quietly, eyes squinting, like she's really trying to figure it out.

Everyone knows which way the ocean is in Hawaii. I don't know how you know it, but you do. You know it even at night, when you can't see the mountains and so don't know how to orient yourself. You know it by the slope of the street beneath you, by the landmarks you grew up with, by the tunnel of trees over Kapiolani bending one way or another. You know it by the way the air moves, and by the particular dark quality of the sky, and by where the clouds hang on the moon. You know it like you know where the parts of your own body reside: your head to your hands, fingers to toes.

I'm yelling, finally. I'm shaking. "Which way is the ocean? Jesus! What are you on? How can you not know where you are?"

"My mouth!" my mother cries, "The pain in my tongue. Can't you see!" She sticks out her tongue and tries to show me the part where it's ripped. "The painkillers!"

Then she's quiet. We've stopped. "Let's just go to the Pagoda." She's holding herself, swaying back and forth. "Call Layla. Let's just go to the Pagoda. We can get a room and I can be with you guys. That's all I really want to do—be with you guys."

She reaches across the well to me. I let her hand stay on my knee but soon I have to shift and her hand is back in her lap and we're on our way again.

I call Layla. "I've got her," I say. "Meet us at the Pagoda."

"Mom?"

"Yeah, she's here. I've got her."

"Okay, okay. I'm leaving right now."

Next to me my mother rolls up her window. It has started to rain.

The definition of tragedy, I read once, is a missing of the mark, a fundamental misapprehension, an inability to recognize something close to you, like Oedipus. I always thought my mother was the tragedy. Her fall from grace, our family's fall. The evil deeds we did to Hawaiians, and to the plantation workers, and to ourselves. Our curse: Mana, where the dead process, the Lady of the Twilight. Our tragedy was so beautiful.

I am the fool. All those years I hadn't seen how close I was to her, and her to me, and how close I was to my home. I used to think she was such a bad mother.

At the Pagoda I try to park. "You don't have to be *perfect,* Tara. Why are you trying to find the *perfect* parking space? Just park here." She points to a tow space. I back into the parking lot of a bar in which some kind of party is happening. Limos purr in front of us, girls in low-rider black slacks arch. All the men have spiky hair. Mom rolls down the window, yells at the attendant.

"No, we're not going to the *party*. We just want to be let through." Then to me: "See what you've done? God. *Stupid.*"

My mother has never once called me stupid.

"You're *stupid*. Why don't you listen to me? No one ever listens to me. No one ever believes me."

"I believe you."

In the parking garage she gets going. She is crying again. We loop up the floors of the garage, wet tires squeaking as we turn.

"You know what Serena said? Serena said to Ron, 'Ah, Karen. Rape. Right. Why do you even believe her?' Can you believe that? That's what she said."

I don't know what to say. You always have to believe a rape victim.

"Oh, Mom. I'm sorry. I'm so sorry."

She narrows her eyes, looks at me from the passenger seat. "Oh, please, Tara. *Oh, Mom, I'm so sorry.* What about, 'That fucking cunt. I can't believe she didn't believe you. What a bitch.' Huh? That's what you should say. 'What a fucking cunt, Mom.' Jesus. Jesus!"

In the lobby she calms down. Hotel lobbies do that to people: the desk, the desire to look admittable. Warm light shines on the check-in woman's parted hair. There is a miniature Japanese garden across from the desk, complete with pagoda and bonsai.

At the pantry we buy water, cigarettes. She still has a sense of the world. "People can't stand to be around me," she keeps saying. "I'm different. I'm different." It's a little too loud, but the man behind the counter smiles. "Anyway, get the cheap ones." To him she manages a grin. "This is my daughter," she points to me. "I'm so proud of her."

Layla arrives, looking worried. Her hair is up in a loose bun, she's in sweats and ready for business. I am happy and relieved to see my sister. She immediately takes out a cigarette.

We go up to the room. Mom sits us down on the polyester bedspread and strokes our hair. She hovers and moans and tries to hug us both at the same time. But she's too close—her sense of distance is off and she's clammy—and both of us duck away.

"I'm so happy to be with you! My daughters! This is what I really wanted. To be together, finally!"

Once, when Mom was dating Terry, Lauren wrote her a letter. *Don't let the candle burn out between us,* Lauren wrote. How do children tell their parents they love them? Often in the most obvious terms. I'm glad my sister is in Texas. No one should have to see this. But there's something here that feels like an ending, too. Like the thing finally burst. Lauren will have to do it her own way.

Mom's unpacking her stuff, ranging around the room, which is late-sixties, weirdly ample. There's a rabbit-eared TV in the corner. Mom sets out her medicines, her bandages, her ointments, her scissors—junkies are the fucking Red Cross—on the expansive vanity, under the mirror. Layla's tucked against the headboard of the bed, scared.

"Oh, Layla," Mom croons and reaches across the bed to hug her. "Oh, honey."

From a chair by the television I watch the scene. It is pathetic and I want it to stop.

"Mom, why don't you take a bath?"

I'm trying to get her to take a bath so I can figure out what to do. I've already called 911—they tell me to take her to Queen's, to Kekela, to the psych ward. "Queen's won't take me in," she says. "I have Kaiser insurance, Tara. *Kaiser.*"

Stupid, she starts calling me.

She's on the edge of the bed now, unwrapping her soiled bandage.

"What's that," I say, pointing.

"I told you. It's a spider bite."

"I don't believe you."

"It's a spider bite! It's a fucking spider bite! You want to see what the doctor says? Stupid. I'll fucking show you. Goddammit. Don't believe me."

A piece of paper unfolds, she points to a few words. *Abscess from insect bite,* indeed. *Bite,* it says, right there in doctor scribble.

"See? The doctor says it's a spider bite. See? *Bitch.*"

She's never called me a bitch before. She's still holding the paper, sitting at the edge of the bed, cheeks swollen, foot treacling pus, but now she's called me a bitch, so everything is different.

"You could have told them anything. You need to go to Queen's."

"Shut up, bitch."

She's left her scissors on the bureau. I take them and wrap them in some of her clothes and put them in a drawer. I'm doing it because I think she might hurt herself, but my thoughts are only of blood.

"Don't trick me," she says. "Don't you even try to trick me."

I trick her, sort of.

"Want to go back to the park, then? I'll drop you back in the park. Is that where you want to go?"

I start stuffing the shit she's so neatly arranged—her clothes and all her medicines and her AA books and her schedule—into her bag.

She's in my face now. "Fuck! You know how long it took me to get that bag together? Homeless people have to have their stuff *arranged!*

Okay? Fuck! Shitface! Fucking bitch! It took me two hours to pack that bag, bitch! I hate you! Stupid! Shithead!"

I could hit her. I could use her scissors and cut her beautiful throat. I could push her and then she'd push me back and then everything would be all over, everything I've always wanted to do would be done. We'd meet—we'd connect, finally, even if it were in violence. I'd know her.

Motherfucking whore cunt fucking asshole shitface crack dickhead. She's not angry at Layla. She's yelling at me. She's stood over Layla with a butcher knife. *Clean up your room!* She's called the cops on Lauren. She's never been that way with me. I've been the good girl, so good she couldn't get mad. Until she finally is.

"I'm going to get the car."

When I come back she and Layla are sitting on the curb. "You're *stupid*," she says again. "You're a shitface. I'll never forgive you. You're not my friend."

I feel like laughing. "I'm not your friend?" I turn to look at her. "We're going to Queen's."

She could run away, but she doesn't. She slumps in the backseat and for a while we're quiet until Layla turns around.

"Mom, stop ashing in the car."

Everything is quiet for a moment while my mother studies her cigarette. Then she looks up and narrows her eyes. She's still so good at making a scene.

"Fuck your *father*. Fuck *him*. He didn't *want* you. He couldn't stand to see you *breast-feed*."

I snort, turn on the radio, but my hands are shaking. "I've heard that one already, Karen."

"I hope this fucking car *blows up.*"

I want to throw her out of the car, kick her fucking face in.

At Queen's, at Kekela, the psych ward, the wait is five hours, like it was that afternoon at Kaiser. Comedy Central's on the waiting-room TV, though the volume is off. At two in the morning a blond psychiatrist who looks like Teri Garr comes in: "I am sorry, girls. I am so sorry I can't do anything. She's not psychotic. She knows her name. She knows the day. I can't make her stay here against her will. You might just have to watch your mom bounce along the bottom for a while."

She looks at her hands, which are pink and small. "Have you tried Alanon?"

She's nice, but it's just so fucking sad. Layla and I cry. Teri Garr leaves. I buy Mom a juice and try to give it to her on the way out. She won't speak to us. "No," she says. "No. No. No.

"Take me to the park."

There's no way I'm taking her to the park. Other than that I have no idea where I'm going.

"Mom, why don't you come back to the hotel with us? Why don't you do that? We'll go to sleep."

Somewhere past the hospital I pull over to the side of the road.

"I'm not going to take you to the park," I say. "Why don't you just come back to the Pagoda with us? Just come back to the hotel."

"No. Take me to the park."

"Mom," Layla cries. "Please, we're begging, Mom. Please. This isn't a joke."

It is a joke. Too late I realize I've pulled over right in front of Central Intermediate, the school where she and Ron sleep. She hadn't even directed me and I did it anyway. She opens the car door and grabs her duffel and jumps out.

Fuck everything being so close here.

She walks fast into the darkness, the school rising up before her white, moonlit. Her shoulders hunch. She carries her bag, her ointments and bandages and scissors and clothes no longer neatly folded. It doubles her over.

"Don't leave me. Don't leave me," I cry, running after her. "You already left me once!"

In fact, I left her. But anyway, that's how I felt.

"Oh, come on," she calls back, though she doesn't turn around. She is a dark silhouette, bearish, walking away from us. Then she's gone.

In the car Layla puts her fingers to her eyes. "This is it. This is it. I can't take it anymore."

Layla and I sleep at the Pagoda that night. We share the double bed, turn on the AC and draw the shit-colored curtains. We sleep till eleven: a dark, sodden sleep. In the morning I'm sorry we have to leave. Even cheap hotels are good for forgetting.

I am going back to New York in a week. I have finally decided to leave. I make my flight and start to say good-bye: to Dad and Deirdre, Debbie on the Big Island, Gail, Margaret in the hospital, Gamma. I've sublet my apartment in New York so I don't have a house to return to, but I can't stay here anymore. Lauren's in Houston now; Layla's moving to Virginia in July. We can still be sisters on the mainland. I don't know what will happen to Mom.

On Christmas Eve I ask Layla to help me find her. One last time, I tell her, as if repetition itself will change things. That I once thought that my mother had disappeared seems a pathetic fantasy now, a fairy tale's ending to a story that's simply too sad.

We find her at Triangle Park. Ron's been thrown in jail. "He beat me up," Mom tells us. "Oh, Mom," we say on cue. Secretly we're thrilled. We make a plan to see her on Christmas. We'll take her to brunch at Kaimana. Pancakes with coconut syrup, sautéed mahimahi with macadamia nuts. I've bought her a wheely bag so she can ditch the duffel. I ask people whether I should and they say, *Well, if it helps*. Layla has gotten her a gift certificate to Safeway. We'll give her the presents, then we'll take her to Sand Island.

Christmas morning she cancels. She calls us from somewhere in Kahaluu, batu central. She can't make it. "Everyone's sleeping here." She's hoarse. "I don't have a ride."

"I'm sick of her," Layla says. "She only calls us when she wants something."

But I want something, too. I want her to get well. So I drive to fetch her. On the phone she starts crying. "I'm scared, I'm scared," she's whimpering. She doesn't quite know where she is. Finally I find her in some suburb backed against the Pali, barefoot.

"Get in." She does.

"I lost my shoes."

"Whatever. We're going to IHS." *They've helped three thousand men, women, and children.* "I'm taking you to IHS."

"No, no! I'm not going there!"

"But you are." I'm trying to be firm. "You are."

Outside the Peanut Butter Ministry the scene is like it was that day in late summer when I first went looking for her. Mothers with strollers, people in line for the pay phone—all behind the yellow line. I forget it's Christmas. No one down here seems that into it anyway.

She's lost her shoes again. She asks me for money so that she can get Orajel. I tell her I'll buy it for her. At a shop down the road I buy her two pairs of slippers and Orajel and some water. When I return I give all of it to her as well as the wheely bag and a few phone cards. She doesn't want any of it.

"Give me twenty dollars, at least."

"No. You need to go to Sand Island. You need to get some rest. You're sick."

"No! No!" she cries. "I'm afraid," she says. "The guards yell at the women here." She sits on the sidewalk and cries.

"Fine." This time I mean it. "Where do you want to go?"

"Not here."

"Good. Let's go. I have to meet my father."

"Fucking Kirk!"

I drive her back to Triangle Park. I wait while she debouches her duffel bag, her wheely bag, her new brown paper bag of slippers and Orajel. I'm finished. It's six o'clock on Christmas Day and my father and I are supposed to eat steak together.

"You're going to leave me? Just going to leave me here alone? On Christmas?"

I leave her under a tree. I drive away and I do not look back.

At the steak house my father is flushed.

"I'm sorry," he says.

"Why? It's not your fault." I feel like I might cry so I look at the menu.

"No. It is my fault."

It's not, but I appreciate him saying so anyway.

In the beginning there's hope. After hope there's courage. After courage, determination. After determination there's something like habit, and desperation, opposite sides of the same coin. I am leaving in a few days. Without my mother to look for I find myself at a loss as to what to do. Sand Island still beckons. I think about locking her in a room and sitting there with her until she's better, but I realize I know nothing about heroin or pills or whatever she's on, or how long detox would take, what it looks like, how sick she would be. I am afraid of her overtaking my life until I realize she already has. The dream of getting better is a hard one to kill.

I call Layla the next morning. "Let's try again."

We spend the day after Christmas pleading with our mother in the park to go to treatment. She's pouting. She's beginning to like the attention.

"No. You left me yesterday. Remember? You left me on Christmas."

Celeste drives up with a blond man in an American sedan, her feet dirty on the dashboard. Mom walks over and leans in. I follow her.

"She wants me to go to *Sand Island,*" she says, pointing back to me. "No *way.*"

Celeste and the blond man snicker. Disgusting junkies. I glare at them until they drive away. Mom walks back defiant, her chin high. She's limping but she's still proud.

A tall handsome black guy comes by. Layla nudges me. "I think it's her pimp."

"Doesn't he look like Michael Jordan?" Karen giggles to Layla loud enough so he can hear. Then to the guy: "Hey, can you come back later? I'm with my daughters."

He stands still, looks at her. "What are you doing later?"

It's weird, how he won't leave.

"I don't know." She smiles, tilts her head toward us. "But come back later." When he finally leaves Layla asks her how she knows him.

"Oh, he's from NA. He's in the program."

"Right." Layla sneers. Then to me: "I'm starting to lose it, Tara. I'm starting to go on overload."

Finally, a dark-haired man in a sports jacket comes over. "Hey, it's Nate the Blade! Nate went to Oxford," she says to me. "He writes poetry. He's deep."

Nate sits down next to us, backpack still on. He tells me he's my mother's best friend. He's taking care of her, he says. I don't have to worry.

"I think I have something that will take care of you really well, Karen," he says ominously, raising his eyebrows. It's all so bizarre and obvious.

"Please come, please come," Layla's saying to our mother. "Please come to Sand Island."

"Hey, I know you, Tara," Nate's saying. "I know you. Your mom has told me a lot about you, and what she needs right now is a friend. A real good friend. I'm a real good friend to you and your mom."

I'm distracted by Nate's eyes. They are pale and blue.

"I know you, Tara. I know you."

"You don't know me. You don't know a fucking thing about me."

I have never said that to anyone before.

When you are trying to survive something disastrous, you look at parts. You memorize details—a curb, a leaf, the color of the sky. You progress from one zeroed-in shot to another. Somehow this lets you clear to the end of the story without ever having to look or think about the gravity of the loss, its meaning, your part in it, the ways you failed. The ways you were failed. I find it harder to think about this. Good girls endured horrible circumstance and came out on top. You either made it or you didn't. And I knew what that looked like.

Here I am in Triangle Park with my sister and my mother, trying to figure out what to do next, and nothing is so clear. Being quiet doesn't help, nor does being angry. I can't cut my mother's hair or buy her enough bags to hold what she constantly seems to be losing. I love her and love is a kind of responsibility but nothing will return her to me in the way that I need. Some things are just lost, and you make do with what remains.

The last day I look for her I'm alone. Layla's in school. She's working on her cosmetology license. She's going to put makeup on people, do their hair, like she used to with Lauren. I am proud of my sisters. I want them to fulfill their dreams.

Lauren is still in Houston, going to school. I have called her and told her about what's happening, but in terms that aren't as confused as I feel. "She's having a hard time," I say, and Lauren is quiet. My sisters have had hard lives and they remain loyal to their mother to the end. Karen made sure of that.

The tradewinds have been gone for a long time and suddenly they are back and it's raining. Fitful, tempestuous rain, temper tantrums of rain.

Inside CHAMP Paula says, "You look good, girl." Paula is bony and haggard but straight. The methadone clinic doesn't look as bad as it used to. The pencil holders, the photocopier in a corner, the stacks of files. A nurse comes into the lobby wearing blue scrubs.

"Did you check over by the river?" Paula says.

"Yeah, I checked by the river."

She rearranges something on the desk, sighs, folds her arms over her chest. Ray comes out to say hello.

"Can I leave my number with you, Ray? In case she calls?"

He nods, pulling out a scrap of paper, and then he pauses with his pen in the air.

"Tara," I say.

He smiles, pats my hand. "Now you don't think I would forget that, do you?"

"No. I didn't think that."

"It's particularly poignant," says Paula, "because your mom's smart. She knows."

She gives me an umbrella that had been left by a client. "Maybe it will help you find your mom," she says, smiling.

I think of the story of Gampa Great; the Hawaiian diviner who found the water to make the sugar to make the profits to make us rich.

"A divining rod!" I say.

Paula laughs. She's being polite.

Two hours up and down Fort Street Mall in the rain. When I finally find Mom she has a new outfit on: light blue jeans and a blue cotton top with a ribbon at the breast, white tennis shoes. She's fifty-two and she's dressed like a teenager. I ask her where she got the clothes. Last time I saw her she had lost her bag.

"I stole the whole thing!" She laughs. "Right now, at Ross's."

"Wow." I'm weirdly impressed.

"Look, I'm ready to go to treatment now. I knew you'd come." She's safety-pinned the back of her pants together. "And look! I'm gaining weight!"

This is not true, but I nod and rub her shoulder anyway.

In front of Ron's post office box, we sit for a while. Mom opens mail. Ron's still in jail and she's looking for his disability check. Then we go to buy cigarettes. She says to the woman behind the counter, "My daughter is writing a book." She said it to a clump of street people earlier, her friends. "About what it means to grow up haole in Hawaii, something like that."

"Now I just have to get my stuff."

She says it just like that. One more rung to climb and we're at Sand Island.

We have to get her stuff from Nate the Blade: the wheely bag, the phone cards, her duffel. He had carried them off to his storage place the day before. If we can just find Nate she'll go to Sand Island.

"Otherwise, no way."

We stop at the library to look for him. *Peau de soie. Cymbidium orchids. Eddie Kinilau serenades.* "No," she says. "I have to find Nate. Otherwise I can't go." Back to Fort Street. I can't remember if I've given her money. I follow her, like a cop. She stops and talks to people along the mall. Is she scoring? I'm that confused. The sun hasn't even hit midsky. I can't believe it's still morning.

Finally she gets in the car. We are heading down Nimitz, toward Sand Island. I'm going to quarantine her. She looks back at the buildings.

"Stop this car." She loosens her seat belt. "I'm not going. I'm not going without my stuff."

"I'm taking you."

She places her hands on the dash, as if to still us. "Stop this fucking car!"

"No." I'm going to do it better this time. I've learned. I'm going to be better once she gets to Sand Island. I just have to get her there.

Traffic intervenes. I have to slow down and suddenly she's opening the door. We're in the middle of the highway. Cars next to us slow down, speed away.

"I don't like the way you do things," she says, and slams the door.

She heads for the curb. There's not much of a sidewalk here. It's an industrial area so she walks as far as she can get and then when the sidewalk runs into a warehouse she crosses the road.

I chase after her. "Please, Mom! Please!"

Cars pass. I've never been to this particular spot in Honolulu before. I'm disoriented and stuck.

She walks down the highway, on the median, heading toward downtown from the harbor. She knows where she's going. She walks quickly. She looks at the cars at her sides. She holds her head up. I sit in the car and watch her till I can't see her anymore.

Gamma says, "Start from the beginning. Tell me logically, unemotionally, what happened." I realize I can't. I don't want to tell the story. I want to forget.

Gamma laughs nervously, readjusts her dark glasses.

"I hear Brad McCorry is living with his mother. Gone crazy. We didn't know in those days about drugs. At Hanalei I picked up a phone and there was Neil Daniels, talking to your mother. He said, 'Can't you just put it in her suitcase?' And poor Karen saying she couldn't. 'I can't do that to my mother,' she said."

Gamma stops. "Out of all my children, she was the one. She just looked at you. She just looked at you and sized you up, and said, 'Well, what about you there?'"

My grandmother pauses. "All of us are born with a full cup, Tara dear. That's ours. No one can take that away from us."

We're sitting in her living room. The chairs have started to lose their stuffing.

I don't know if this is true. I would like to think it is.

At Stinger Ray's, the airport bar, a waitress named Shellsea serves me a gin and tonic and shrimp Louie. The flight is uneventful. In New York it has snowed.

Two days after New Year's my mother calls me from the psych ward at Queen's. "I went to Kekela and they called me a junkie and wouldn't let me in, until I started talking about Gampa Morgan, and the wing named after him and then they were really nice. Isn't that sick?" She laughs. Her voice is almost gone.

"Yeah, that's pretty sick." I'm thinking, Thank god.

Why now, though? Why after I'm gone?

She's talking about her spider bites again. Two on the tops of her feet, one just above each elbow.

"God, this methadone is strong. Terrible stuff."

"I know," as if I do. "How are you feeling?"

"I've got cellulitis. I know it sounds scary but they're just little sores."

I read in the DSM-IV that when the veins calcify you start shooting into the subcutaneous skin, and cellulitis and buboes and abscesses appear. Over in the dialysis ward of Queen's Margaret has cellulitis of her toes. They might have to cut them off. I send my aunt socks and peppermint lotion. I write my mother a letter.

"Sand Island is coming to pick me up," she says. "I hope they come. I hope that's what's meant for me."

She sounds tired on the phone.

"Definitely, Mom, definitely."

She writes Layla first. My sister reads me the letter over the phone. I'm back, she writes. "And she underlined it," Layla says.

I start crying.

When she gets out I'll go down to Sans Souci with her. Kaimana. Dig Me Beach. I love thinking about her there, framed by blue, the natatorium and the palm trees, and Waikiki and the park in front of us and the whole ocean behind us. We'll go down there in the morning right when the sun's up and it's just us and the surfers and we'll jump in the water and turn our backs to the shore and we'll go swimming.

Karen, 1969

Epilogue

February 2004   New York City

HERE THEY ARE: THE LITLE BITS OF YOU I'VE CARRIED around since we parted. They are small and in pieces but they are from the very beginning, and they make a story, and that's what I always wanted, a story. Now I have all these stories and they don't go together in the way I wanted to make me understand. What explains us? Nothing. I wanted to know how you could have given me up before I was ready to be given up. I wonder if that's explainable anymore.

But then memory itself lies. Take this: my first is of a swimming hole. Blond skinny hippies with beards, mud. Everyone's naked. I carry the memory around with me like a little charm, all through my childhood, after I'm taken from you, all the way until I get to college, when I find it's not a memory at all: it's the opening sequence of the *Woodstock* movie.

Never mind. They're having fun. I'm having fun. We are in a tent of leaves, the sun shines through the branches and sets the water aglitter.

Margaret passed away in September 2003, very brave until the end. I was in Italy—a place I know hardly anything about—so far away from

Hawaii that I felt as if I had touched down on a different planet. Different sky, different color of leaves, mountains made of different stone.

The night my aunt died I was in a courtyard at a party. Music played. I had been listening to a concert—two women sang. Margaret was in her heart a musician and that's what I felt that night under that foreign sky, a foreigner again, but more comfortable with the role now.

Hawaii is still the same, though it changes every time I go back. And these changes, because it really is such a beautiful place—maybe there was a paradise here, after all—are frightening. Humans know what they sometimes do to things they love too much.

I am more used to New York now, but I live across the river in Brooklyn so I'm happier. At night the lights and the shadows of the buildings give the city an odd resemblance to the jagged mountains of my childhood, made of lights and glass. And perhaps this is what happens in any case to our childhoods. We transform them into shining things so that we can move on.

My mother still struggles. She calls it "partying," the companion of the eternal flower child, as if time hasn't passed, children have not been born and lost, wrinkles not formed, faces not dropped.

The story continues, as real life does.

The coiner of the term *manifest destiny* was obsessed with the idea that America was new, unburdened by history. In Hawaii the past is not extinct. Ghosts just want to be heard, which is why we remember them.

Still, I have hope for the living.

Pronunciation Key and Glossary

The consonants *p, k, h, l, m, n* are pronounced as they are in English; *w* after *i* and *e* is pronounced like *v,* after *o* and *u* like *w,* after *a* and initially like either *w* or *v;* the glottal stop (') is similar to the stop in English *uh-oh.* Vowels, unstressed: *a* as in *above; e* as in *bet; i* as in *city; o* as in *sole; u* as in *moon.* Vowels, stressed: *ā* like in *far; ō* as in *bowl; ī* like in *see; ū* as in *moon; ē* as in *play.* Dipthongs *ei, eu, oi, ou, ai, ae, ao, au* are always stressed on the first letter, but the two are not as closely joined as in English.

'ahi, yellow-fin tuna
ahupua'a, land division usually extending from the uplands to the sea
'āina, land, earth
aku, bonita, skipjack
alaia, small thin surfboard
'alalā, Hawaiian crow
ali'i, chief, chiefess
aloha, love, affection, compassion, mercy
'aumakua, family or personal god
bango, metal tag
bufo, cane toad

buke, book

daikon, turnip

dala, see **kālā**

ʻehu, reddish tinge in hair

hanabata, booger

hana ʻōkolele, a taunt

haole, white person, American, Englishman, Caucasian

hapa, portion, fragment, part

hapa haole, part haole

hāpai kō, haul cane

hasu, lotus root

hau, a lowland tree related to the hibiscus

hauna, stench

Hawaiʻi nei, this (beloved) Hawaii

hoaʻāina, tenant or caretaker, literally friend of the land

hui, club, association, society

huipa, whip

humuhumunukunukuāpuaʻa, variety of triggerfish

ʻiwa, frigate or man-of-war bird

kahuna, priest

kai, sea, ocean

kaimana, diamond

kālā, dollar, money

kalo, taro

kamaʻāina, native-born, one born in a place, host, literally land child

kanaka, human being, man, person, individual

kanaka maoli, full-blooded Hawaiian person

kane, man

kapa, cloth made of the paper mulberry tree

kapu, taboo, prohibition

kasuri, Japanese weaving process in which portions of yarns are left undyed and then woven to create a pattern against a darker dyed background

kauwa, outcast, pariah, slave

kiawe, algaroba tree

kō, sugar cane

koa, largest of native forest trees with light gray bark, crescent-shaped leaves, and white flowers in small, round heads

konohiki, headman of an ahupua'a under the chief

kua'āina, person of the country, literally backbone of the land

kū'ē, to oppose, resist, protest

kukuī, candlenut tree

kuleana, right, privilege, concern

lānai, porch, veranda, balcony

lani, sky, heaven, heavenly

laulau, packages of ti leaves or banana leaves containing pork, beef, salted fish, or taro tops

lei, garland of flowers

liliko'i, passionfruit

lū'au, Hawaiian feast

luna, headman, overseer

mahimahi, game fish popular for food

māhū, homosexual of either sex

maka'āinana, commoner, populace, people in general, literally eyes of the land

makai, toward the ocean

malasada, Portuguese fried dough dusted with sugar

malihini, newcomer

mana, supernatural or divine power

mauka, toward the mountain

mele, song

milo, a tree found on coasts of the eastern tropics

mochi, sticky rice cake

moekolohe, adultery, sleeping rascally

moke, local male

mu'umu'u, loose gown

naupaka, native shrub found in mountains and near coasts

nīele, inquisitive, curious, nosy

nō ka 'oi, the best

'okina, glottal stop

'ole, without

oli, chant

'ō'ō, black honeyeater with yellow feathers in a tuft under each wing

oof, engage in sexual intercourse

'ōpae, shrimp

pakalana, Chinese violet

pakalōlō, marijuana

Pākē, China, Chinese

palaka, a checkered shirt, usually blue and white, of block-print cloth

palapala, paper

pali, Pali, cliff, especially those along the Koolau range on Oahu

pānānā, compass

paniolo, cowboy

pareu, Tahitian wrap

pau hana, end of the workday

pepa, paper

pīkake, jasmine

poi, Hawaiian staff of life, made from cooked taro corms, pounded and
    thinned with water

po'o kanaka, skull

puka, hole

pūne'e, movable couch

pu'uhonua, place of refuge

saimin, Japanese noodle soup

see moi, Chinese dried and preserved fruits

tī, kī, woody plant in the lily family, native to tropical Asia and Australia

tiare, Tahitian gardenia

tita, local female

'uku, louse, flea

'ulu, breadfruit

ulua, crevalle, jack, or pompano fish

vog, volcanic fog

wahine, woman

Definitions and pronunciation guide are adapted from *Hawaiian Dictionary,
Revised and Enlarged Edition,* Mary Kawena Pukui and Samuel H. Elbert.

Acknowledgments and Sources

I am deeply grateful for the help and encouragement I have received over the six years spent researching and writing this book. My first and most heartfelt thanks is to my family, who have been unwavering in their support, generosity, and love. Kirk Smith, Debbie Baker, Layla Pierson, Lauren Stewart, Peggy Faye, Eleanor Faye, Gail Morgan, Brewster Morgan, Margaret Morgan, Charlotte Faye, and most of all, my beloved mother, Karen Morgan, shared their lives and stories with me and endured my attention with courage, understanding, and humor. Audrey Higuchi, Ross Wilson, Betty Dentry, Laura Aquino, Linda Collins Faye, Michelle Collins, and the Stewart/Fleming clan opened their homes and hearts and made me laugh; while Christine Faye, Marc and Gerda Faye, Michael Faye, Elizabeth Faye, Sally Muirhead, David Penhallow, Axel Faye, and the late Isabel Faye worked much of their lives to elucidate and preserve a history that has sustained, interested, and inspired many generations. Special thanks in this regard goes to Linda Collins Faye and the Faye family, as well as to Liz Hahn, Roland Sagum, and all of the staff and employees at Kikiaola Land Company and Waimea Plantation Cottages.

Hawaii's history has been carefully and painstakingly researched, recorded, and rendered by countless people who love these islands. In addition to the many sources listed below, I am indebted to those who shared their knowledge and gave me guidance: Carol Wilcox and the Wilcox family; Robert Schleck, Ruth Smith, Barnes Riznik, and the staff at Grove Farm; the archivists at the University of Hawaii Special Collections HSPA Plantation Archives; Wilfred Ibara at Gay & Robinson; Judd Malkin at JMB/Amfac; Margaret at the Kauai Museum; Bob Osgood at the HSPA; Warren S. Nishimoto at the University of Hawaii Center for Oral History; the Kauai Historical Society; the Bishop Museum; W. S. Merwin, David Alexander; Gordon Poiré; and Doug Arnott.

I couldn't have started, much less finished, this book without the support and wisdom of the readers and writers in my life, especially my first teacher, Cynthia Huntington, and those I met through Columbia University's MFA program: Lis Harris, Patricia O'Toole, Richard Locke, Susan Thames, Patricia Bosworth, Nic Christopher, Michael Scammell, Lawrence Weschler, and Vivian Gornick. Jana Ragsdale, Erik Olsen, and Dennis Smith gave me the wherewithal those first years to support myself, and fellow writers and first readers Jeff Tietz, Randy Hartwell, Donna Moreau, Linda Burnett, Rachel Wenrick, Nelson Eubanks, John Bowe, Eric Konigsberg, Eden Elieff, Elizabeth Gold, and Doug Lavin continue to astound me with their love, patience, sensitivity, humor, and intelligence. Thanks especially to Maia Palileo, Michael Gangemi, Chris Milenkevich, Megan Clark, Darcie Wilcox, Jennifer Bosworth, Emily Melnick, Dan Raeburn, Ben and Kirsten Scobie Southworth, Karen Shakman, Karen and Bob Sheridan, Jerry and Kelley Lavin, Andrew Urtz, Shauna Lyon, Ramin Serry, and Andrea Russell for their friendship and help, and to Emily Garrod for her insight and empathy.

I was blessed with the best agent and editor a writer could hope for. Richard Abate and Marysue Rucci made this book real. They also nurtured and cared for me; to them I owe my most profound thanks. I am grateful also to everyone at ICM—especially Kate Lee for being consistently fantastic—and to Simon & Schuster for shepherding an unusual story to completion: David Rosenthal, Tara Parsons, Victoria Meyer, Alexis Welby, Mara Lurie, and the copyediting and art departments, and Griffin Hansbury for lending his style to the catalog copy. Thanks finally to Caren Lobo and Kristina Garcia for helping to spread the word.

In telling the stories and anecdotes in this book I used many sources. I list some of them here in part to give credit, but also in part to encourage anyone interested in Hawaii's history to read and study further. Many people from all over the world have been captivated by these islands and the people who have inhabited them. I humbly offer this book in the spirit of love—aloha—and gratitude to them and to my home.

All part epigraphs were taken from *'Ōlelo No'eau: Hawaiian Proverbs and Poetical Sayings,* by Mary Kawena Pukui. All Hawaiian word and place name definitions are from *Hawaiian Dictionary, Revised and Enlarged Edition,* by Pukui, Samuel H. Elbert, and Esther T. Mookini, and *Place Names of Hawaii, Revised and Expanded Edition,* Pukui, Elbert, and Mookini.

Other sources are as follows (listed alphabetically by author):

Lā'au Hawai'i: Traditional Hawaiian Uses of Plants, Isabella Aiona Abbott; *The Journals of Captain James Cook on His Voyages of Discovery, Vol. III, The Voyage of the Resolution and Discovery, 1776–1780, Part One and Part Two,* ed. J. C. Beaglehole; *Hawaiian Mythology* and *The Kumulipo: A Hawaiian Creation Chant,* Martha Warren Beckwith; *The Niihau Incident,* Allan Beekman; *Last Among Equals: Hawaiian Statehood and American Politics,* Roger Bell; *Six Months in the Sandwich Islands,* Isabella L. Bird; *Hula Moons,* Don Blanding; "Kanaka Maoli Self-Determination and Reinscription of Ka Pae' Aina (Hawai'i) on the U.N. list of Non-Self-Governing Territories," Kekuni Blaisdell; *Kauai's Geologic History: A Simplified Guide,* Chuck Blay and Robert Siemers; "Battle of Niihau," Burl Burlingame in the *Honolulu Star-Bulletin; The Gifts of Civilization: Germs and Genocide in Hawai'i,* O. A. Bushnell; *Shaping History: The Role of Newspapers in Hawai'i,* Helen Geracimos Chapin; *Da Kine Talk: From Pidgin to Standard English in Hawaii,* Elizabeth Ball Carr; *The Sandalwood Mountains: Readings and Stories of the Early Chinese in Hawaii,* ed. Tin-Yuke Char; *America in Hawaii: A History of United States Influence in the Hawaiian Islands,* Edmund James Carpenter; *The Great Mahele: Hawaii's Land Division of 1848,* Jon J. Chinen; *Remember Pearl Harbor!,* Blake Clark; *Rediscovering Water,* Tom Coffman; *Kaua'i in History: A Guide to the Resources,* compiled by Christopher Leland Cook, ed. Marie D. Strazar; *Koamalu,* Ethel Damon; *Two Years Before the Mast: A Personal Narrative of Life at Sea,* Richard Henry Dana, Jr.; *The Norse Migration: Norwegian Labor in Hawaii,* Carl and Eleanor H. Davis; *Shoal of Time: A History of the Hawaiian Islands,* Gavan Daws; *A Hawaiian Reader, Mad About Islands: Novelists of a Vanished Pacific,* and

Mark Twain's Letters from Hawaii, A. Grove Day; "We'll Always Have Honolulu," Joan Didion in *Travel + Leisure; O'iwi: A Native Hawaiian Journal*, ed. Māhealani Dudoit; "Kanaka World Travelers and Fur Company Employees, 1785–1860," Janice K. Duncan in *The Hawaiian Journal of History, Vol. 28*; "The American Raj," John Gregory Dunne in *The New Yorker; Memoirs of Henry Obookiah*, E. W. Dwight; *Hawaiian Treasures*, David Forbes; *Kauai Movie Book*, David Forbes and Chris Cook; *Roaming in Hawaii: A Narrative of Months of Wandering Among the Glamorous Islands that May Become Our 49th State*, Harry A. Franck; *The True Story of Kaluaikoolau: As Told by His Wife, Piilani*, trans. Frances N. Frazier; *Hawaii Pono: Hawaii the Excellent*, Lawrence Fuchs; *Anatomy of Paradise*, J. C. Furnas; *Hawaii: Tales of Yesteryear*, Roland L. Gay; *Women and Children First: The Life and Times of Elsie Wilcox of Kaua'i*, Judith Dean Gething Hughes; *Hawaii: The Sugar-Coated Fortress*, Francine Du Plessix Gray; "Grog Shops and Hotels," Richard A. Greer in *The Hawaiian Journal of History, Vol. 28; The Geology of Kauai and Niihau*, Norman E. A. Hinds; *Old Honolulu: A Guide to Oahu's Historic Buildings*, Historic Buildings Task Force; "Remembering Mana: An Historical Review," Historic Hawaii Foundation; *The Specter of Communism in Hawaii*, T. Michael Holmes; *Stories of Long Ago*, Ida von Holt; "The Haoles," Bernhard L. Horman in *Social Process in Hawaii 29; Blue Latitudes*, Tony Horwitz; *Kauai: The Separate Kingdom*, Edward Joesting; *Nā Mo'olelo a ka Po 'e Kahiko*, Samuel Mānaiakalani Kamakau; *Native Land and Foreign Desires: Ko Hawai'i 'Aina a me Na Koi Pu'umake a ka Po 'e Haole*, Lilikaka Kame'eleihiwa; *The Kauai Papers*, Kauai Historical Society; *Kanuka of Kauai*, Eric Knudsen; *Hawaiian Flowers and Flowering Trees*, Loraine E. Kuck and Richard C. Tongg; *Grove Farm Plantation*, Robert Krauss; *Hawaii, a History: From Polynesian Kingdom to American Commonwealth*, Ralph S. Kuykendall and A. Grove Day; *Hawaii: A Literary Chronicle*, ed. W. Storrs Lee; *On the Makaloa Mat: Island Tales*, Jack London; *Revolt in Paradise: The Social Revolution in Hawaii After Pearl Harbor*, Alexander MacDonald; *One Drop of Blood: The American Misadventure of Race*, Scott L. Malcolmson; *Hawaiian Antiquities*, David Malo; *Manual of Hawaiian Securities, 1924–1925; Trembling of a Leaf*, Somerset Maugham; *Moby-Dick, or The Whale* and *Typee*, Herman Melville; *Hawaii: America's Sugar Territory 1898–1959*, H. Brett Melendy; *Hawaii*, James A. Michener; *The Folding Cliffs: A Narrative of 19th-Century Hawaii*, W. S. Merwin; *Whaling Days in Old Hawaii*, Maxine Mrantz; *The Apotheosis of Captain Cook: European Mythmaking in the Pacific*, Gannath Obeyesekere; "Empire Can

Wait": American Opposition to Hawaiian Annexation, 1893–1898. Thomas J. Osborne; "History and Heritage of Civil Engineering," C. S. Papacostas in Wiliki o Hawaii; "A Yank in the RAF," interview with Brewster Morgan by Robert L. Popp; "Poli Hiwa Hiwa," Arthur Price; Nā nā I Ke Kumu, Look to the Source, Vol. I, Mary Kawena Pukui; Survey of the Birds of Kauai, Hawaii, Franck Richardson and John Bowles; "From Barracks to Family Homes: A Social History of Labor Housing Reform on Hawaii's Sugar Plantations," Barnes Riznik, The Hawaiian Journal of History, Vol. 33; How "Natives" Think: About Captain Cook, For Example, Marshall Sahlins; State of Hawaii Data Book, Bob Schmitt; "Death in Hawaii: The Epidemics of 1848–49," Robert C. Schmitt and Eleanor C. Nordyke in The Hawaiian Journal of History, Vol. 35; Dynasty in the Pacific, Frederick Simpich; Before the Horror: The Population of Hawai'i on the Eve of Western Contact, David E. Stannard; "Unlucky Star: Princess Ka'iulani," Marilyn Stassen-McLaughlin in The Hawaiian Journal of History, Vol. 33; The Happy Isles of Oceania: Paddling the Pacific, Paul Theroux; U.S. Congress, "The Blount Report," in Executive Documents of the House of Representatives, 53rd Congress, 3rd session, (1894–1895), v. 1.; Pau Hana: Plantation Life and Labor in Hawaii, 1835–1920, Ronald Takaki; From A Native Daughter, Haunani Kay Trask; "600 Living on a Private Hawaiian Island," Wallace Turner in the New York Times; Kauai and the Park Country of Hawaii, Robert Wenkam; The Hawaiian Guide Book, Henry Whitney; The Mainland Haole: The White Experience in Hawaii, Elvi Whittaker; Kaua'i: Ancient Place-Names and Their Stories, Polihale and Other Kaua'i Legends, Tales of Kaua'i, and Touring the Legends of Kōkee, Frederick B. Wichman; Sugar Water: Hawaii's Plantation Ditches, Carol Wilcox; The Kauai Album, Wilcox, Wehrheim, and Kunichika; Big Sugar: Seasons in the Cane Fields of Florida, Alec Wilkinson; The Wilders of Waikiki, Kinau Wilder; Reimagining the American Pacific, Rob Wilson; Displacing Natives: The Rhetorical Production of Hawaii, Houston Wood; "The Significance of Local," Eric Yamamoto in Social Process in Hawaii 27.

The following were also helpful: "Waimea, 80 Years Ago," Atsushi Yasutake, Waimea High School; Oral history of Waimea, Christine Fayé; "The People Tell Their Story, Vol. 1," and "The 1924 Filipino Strike on Kauai, Vol. II," Ethnic Studies Oral History Project, University of Hawaii Oral History Archives; Margaret Faye Reminisces, interviewed by David Penhallow; Isabel Faye Oral Histories interviewed by David Penhallow; and the Isabel Faye Archive at Marc and Gerda Faye's.

Tara, 1973

About the Author

✦

Tara Bray Smith was born and raised in Hawai'i. Today she lives and writes in New York City. *West of Then* is her first book.